Koreatown, Los Angeles

ASIAN AMERICA
A series edited by Gordon H. Chang

Koreatown, Los Angeles
Immigration, Race, and the "American Dream"

Shelley Sang-Hee Lee

STANFORD UNIVERSITY PRESS

STANFORD, CALIFORNIA

STANFORD UNIVERSITY PRESS

Stanford, California

Printed in the United States of America on acid-free, archival-quality paper

Library of Congress Cataloging-in-Publication Data

Names: Lee, Shelley Sang-Hee, 1975– author.

Title: Koreatown, Los Angeles : immigration, race, and the "American dream" / Shelley Sang-Hee Lee.

Other titles: Asian America.

Description: Stanford, California : Stanford University Press, 2022. | Series: Asian America | Includes bibliographical references and index.

Identifiers: LCCN 2021048631 (print) | LCCN 2021048632 (ebook) | ISBN 9781503613737 (cloth) | ISBN 9781503631823 (paperback) | ISBN 9781503631830 (ebook)

Subjects: LCSH: Korean Americans—California—Los Angeles—Social conditions—20th century. | Immigrants—California—Los Angeles—Social conditions—20th century. | Minorities—California—Los Angeles—Social conditions—20th century. | Racism against Asians—California—Los Angeles—History—20th century. | Koreatown (Los Angeles, Calif.)—History—20th century. | Los Angeles (Calif.)—Race relations—History—20th century.

Classification: LCC F869.L86 K675 2022 (print) | LCC F869.L86 (ebook) | DDC 979.4/94—dc23/eng/20211007

LC record available at https://lccn.loc.gov/2021048631

LC ebook record available at https://lccn.loc.gov/2021048632

Cover design: Derek Thornton, Notch Design

Cover photography: (Top) Artem, Flickr; (Middle, b/w) Collection of J. Eric Lynxwiler; (Spine edge and bottom) Los Angeles from Koreatown, Daniel Schwarz, Stocksy.com

Typeset in 11/14 Garamond Pro

To Cha Bok-Hee

Contents

Acknowledgments

Working on this book has truly been a journey. I thank my guides and eyewitnesses to Los Angeles's Korean American community and history, who generously shared their time, insights, and at times their material: Ralph Ahn, Larry Aubry, Steve Chanecka, Grant Din, Kathy Dunn, Warren Furutani, Randy Hagihara, K. W. Lee, Jai Lee Wong, Do Kim, Katherine Kim, Sophia Kim, Pyong Yong Min, Cooke Sunoo, and Eui-Young Yu. A 2015 summer fellowship at the Huntington Library in San Marino, California was pivotal for getting this project on track, so I am grateful for the support and opportunity. Over the last few years, I spent countless hours in conversation with colleagues and friends who inspired me with their intellectual comradery, good cheer, and moral support. Thank you especially to Ana Burgos Diaz, Cindy Cheng, Meredith Gadsby, Rachael Joo, Wendy Kozol, Pablo Mitchell, Sergio Negron, Tamika Nunley, Gina Perez, Celine Shimizu, Ann Sherif, Len Smith, Danielle Terrazas Williams, Judy Wu, and David Yoo. Thank you to the students of CAST 200, Fall 2021, who read and gave their generous feedback on a nearly final version of the book. From start to finish, I worked on this book about Los Angeles while employed at Oberlin College, in Ohio, and though I was far away from my subject, I was lucky to be surrounded by students and colleagues whose curiosity, energy, and creativity sustained my engagement and ability to see this project through. Jeong Hyung Hwang deserves special acknowledgement for his help translating Korean-language material. I received institutional support from Oberlin College in the form of a paid research sabbatical, and despite its interruption by a global pandemic, this was critical for bringing the book to completion. Thank you to Pam Snyder, David Kamitsuka, and Marvin Krislov for the help. I would also like to give special mention to my colleagues in the Comparative American Studies and History Departments, and especially Gina Perez and Wendy Kozol, two models for how to sustain productive scholarly careers while working at a liberal arts college. I've learned so much from Gina and Wendy's selflessness and collegiality and can only hope that I am able to return a small fraction of what I have received from them.

Thank you to Gordon Chang and Margo Irvin at Stanford University Press for their support and enthusiasm. Being included in the Asian America series feels as though we are closing a circle in my academic journey that started when I entered graduate school in 1998 to study with Gordon in the History Department at Stanford. His influence runs through this work, and I just hope it does justice to the tremendous series he has built. Working with Stanford also allowed me to follow Margo from another press, where she was an editor on a previous book. It has been a pleasure getting to work again with such a capable, knowledgeable, and professional editor.

Though there is nothing directly autobiographical in this book, it is the most personal work I have written, so I finish these acknowledgements with overwhelming feelings of gratitude for my family and the greater Korean American community. The person I thought about most as I wrote this was my mother, Vicky Lee (Cha Bok-Hee) who came to the United States in 1978 at the age of twenty-six, married with two young children. She remains my hero, my model of grit and resilience, and the person whose respect I still strive to earn. She also helped me with translations of Korean-language material, so this book was also collaboration with her. Thank you, *eomma*.

Rick and Kaya Baldoz were there throughout and sacrificed the most. They traveled with me to Los Angeles numerous times, gave me their blessing to go on writing retreats, and bolstered my resolve to keep going. I often worried that my work, and this book especially, took too much out of everyone, so for that reason I am very glad this is done. I will continue to try to find the words to express what they mean to me and the depth my gratitude, but for now *sarang-hae* will have to suffice.

Koreatown, Los Angeles

Introduction

On Thursday, October 13, 1983, a warm and fair fall day in Los Angeles, the Southern California Korean Grocery and Liquor Retailers Association held its first annual awards banquet at the Ambassador Hotel. Formed the previous November with forty-two charter members, the association was growing rapidly and by 1986 had 1,089 members.[1] In attendance at the banquet was a veritable who's who of local officials and Korean American community leaders, including the city councilman David Cunningham, the state assemblyman Mike Roos, the association's president Yang Il Kim (who went on to be the president of the National Korean American Grocers Association), and the Korean American Coalition (KAC) president Tong Soo Chung.

Among the meeting's notable aspects was its setting. The Ambassador Hotel, located at 3400 Wilshire Boulevard, was a relic of the golden age of Hollywood, originally opening in 1921 and becoming a favorite spot for movie industry luminaries. Its association with glamour and celebrities, however, had faded by the 1950s, as the mid-Wilshire area entered a period of decline amid white and capital flight to the suburbs. Nonetheless, the Ambassador remained a recognized Los Angeles institution and event venue, though tragedy would attach to its legacy in 1968 when the Democratic presidential hopeful Robert F. Kennedy was assassinated in the hotel's kitchen during a victory celebration for the California primary. Over the next few years, the Ambassador sat like a haunted behemoth, a reminder of the glory days of the 1920s and 1930s as well as the turbulent events of the late 1960s. While the public's awareness of the hotel and concern for the struggles of central Los Angeles waned, the Ambassador became a locational anchor for the growing Korean immigrant community due to its location, which by the mid-1970s people were calling Koreatown.

The president of another recently formed group, the KAC, Tong Soo Chung, a young activist and student at UCLA law school, spoke at the banquet about the potential of Korean retailers to do good, not just for their own pocketbooks but also for the local communities they served. Estimating that Koreans controlled 30 to 40 percent of the retail market in groceries and liquor in Southern California, he said, "Your judicious exercise of control over purchasing power and shelf space can be directly translated into economic gains for you." With this presence and power, Chung thought retailers could play a decisive role in the advancement of Korean Americans in Los Angeles's social and civic life. "KAC and Korean retailers can set the pattern for the rest of the Korean community in creating unity and working together," he said.[2] Chung called on Korean retailers to think and act beyond their business ambitions, which he felt were overly fixated on climbing the ladder into wholesale, distribution, and manufacturing. They should also consider creating or participating in "fair share" programs— similar to those found in the Black community—in partnership with community members.

Chung also stressed the pivotal role that retailers could play in relations between Koreans and Blacks in Los Angeles. These communities, he said, "have a great deal to offer each other and [can] learn and benefit from each other." With Korean-owned shops opening throughout Southern California, including in impoverished inner-city neighborhoods with disproportionate concentrations of Blacks, the Korean merchant and Black customer had become by 1983 figurative stand-ins for Korean-Black relations more generally. As non-whites and recent immigrants, Chung pointed out, Koreans had a debt to pay African Americans. He thanked "black Americans for their civil rights struggle in the last 30 years, which has made America a better place to live for all Americans, including Korean immigrants . . . Without their sacrifices and struggles, you and I, the Korean immigrants of today, could not possibly enjoy the civil rights and freedom of activity as we do." The struggle was ongoing, however, so Chung expressed his wish that "Korean and black communities will join forces to make America a better place to live for all of us."

The wistful and hopeful notes of Chung's remarks contrasted with worrying local developments likely on the minds of some attendees. Koreans and Blacks might have shared a status as racial minorities in Los Angeles, but their encounters were also mediated by their distinct identities and structural positions that could fuel antagonism instead of affinity: merchant versus customer, foreigner versus American, non-Black versus Black. Stories of shoplifting, accusations of shoplifting, rude store owners, rude customers, robberies, assault by customers, and assault by store workers circulated and raised people's guards. Korean merchants reported being frightened to go to work. Black residents complained Koreans were draining their already strapped and vulnerable communities. Chung aligned himself with other Korean and Black activists appealing for interracial solidarity and cooperation and hoped this outreach to retailers would prompt introspection and action to reduce the tensions and reframe Korean-Black relations around their shared struggles and concerns.

That Chung was delivering these comments at a retailers' conference attended by local power players in what had become a gathering place for Korean America's elites reflected the contradictory positions that Korean Americans held. As they pursued their personal fortunes, distinguished themselves as entrepreneurs, and built Koreatown, they were extolled for proving that the American dream was still in reach for anyone. Or as a 1985 headline in the *Wall Street Journal* stated, "The American Dream Is Alive and Well in Koreatown."[3] Their achievements were all the more notable at a time when the working poor—particularly the African American working poor—was losing ground economically. Relations between Korean merchants and Black customers, and between the Korean and Black communities more generally, might be pressing in the face of a concerning event or negative story, but they could otherwise be treated as incidental to the greater cause of generating profit and accumulating capital.

Koreatown, Los Angeles seeks to tell a story of Korean Americans against larger stories of Los Angeles and the United States during the late twentieth century. Korean Americans, until after the 1960s a very small group even within the Asian American population, have grown their numbers markedly in recent decades with new immigration. Though often equated with socioeconomic achievement and assimilation, their experiences as racial minorities and immigrant outsiders illuminate key economic and cultural developments in the United States since 1965. *Koreatown, Los Angeles* examines the social and cultural history of Korean Americans in the city and includes the perspectives of US-born Koreans and non-Koreans, government officials, local activists, other minorities, and the media. It argues that building Koreatown was an urgent objective for Korean immigrants and US-born Koreans eager to carve out a spatial niche within Los Angeles to serve as an economic and social anchor for their growing community. More than a dot on a map, Koreatown was also an idea and a set of aspirations, and for Koreans all over the United States, it held profound emotional significance as a symbol of their shared bonds and place in US society. At the same time, Korean Americans' lives were constrained and shaped by external factors such as the global aspirations of Los Angeles, patterns of racial segregation and urban poverty, and legacies of anti-Asian racism and orientalism. Koreatown, as with all communities, was an inward and outward facing entity, formed by what it meant for others as well as notes the needs it served for Korean people.

Koreatown, Los Angeles explores well-trodden themes in Asian American history, such as migration, belonging, citizenship, and racism. Its chronological focus sets it apart from the existing scholarship in that it deals with immigrants arriving after 1965. This focus allows it to highlight Korean American figures that have received scant scholarly attention, from the journalist K. W. Lee to real estate investor Sonia Suk. The book also contextualizes its subjects against a broader national backdrop of cultural malaise, urban turmoil, liberal multiculturalism, and economic transition. These contextual considerations shape the book's interests in intraethnic relations; Korean Americans' pursuit of economic and political power in a post–civil-rights-movement, postindustrial society; Koreatown's meanings as a spatial community and emotional home for diasporic Koreans; and the strategic and fraught position of Koreans in a city coming into its own as a global metropolis.

The book consists of six chapters that are topically and chronologically organized. The first provides an overview of Korean immigration to Los Angeles, situating the phenomenon against a larger surge of post-1965 immigration in the wake of legislative reform and growing social and economic malaise in the United States. The second chapter examines the birth and development of Koreatown in the 1970s and 1980s with respect to the leadership of immigrant place entrepreneurs and their ambitions for ethnic and commercial dominance in the area. The third chapter considers Korean immigration from the point of view of the "BK" (before Koreatown) or

Americanized Koreans who felt distanced from the newcomers but were otherwise profoundly transformed by their presence. The fourth chapter discusses how Los Angeles's bid for economic growth and urban renown as a global city created opportunities and dilemmas for Korean Americans. The fifth chapter examines Korean-Black relations in South Central LA, the escalating of anti-Korean sentiment, and the destruction of Koreatown and Korean-owned businesses in the Los Angeles uprising of 1992. The final chapter traces how Korean Americans resolutely "moved on" by rebuilding Koreatown and leaving South Central.

Throughout its chapters, the book underscores and examines the ironies and extremes of experience that have characterized Korean American history since 1965. In a time of growing wealth inequality and diminishing opportunities, the example of Korean small business entrepreneurs purportedly showed that the American dream still worked, but the destruction of their businesses in the 1992 uprising showed how those dreams were intertwined with larger questions of racial conflict, uneven development, and political power. Koreatown has been a neighborhood development initiative, a rallying symbol for people desiring a sense of community, a marker of recognition, a concentration of unwelcome foreign intruders, a phoenix rising from the ashes, and a reminder of political voicelessness despite neighborhood visibility. The book follows Korean Americans through these trials and tribulations and reveals how their story reflects the promises and pitfalls of the immigrant narrative and valorization of the American dream.

With its chronological focus from the late 1960s to early 2000s the book joins the growing works of historical scholarship on the recent past. Moreover, its attention to Korean Americans sheds light on the experiences of a group in the Asian American population that has been understudied compared to Chinese and Japanese. Further, *Koreatown, Los Angeles* takes a historical approach to understanding the emergence of "global" cities and the importance of Pacific connections and Asian immigration in their rise and transformations, interests that also informed my first monograph on Japanese in Seattle. Explaining connections between local experience and global connections has been a salient concern in the social sciences and has animated much of the research about Asian migrants. Concepts like the *Pacific world* or *global city* for understanding conditions in the twentieth century have been important in the study of political economies and international diplomacy but have been less central in domestic histories of US migration and race relations, particularly for the mid-twentieth century onward.

This book illustrates some distinct joys and challenges of researching and writing about the recent past. While many of the historical events recounted in *Koreatown, Los Angeles* have been and continue to be preserved and cataloged in institutional archives—particularly as they concern the 1992 uprising and the mayorship of Tom Bradley—I have also gone "outside the archive" and relied on interviews, obscure memoirs, and online sources. Moreover, for the historian trying to make sense of the 1970s to 1990s, contemporaneous social science research—of which a great deal exists about Korean immigrants—comprises remarkably rich primary material. As far as the content and analysis in the chapters that follow, I have chosen to prioritize narratives and to present a multifaceted story of Korean Americans told from different points of view. Invariably because of those choices and the fact that the book is not an exhaustive history of Korean Americans, some perspectives, organizations, and histories will not be reflected. Hopefully, however, the reader will find a cogent yet complex story that sheds light on the recent history of US immigration, the unique aspects of Korean American experience, and the troubled times of the late twentieth century.

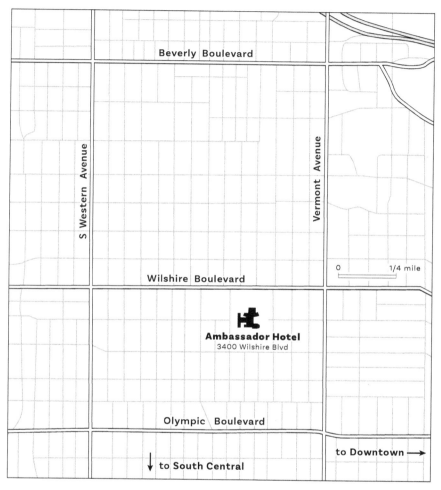

MAP 1   This map shows Koreatown, Los Angeles, and the location of the
Ambassador Hotel, an "old Hollywood" which was built in 1921 and subsequently
became an important meeting venue for the Korean community by the 1970s. The
Ambassador closed in 1989 and was demolished in 2005.

CHAPTER I

The Changing Face of LA

LIKE HIS NATIVE KOREA, David Hyun seemed to have lived several lives in the course of a few decades. Born in Seoul in 1917, he was the son of Reverend Soon Hyun, a leading activist in the movement to liberate Korea from Japanese control. In 1924, after five years in Shanghai, home of the Korean Provisional Government protest state, the family went to Hawaii, where a sizeable Korean community existed. Hyun labored on sugar plantations and pineapple canneries, graduated from the University of Hawaii, and during World War II worked for the US Army Corps of Engineers. In 1947 he moved to Los Angeles and spent much of the 1950s and 1960s fighting deportation orders stemming from charges that he was an alien subversive and member of the Communist Party. Hyun's persecution, which he originally attributed to his stint as a labor activist in Hawaii in the 1940s, escalated with the Korean War (1950–1953) and Syngman Rhee's rise to the presidency (1948–1960) of the newly formed Republic of Korea. In general, the 1950s and 1960s were precarious times for immigrants from nations that became Communist, as they could come under intense scrutiny by the US government. Hyun, however, faced additional danger because he came from a prominent family with outspoken critics of the Rhee regime, so had good reason to fear harsh punishment if deported to Korea. Pro–civil liberties and leftist groups, most notably the Los Angeles Committee for the Protection of the Foreign Born, assisted Hyun in his fight to stay in the United States, which stretched over sixteen years and became a progressive cause célèbre.[1]

8

While he was fighting deportation, David Hyun embarked on a career in architecture and entrenched himself in his adopted city of Los Angeles. By the time the INS withdrew its case against him in 1966, he was an established architect with his own firm and an essayist with expansive literary interests. The late 1960s to 1980s brought another set of profound changes to Hyun's life. New immigration, globalization, and urban redevelopment were transforming Los Angeles and in the process Hyun's own outlook as a Korean, Asian American, and architect. With his characteristic grandiosity and sense of historical gravity, he wrote in 1983 that these forces had made Los Angeles nothing short of an "East-West Ethnic Miracle." And as one of the fastest growing immigrant communities connected to one of East Asia's most rapidly developing economies, the city's Korean residents held a key position in this "wondrous meeting."[2] Hyun also noted that, in contrast to the Chinese and Japanese immigrants of the late nineteenth and early twentieth centuries, modern-day Korean immigrants were "no longer stifled in ghettos." Instead, they were making a positive impact on the city, even "[reversing] urban decay . . . without federal aid." Through their labor contributions, business activities, and civic engagement, Hyun predicted, Korean immigrants would enrich the city, promote US–South Korean trade, and encourage investment, in turn, making Los Angeles "the greatest cosmopolitan metropolis of the world—a gateway for the passage of trade, goods, culture, and peoples."

Hyun's voice was distinct, given his tendency to fold his life story and saga of the Korean people into commentaries about Los Angeles's remarkable demographic and economic trajectory, but he was far from the only one noticing and seeking to make sense of the astonishing changes in the city. As one April 1980 *Los Angeles Times* article title proclaimed, "Exploding Ethnic Populations" were "Changing the Face of LA." Immigration to the United States had been rising following implementation of the Hart-Celler Act of 1965, which abolished a restrictive and racist system that favored northern and western Europeans and effectively excluded Asians. Under the new system, annual immigration reached unprecedented heights and was dominated by newcomers from Latin America and Asia.[3] "By the thousands they have come," wrote Richard Meyer in the *Los Angeles Times*, "Rosarios, and Liens and Sus."[4] Having overtaken New York as the leading immigrant port of entry, Los Angeles was anointed the "melting pot of the 1980s" and the "new Ellis Island."[5] Related to its rise as a preeminent urban melting pot was the city's emergence as a leading hub of the globalizing economy, especially in the Asia-Pacific region.

The reactions to these developments varied, with optimism and excitement on one end, as captured in David Hyun's essay. On the other end were more sobering and concerning views. For example, in 1979, a representative at the Los Angeles County assessor's office sounded alarm over foreign companies' increased development of and investments in downtown properties, warning that should trends continue, "U.S. firms would find themselves crowded out of key locations, would lose business, and ultimately have to eliminate jobs."[6] Meanwhile, on the subject of immigration, a reader of the *Los Angeles Sentinel*, the city's largest Black newspaper, bemoaned what they deemed a foreign "takeover" of parts of the city, reserving special ire for Korean business owners. "The Korean people have taken over Olympic Blvd." remarked the reader, "and their signs are out there to let you know. You would think you are in a foreign country."[7]

This chapter examines aspects of the "changing face of LA" in the 1970s and early 1980s with regard to immigration, globalization, and urban conditions, arguing that these forces profoundly altered daily life in the city and resulted in a newfound prominence for the growing Korean community. These were very fluid and unsettled years in the nation and world, which saw the end of a sustained period of economic prosperity after World War II. This chapter describes how Americans endured these difficult times, the critical adaptations made in the public and private sectors, and how those adjustments meshed with the shifting politics of race and ethnicity. Along with the rest of the nation, Angelenos entered the late twentieth century committed to a neoliberal economic and ideological order in which they could extol racial and ethnic diversity, accede to the existence of class inequality, and pledge allegiance to the private sector. In these circumstances, the Korean immigrants settling in Los Angeles seemed remarkably well-suited to the times and its challenges. Not only did they contribute to the diversity evoked in discussions about the "changing face of LA" but they also showed adaptability in the face of hardship, a knack for entrepreneurship, and an abiding belief in the American dream, which intrigued and awed observers.

Bad Times

Immigration after 1965 surged amid recession, and magnifying Americans' sense of calamity during these years was the stark contrast to the preceding era. The years from 1947 to 1973 bookended the most sustained period of economic growth in world history, during which millions of Americans prospered. Their incomes rose, they joined the middle class in un-precedented numbers, and they enjoyed improved standards of living in their new suburban subdivisions. Factors underpinning and sustaining the golden era of economic growth included US dominance in manufacturing, the availability of abundant and inexpensive energy, and an understanding between labor and management of the mutual benefits of free trade and growing exports. The expansion of social welfare, driven especially by poli-cies of the New Deal and Great Society, helped bring poverty to its lowest level of 11.1 percent in 1973.[8]

By contrast, the United States that immigrants of the late sixties and sev-enties entered was in the throes of deindustrialization and stagnation. The economic statistics of the 1970s were sobering. In 1971, for the first time since the nineteenth century, the United States became a net importer, largely re-maining that way since. The national economy never recaptured its buoy-ancy of the 1940s to 1960s, with GDP growth either sluggish or negative.[9] As Barry Bluestone explains, a "near complete collapse in the rate of productivity growth" occurred, with output per US worker declining across industries.[10] The end of the decade brought little relief. The second quarter of 1980 saw the steepest decline in GNP in history, and in 1982, unemployment reached 10.8 percent, the highest monthly level since the Great Depression. The 1970s endured an unrelenting barrage of setbacks, with two oil crises, runaway inflation, and several deep recessions. The economic orthodoxy that mod-eled an inverse relationship between inflation and unemployment faltered under stagflation when both remained high.[11] Skyrocketing prices and long gas lines—two especially indelible associations with the 1970s economy—underscored how dependent Americans had become on cheap imported oil and the unsustainability of a "good life" built on automobiles and massive suburban sprawl.[12] Many of the cultural references and argot of the 1970s also underscored the era's malaise. President Jimmy Carter, for instance, told Americans that they were having a "crisis of confidence," and a prominent economist developed a tool called the "misery index." The era's popular cin-ema—in movies like *Taxi Driver*, *The Warriors*, and *Death Wish*—presented pessimistic and violent perspectives on American life.

US producers were losing ground in durable manufacturing—the "metal banging" sectors—to countries like Japan and Germany. Japan's industri-alization, which would have enormous implications for Los Angeles, re-lied significantly on US support and investment after World War II. By the

1960s, it was in the midst of a "postwar economic miracle," and the following decade, some of its industries were competing directly with US producers. No longer was US steel king. Nor could consumers be confident that RCA made the best televisions or that Maytag produced the highest quality dishwashers. As if to concede defeat, companies laid off workers in droves, shuttered their plants, and relocated operations where cheap and nonunionized labor was available.

In this globally competitive environment, ordinary working people suffered disproportionately. Barry Bluestone estimates that private disinvestment in industry and relocation resulted in the disappearance of thirty-two to thirty-eight million jobs in the 1970s.[13] Manufacturing employment, once a reliable path into middle-class security, peaked in 1979 and declined precipitously thereafter. The growth of real wages, to which Americans had grown accustomed since World War II, halted and then drifted downward over the 1970s and 1980s, never returning to their 1973 peak.[14] Unemployment nearly doubled between 1973 to 1975, reaching 8.3 percent, and by 1982, 15 percent of Americans lived in poverty. As their purchasing power diminished and improvements in the standard of living lagged, families had to adjust to new norms, such as all adults working outside the home.

No regions were spared by the economic downturns. The industrial heartland of the Northeast and Midwest saw the decimation of its manufacturing industries while the Sunbelt and West bore nearly half of all job losses.[15] Los Angeles also experienced the turbulent decade's extremes. It had been an economic powerhouse from the 1940s to early 1960s, home to a large industrial manufacturing base as well as entertainment, food processing, and furniture production, among other sectors. According to historian Josh Sides, by 1963, only Chicago produced more.[16] Thus, when a wave of closures during the 1970s and 1980s hit such major Los Angeles employers as BF Goodrich, Norris Industries, and Goodyear, the effects were widespread and devastating.[17]

Compounding matters and impeding recovery were cuts in federal funding for social welfare programs and the hobbling of organized labor. From the New Deal to the Great Society, the federal government increased its spending to provide Americans with jobs, services, and other forms of direct assistance. It also passed legislation protecting labor unions. These measures, economists and policymakers argued, lifted the entire economy by boosting productivity and consumption, but the scarcity of the 1970s chipped away at support for them or anything that threatened the wealth of the private sector. Taxes would become a particular target. The priorities of the state then, by the end of the 1970s, were to reduce social welfare spending and unshackle businesses from regulations. In this environment, unions—often blamed for the high costs of labor—were crushed, and priorities such as expanding public housing fell by the wayside. Some cities increased their spending to offset federal cutbacks, but Los Angeles was not one of those, as its government did not contribute revenue to programs for the poor. Thus, already underserved communities—the elderly, homeless, and jobless—found themselves even worse off.

In this time of economic setback and social change, blue-collar African Americans experienced the one-two punch of race and class disadvantage. Many had achieved mobility and security through manufacturing and defense jobs, but these gains proved fleeting when they were disproportionately targeted by layoffs. In light of their long and incomplete struggle against employment discrimination, the materializing of the adage "last hired, first fired" was especially cruel and painful.

Racial segregation in metropolitan areas and the spatial concentration of poverty intensified from the 1960s and would both guide and haunt Los Angeles's development. Across the nation, middle-class Americans—whites, upwardly mobile Blacks, and others—fled central cities for the suburbs, leaving behind urban populations that grew poorer, Blacker, and Browner. These communities faced severe disadvantages in adapting to an economy transitioning from producing goods to services (discussed in the next section). Trapped in cities where nodes of administration and information exchange replaced centers of manufacturing, residents lacked access to the education and training necessary to lift them out of their circumstances.

Los Angeles's population from the 1960s on was a paradox, becoming simultaneously more segregated and diverse. As the *Los Angeles Sentinel* put it in 1971, "Minorities' Influx Continues as Whites Leave."[18] During the 1960s, the number of "non-Anglos" doubled to reach a third of the county's population—with pronounced growth among Asians, Blacks, Latinos, and Native Americans—while the white population decreased from 81 to 68 percent of the county. This trend foretold emerging patterns of racial and ethnic segregation, as well as the ravaging economic repercussions of the 1970s and 1980s. The closure of auto, rubber, tire, and steel plants in South Central and the Alameda corridor devastated African American households whose livelihoods depended on the manufacturing industries. In the predominantly Black South-Central area, unemployment rose by nearly 50 percent and purchasing power dropped by a third over the 1970s and 1980s.[19] Meanwhile, rates of criminality, teenage pregnancy, and other social problems rose above those of the general population.

Outbreaks of civil unrest in US cities during the 1960s brought national attention to Black urban poverty, isolation, and disfranchisement, but ultimately, these crises would be a lost opportunity to understand and alleviate problems of systemic inequality. In Los Angeles, the Watts uprising of 1965 climaxed mounting local frustrations toward police and greedy merchants amid growing poverty. In its wake, middle-class flight accelerated, and parts of South Los Angeles continued their descent as a "deindustrialized twilight zone,"[20] where, in the words of William Julius Wilson, only the "truly disadvantaged" remained.[21]

Renewal and Restructuring

The setbacks discussed above might have suggested that US capitalism was in a crisis, but the end of the 1970s showed that it was remarkably adaptable and resilient. With the rising costs of labor and production and emerging competition from imports, how would US companies continue to grow, expand their markets, and generate earnings? As mentioned, a solution to reduce expenditures and recover profits was to relocate plants where wages and regulations were less burdensome (i.e., out of city centers and into the suburbs, the Sunbelt, or abroad). Those unable to meet the challenges had little choice but to shut down. From one vantage point, such actions were signs of crisis; but from another—and this became clear over time—they were part of an adjustment, or restructuring, of capitalism.

Among the most significant aspects of economic restructuring were the international fragmentation of production and internal reconfiguration of labor. To stay competitive against emerging powerhouses like Germany and Japan, some US companies shifted their production offshore to the developing world. Two of those developing countries, South Korea and Taiwan, achieved remarkable economic growth and industrialization by the 1970s. Alongside Singapore and Hong Kong, they were called the Four Tigers of Asia. With the balance thrown off again, US companies searched for new sources of cheap overseas labor, finding it in places like Guatemala and Vietnam.

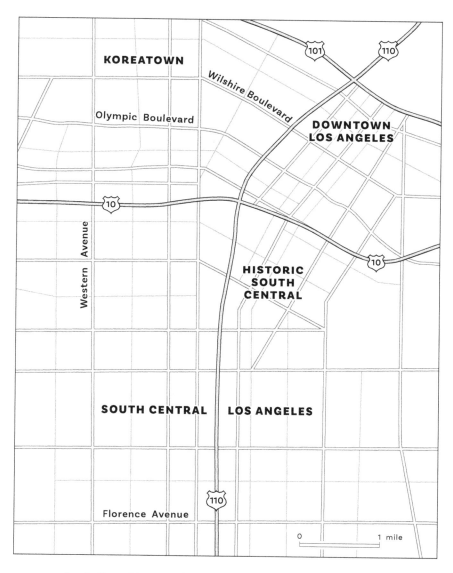

MAP 2 South Central Los Angeles. Neighborhoods in Los Angeles that became known by the 1980s as South Central, which is distinct from Historic South Central. South Central referred to dozens of neighborhoods, including Crenshaw, Watts, and West Adams, in a vast sixteen-square-mile area south of the 10.

Los Angeles underwent both deindustrialization and what Josh Sides has called "re-industrialization," and entered the 1980s as an exemplar of postindustrial adaptation. The decline of durable manufacturing entailed massive job losses but was offset to a degree by a strong aerospace industry and the creation of jobs in high-tech and nondurable production (e.g., apparel, food).[22] As Manuel Pastor noted, Los Angeles was "bleeding good jobs"; unionized positions with good pay, security, and benefits disappeared and were replaced by low-wage jobs with none of those advantages.[23] Reflecting the declining fortunes of blue-collar workers was the drop in unionization among manufacturing employees from 34 percent in 1971 to 19 percent in 1987.[24] Between 1990 and 2005, Los Angeles County lost over 40 percent of its manufacturing jobs, but in nondurable manufacturing, employment rose from 34.4 to 44.1 percent.[25] The rise of immigration coincided with this transition, and employers found new arrivals from Latin America and Asia to be cheap and easy to exploit. As a result, they held many of the jobs in the growing manufacturing sectors. For example, they quickly became the backbone of LA's garment workforce, ironically making goods to compete with products from Mexico, Hong Kong, and China.[26] Employers also hired immigrants to perform service jobs in restaurants, hotels, and corporate offices. Because of their dominance in low-wage industries and vulnerability against unscrupulous companies (especially the undocumented), immigrants fueled what was effectively the "third world sector" of the US economy.[27]

Rounding out the workforce were white-collar professionals. In an economic system dedicated to generating and expanding market shares, developing plants and equipment and growing productive capacity were not the only ways to pursue these ends. Companies could also create and harness innovations in technology, organization, and finance. These approaches underpinned the rise of the high-tech and financial services industries, which relied on an educated professional and managerial class. The rise of financial services signaled a transformation in which speculation replaced industrial production as an economic driver, making *mergers, takeovers, debt,* and *bonds* the lingo of growth. It also made bankers, fund managers, and traders with specialized knowledge integral to the entire economy. As the professional and managerial classes expanded, so did their demand for services that would be met by low-paid immigrant workers who cleaned offices and homes, tended gardens, and cared for children. The skilled blue-collar sector, meanwhile, continued to languish.

Complementing Los Angeles's pursuit of global prominence was a turn in local politics in which leaders staked the city's well-being on downtown revitalization. From about the 1940s, "urban renewal" spread as a mantra in US cities struggling with an exodus of downtown retail and commerce, growing concentrations of poor people, and physical blight. A common vision of midcentury urban renewal, as shown by historian Alison Isenberg, was presented in 1955 by Jim Downs at the International Downtown Executives Association (IDEA) conference. The goal, he said, was "to raise the number and quality of the people that are downtown."[28] Toward this end, downtown associations worked to develop "better markets" that would keep businesses from leaving or would lure them back. Better markets, moreover, usually referred to those white middle-class consumers who were fleeing for the suburbs.[29]

In Los Angeles, the Community Redevelopment Agency (CRA), formed in 1948, undertook dozens of projects that changed the face of the city. The CRA and similar agencies elsewhere were public-private entities arising from the belief that either sector alone could not solve the problem of urban blight. Nor could a federal agency, as deterioration and housing required the direction only a local agency could provide. Typically, the CRA would adopt a development area identified as blighted, and then acquire and prepare the land for improvement. Improvement often meant evicting tenants and demolishing buildings, which the CRA had the legislative and financial authority to do. Such work cleared costly obstacles that would have deterred private investors, who were now more likely to be interested in the parcels to build offices, retail space, and condominiums, and the CRA could sell these below market value. The first project the CRA undertook was Bunker Hill, a once wealthy neighborhood that by the 1930s had become one of the city's most run-down areas, and then by the late 1960s was reborn as a signal achievement of downtown redevelopment.

After years of delay due to political deadlock and litigation, redevelopment in Los Angeles entered its boom period, from the mid-1970s through 1980s, when the CRA "was able to influence the scope and direction of development in Los Angeles—offering attractive investment opportunities to private sector interests, low-cost housing developments to affordable housing advocates, and showcase projects to pro-growth politicians."[30] The redevelopment boom owed to several decisive factors, including the 1972 mayoral election of Tom Bradley. Bradley aspired to turn Los Angeles into a world-class city, which he believed hinged on downtown redevelopment, especially commercial development. Another factor was the 1965 Watts uprising, after which retailers and city leaders rallied around the imperative to "save" downtown from further ruin by unruly Blacks.[31] The CRA's mandate subsequently encompassed all of downtown, and the agency enjoyed broad support from Democrats and Republicans alike and a coalition that included organized labor. In the decade after Bradley's election, almost $2.5 billion of new investments poured into downtown projects supervised by the CRA.

Though the CRA was a government agency charged with serving the public interest, its priorities leaned toward businesses and commercial development, particularly from the 1970s and 1980s. The appointed board members were invariably people in good standing with the business community. During the pro-growth Bradley years, the City Council and Mayor's Office, argues Mike Davis, effectively abdicated their oversight on redevelopment to the CRA and Department of City Planning. As policies such as Richard Nixon's moratorium on nearly all federal housing subsidies and redevelopment programs, Ronald Reagan's permanent cuts to the Section 8 housing program, and California's Prop 13 sharply reduced public funding for redevelopment, the CRA turned to financing methods that further alienated local communities and the public good. Of particular importance was something called tax increment financing. By this method, the assessed value of taxable property in a redevelopment area at the time of adoption served as a baseline. For the duration of the project, taxing entities could not collect property taxes above the benchmark even if the value appreciated. In other words, this baseline limited the taxes a city could collect on an area even as its value rose. That additional revenue—tax increments—went straight to the CRA to pay debts incurred in the redevelopment process and subsidize further development.[32]

By its measures, CRA was extraordinarily successful, though it also drew criticism. By 2004 its projects encompassed more than twenty-one thousand acres (7 percent of the city's land area) and raised assessed valuations by more than $10.5 billion, mostly from downtown appreciation.[33] Los Angeles's modern skyline is an achievement of the CRA, as are numerous retail and entertainment establishments, housing, hotels, parks, and aesthetic improvements. In 1959, Bunker Hill was contributing just $463,000 per year in property taxes, and by 2004, it was generating $4.4 million in tax increments and raised its assessed valuation fortyfold.[34] Critics of increment financing and the CRA assailed what they called a "plush welfare state" for business and private developers.[35] Others, touting the banner of "slow growth," lambasted the rapid cycles of adoption, development, and sales encouraged by the CRA. For example, downtown redevelopment resulted in nearly a third of the land changing hands between 1976 and 1982.[36]

The prominence of international capital in Los Angeles gave it an outsize influence in downtown redevelopment and the city's economic rebound. Becoming a global city, explains sociologist Jan Lin, represented "one vaunted route out of deindustrialization and urban decline."[37] Seizing the opportunity of a relatively weakened US dollar, foreign investors acquired holdings in US companies and real estate. By the late 1970s, firms headquartered in countries from the Netherlands to Curacao had poured hundreds of millions of dollars into downtown Los Angeles, so much that by 1987 foreign companies controlled as much as 90 percent of the area. Some of the most high-profile transactions involved Japan, such as the purchase of the forty-two-story Crocker Plaza by Mitsui Fudosan, a subsidiary of Mitsui Real Estate Development Company, for $79 million. Flush with liquid resources from their country's massive trade surplus with the United States, Japanese companies and investors led a "tsunami of East Asian finance and flight capital" into Los Angeles. Other major transactions included the 1974 Bank of Tokyo purchase of the Lincoln Savings & Loan building and Mitsubishi's contribution to financing the construction of the landmark Bonaventure Hotel, which opened in 1976.[38]

By the 1980s, Los Angeles embodied the contradictions of economic restructuring and postindustrialism. On the one hand, its "yen-fueled highrise developments" represented the stunning wealth in the city. On the other hand, run-down, neglected, and overcrowded neighborhoods highlighted the unequal distribution of this wealth. As commercial buildings and luxury condos replaced dilapidated housing stock, available and affordable units fell far short of the demand. Los Angeles already had a poor track record on public housing, having failed to build any new units since the 1950s, and in the 1980s conditions worsened with drastic cutbacks in federal support for Section 8 housing. To be sure, housing was a concern for the CRA, which spent more than $330 million of Bunker Hill tax increments to construct or rehabilitate over fourteen thousand affordable housing units. All told, redevelopment helped to produce over twenty-eight thousand units of affordable housing citywide, but this was not nearly enough to meet the need.[39] Nor was the city able to adequately house its growing immigrant population. People had few options but to cram into older Black and Chicano neighborhoods, forming "a continuous ring of slum housing around Downtown."[40]

Development often started from the unexamined and insidious assumption that whiteness raised property values while non-whites, especially Blacks, degraded them. "Redevelopers," explains Alison Isenberg, claimed they were saving "a downtown under siege—threatened by a surrounding 'ring' of blight associated with the much-discussed migration into cities of poor African Americans, Puerto Ricans, Native Americans, and Appalachian whites."[41] They fostered the fear that without aggressive urban renewal, downtown districts would become "lower class ethnic islands" of "inferior forms of commerce."[42] While the dominant response to the Watts uprising was a strengthened commitment to protecting downtown against Black encroachment, the disturbance did raise awareness about the deficient state of retail in impoverished minority communities. The economist Frederick Sturdivant called for an "investment guarantee" to draw large retailers like JCPenney and Sears into areas deemed "abnormal risks."[43] Ultimately, the city and developers showed little interest in putting resources into Watts, Compton, South Central or any other part of Black Los Angeles. Aside from a shopping complex near Watts, the CRA neglected the Black neighborhoods in South Los Angeles. It instead helped to destroy the Crenshaw Shopping Center, the leading retail district for the Black community, by granting redevelopment subsidies for the construction of Fox Hill Plaza, which was located on the neighborhood's periphery.[44]

Factoring Race and Ethnicity

The racially polarizing and detrimental forces of restructured capitalism might have been mitigated by the progressive impulses of the labor and civil rights movements. After all, Americans disavowed the overt racism of Jim Crow and codified this in such landmark laws and court decisions as *Brown v. Board (1954)*, the Civil Rights Acts of 1964 and 1965, and the Fair Housing Act of 1968. Further, underpinning reforms like affirmative action, public housing, and free childcare programs of the 1960s was the idea that the state should ensure the equality, rights, and welfare of its citizens. A heightened value placed on racial and ethnic representation and minority participation touched numerous facets of life, from television programming with multiracial casts (e.g., *Star Trek*) to the election of an unprecedented number of Black mayors in large cities, starting with Carl Stokes in Cleveland in 1967 (and including Tom Bradley's victory in Los Angeles). If the hard-fought progress toward racial equality—or at least the championing of the idea—could not be easily ignored or rolled back, then the principle of equal opportunity could be harmonized with the capitalistic imperatives of profit and productivity.

In the dizzying age of civil rights reform during the 1960s, immigration policy too came under scrutiny. Lawmakers said the Hart-Celler Act was a necessary moral corrective to a legacy of state-sanctioned xenophobia; President Lyndon Johnson proclaimed it would "repair a very deep and painful flaw in the fabric of the American Nation." Economic and political priorities also necessitated reform. Maintaining a nativist system discredited US leadership in the fight against global Communism and made hypocrites of the US companies with operations and investments in the countries that were subject to harsh restrictions. Additionally, in the booming postwar economy, the demand for workers with technical and scientific expertise outstripped the domestic supply.[45] For example, health care evolved into an extensive and centralized system of large hospitals and group plans such as Medicaid and Medicare. Meeting a growing population's needs required more medical personnel than was available domestically. Immigrants—doctors from South Korea to nurses from the Philippines—could help to fill the demand.

Signed into law in 1965 and fully taking effect in 1968, the Hart-Celler Act raised the overall annual immigration ceiling to 290,000, with 170,000 allotted to the Eastern Hemisphere and 120,000 to the Western Hemisphere. Eastern Hemisphere nations received up to 20,000 yearly visa slots, to be allocated by a preference system, with most categories favoring family reunification. The principle of family reunification was that resident immigrants long separated from family members should be able to reunite with them.[46] Close relatives of citizens were not subject to the per country quota, and other types of relationships, from adult children of citizens to siblings of permanent residents were tiered within a preference system. Employment preferences ensured that any nonfamily-based immigration would add to the US economy and not hurt American workers' wages.[47] A prospective employer would sponsor the applicant and secure certification from the Department of Labor verifying there were insufficient domestic workers in the field of employment. Those who were considered members of "professions, scientists, and artists of exceptional ability" could bypass the labor certification process.[48]

The predictions that Hart-Celler would result in only minor changes on the volume and origins of immigrants proved wildly off the mark. Moreover, as described earlier, new immigration moved the nation's demographic center of gravity to the West and led to Los Angeles's rise as "the Ellis Island of the 1980s." Researchers and policymakers grappled with the consequences of these shifts. In a published version of a 1982 speech to the Southern California Roundtable at the Los Angeles Chamber of Commerce, Kevin F. McCarthy of the RAND Corporation explained that over the 1970s California had absorbed over two million immigrants and owed half of its population growth to immigration. Though it accounted for just 10 percent of the total US population, the state received nearly 30 percent of newcomers. The prominence of Asians, Central Americans, and Mexicans in this growth put California on track to become the nation's first majority-minority state. Accordingly, McCarthy said that employers should expect immigrants and their children to make up a larger share of the workforce in coming years. Though he cautioned against stereotypes that immigrants drained public coffers, he still worried that in a time of cutbacks, California lacked the resources to support them in their full range of needs. He also warned that continued immigration would strain an already tight job market and create a mismatch between low-skilled immigrants—particularly among refugees and undocumented immigrants—and the rising demand for skilled workers.[49] McCarthy concluded by posing a choice he believed Americans would have to confront:

> Either we decide to let current and future immigrants make it on their own—a decision which may have little effect on most immigrants, but could create the potential for an underclass among the most needy—or we decide to facilitate the adjustment process by providing the necessary services and increasing our taxes. If we decide on the latter, then we risk fostering resentment and conflict among the native born poor who will question why—in a time of economic trouble—immigrants are getting special help while they are not.[50]

Another political and ideological challenge facing Americans was how to balance championing racial equality with the goals of private-sector–led capitalism. The CRA's incorporation of minorities into urban redevelopment was instructive—and ironic—in showing how racial equality could be decoupled from social and economic justice, all without upsetting the interests of business and commerce. In 1972, the CRA pledged its support for affirmative action by signing an agreement with the newly formed American Federation of Minority Contractors (AFMC) that assured equal opportunity to minorities in any jobs, contracts, and services in its jurisdiction. The AFMC was a multiracial organization established with the assistance of city officials that combined existing minority contractors' associations "for mutual gain" and consolidated the following groups: "Indian, Latin-American, blacks, Chinese, Japanese, Korean, and Polynesian."[51] The *Los Angeles Sentinel* said the AFMC's formation accorded with the city's "longtime advocacy . . . of a program to help ethnic groups by recruiting them for city jobs, encouraging them to train for promotions, and recognizing their talents and abilities by appointing citizens of these groups to city boards of citizen commissioners."[52] The agreement between the CRA and AFMC exemplified the institutionalization and incorporation of minority identity in city, county, and state government during the 1970s, often in the form of dedicated offices and liaisons or special commissions on race and intergroup relations. It also represented an unprecedented state responsiveness to and support of historically marginalized groups, all while ensuring that the wheels of private investment and tax revenue kept spinning.

Also illustrating the possibilities and constraints of minority and racial politics during the 1970s was a 1976 state commission on intergroup relations. As with the AFMC, it encouraged people to organize by their racial or ethnic affiliation while also strategically coming together as a minority bloc. It also engaged an ascendant style of minority politics that was potentially transformative but limited in what it could accomplish. The commission was formed under the leadership of Trinidadian-born Lieutenant Governor Mervyn Dymally and was prompted by projections about California's coming majority-minority. If the state's minorities improved their communications and consolidated into one force, he said, they could maximize their influence and "become politically more active and more skillful."[53] Forty-one people representing "Samoans, Filipinos, Chicanos, Japanese, Chinese, Koreans, Vietnamese, Blacks, Lebanese, Arabs, Greeks, Irish,

Native American Indians, East Indians, Cambodians, Laotians, Costa Ricans, Guatemalans, Puerto Ricans, Guyanese [*sic*], Jamaicans, Italians, Jews, Armenians, as well as persons from nations in Africa and South America," gathered to discuss issues such as data collection, educational opportunities, and immigration. Despite the interest and attention the commission's creation generated, leaders were careful to point out that it would not spend any public funds or seek any funds beyond "voluntary contributions."[54] "Because of [the] taxpayer revolt and changing immigration policies," the *Los Angeles Sentinel* reported, "[state senator] Petris urged caution in seeking public funds, urged the groups to help educate Americans in the great benefits of cultural diversity."[55]

Touting "the great benefits of cultural diversity," or "[helping] ethnic groups," by hiring people for government jobs or awarding contracts signaled important change, but observers noted that these actions treated symptoms rather than causes. For example, the sociologist William Julius Wilson said that affirmative action, while noble in intent, tended to benefit minorities who were already advantaged. A job in the city government might uplift an individual, but it also removed them from a neighborhood in need of the social and economic capital that members of the professional and working classes would bring to a community. In this way, affirmative action could create wedges between the haves and have-nots among minorities while exacerbating "inner city social isolation."[56]

Another challenge of minority and ethnic politics in the late twentieth century was parsing the details of inclusion and justice in a society composed of numerous distinct groups. Questions of who counted as disadvantaged and how they should advocate for themselves eluded easy answers yet demanded clarity. To these issues, Asians and Asian Americans were an especially vexing case. In a 1966 column "Orientals Are Non-Political," Ray Zeman of the *Los Angeles Times* wondered why, when "Negroes and a few Mexican Americans" were "organizing political groups in hopes of exerting bloc pressure at the polls," Asians were "making no wholesale efforts to grab political power."[57] The article overlooked histories and instances of activism by Asians in the United States and ignored how their classification as aliens ineligible for citizenship impeded their engagement with electoral politics. Nonetheless, the image of Asians as apolitical and privileged stuck and often confused people—including policymakers—about whether they counted as disadvantaged minorities.

In 1972, in pledging to help minority contractors, Los Angeles city officials construed *minority* broadly to include Native Americans, Blacks, Chinese, Filipinos, Japanese, Koreans, and Polynesians. On the other hand, in 1979 a US House subcommittee removed Asians from the list of "socially and economically disadvantaged" groups eligible for the Small Business Association's 8-A program. The stakes were high, as the Small Business Administration (SBA) contracted with other federal agencies on everything from construction projects to decor for government offices. Representative Millicent Fenwick (R-NJ) said, "I'm surprised the Asians are upset. I don't remember any anti-Asian bias. Between you and me, I find they are magnificently successful—particularly the Chinese."[58] Wilbur Woo, an officer at the Los Angeles Cathay Bank and president of the Chinese Chamber of Commerce, expressed his exasperation, saying, "The resentment stems more from a feeling that Asian Americans have been overlooked in this area. It's very hard not to classify the Asian groups as a minority. If we're not a minority, what are we?"[59]

While, according to Harold Brackman and Stephen P. Erie, Asian Americans took "a backseat to African Americans and even to Latinos" in Los Angeles politics, they nonetheless made a more significant impact than these other groups on the politics of downtown redevelopment.[60] The influx of foreign capital into Los Angeles coincided with the city's promotion of ethnic spaces. This gave Asian Americans a strategic position from which to participate in local politics and advocate for their communities. It also gave rise to new intraethnic divisions and threw into question what it meant to be Asian American and a minority. Regarding Chinatown and Little Tokyo, Jan Lin states that "new central-city ethnic places" were "purveyors of transnational commerce as well as culture, articulating closely with the world trade functions characteristic of global cities."[61] In the city's Master Plan for 1965, officials envisioned a revitalized "International Zone" anchored by Little Tokyo and Chinatown that would boost downtown and draw tourists. Activists who were wary of the CRA and foreign investors but eager to upgrade their ethnic spaces received assurance that any projects would include affordable housing, assistance for small business, affirmative action in construction hiring, and community centers. Funding delays and cutbacks delayed progress on revitalization plans for Chinatown and Little Tokyo, and they were eventually able to proceed thanks to investments from Hong Kong, Taiwan, and Japan.

In Little Tokyo, redevelopment revealed fissures among Japanese and Japanese American stakeholders over commercial versus community-oriented ideas of development and local versus transnational conceptions of community. With hopes to revitalize the area, a group of Japanese Americans formed the Little Tokyo Redevelopment Association in 1969, and the following year, the CRA adopted Little Tokyo as a development area. While some community leaders wanted to boost businesses and tourism to promote Little Tokyo's economic viability, others argued for keeping grassroots concerns and the needs of low income and elderly residents at the forefront. When Japanese firms entered the fray by forming the East-West Development Corporation to fund the new Otani Hotel, many local Japanese Americans saw this as an unwelcome intrusion. The Little Tokyo People's Rights Organization led an effort to stop construction, but the hotel was completed and opened in 1977. Some explained the conflicts over redevelopment as a struggle between Big Tokyo versus Little Tokyo, and by the 1980s, the area represented an uneasy but necessary coexistence of these stakeholders. A new shopping center supported local merchants, and the Little Tokyo Towers and Miyako Gardens Apartments provided affordable housing, while new offices, hotels, and retail met the needs of Japanese nationals and firms. Other institutions, such as the Japanese American Culture and Community Center, tried to integrate Japanese and Japanese American interests and identities. Financing the $12 million facilities were the Department of Housing and Urban Development (HUD), US and Japanese corporations, and the Japanese government. Local activists objected to the original name, the American Bicentennial Commemorative Japanese Center, arguing it represented Japan rather than Japanese Americans.[62] Eventually, stakeholders agreed to change the name to the Japanese-American Cultural Community Center, and it opened in 1980.

The politics of redevelopment presented an opportunity for certain minorities to participate in the city and shape its future. But it also wedded them to a system that waged injustice and perpetuated economic inequality. By the 1980s, the CRA and private developers were eyeing Skid Row, which neighbored Little Tokyo, for revitalization. The area sat on prime real estate, and its improvement would be necessary to maintain the flow of Japanese capital.[63] Resolved to clean up Skid Row, the city embarked on a plan to dismantle the homeless camps that crowded the sidewalks and remove their residents. With Tom Bradley's support, police chief Daryl Gates issued a controversial directive in 1987 ordering homeless people to clear the streets or face arrest.[64]

An Unquiet Odyssey

"Thousands of other Asian immigrants have poured into Los Angeles during the same period, but no other group has yet had such a visible impact on the city," wrote *Los Angeles Times* reporter William Overend in September 1978.[65] The article was one of many on the seemingly sudden presence of Korean immigrants—most strikingly in Los Angeles but also in other large cities such as New York, Washington, DC, and Chicago. More than just participants in a historic wave of immigration, they were at the forefront, entering at a rate of 30,000 people per year during the mid-1970s through the 1980s, exceeded only by people from Mexico and the Philippines.[66] The number of Korean immigrants in the United States jumped from about 11,000 in 1960 to 69,130 in 1970 and then rose to 290,000 in 1980.

An effluence of research and reporting about Korean immigrants from about the mid-1970s through the 1980s illustrated the public's growing awareness of this group. According to a 1975 report by the Los Angeles County Department of Community Services, two hundred new immigrants were arriving from Korea on airliners daily in California.[67] The astonishing growth of the Korean population could perhaps shed light on the interlinked processes of globalization, economic restructuring, and race relations in the context of Los Angeles's rise as a world city. Their dramatic lives, moreover, made them compelling subjects of human-interest stories. For example, a 1976 profile in the *Los Angeles Times* of Hi Duk Lee detailed his journey from blue-collar worker to successful entrepreneur.[68] A college graduate, Lee came to the United States in 1967 after a brief time in West Germany where he worked as a miner. In Los Angeles, he found employment as a can inspector and welder. By dint of hard work and frugality, Lee was able to quit his jobs and purchase the Olympic Market at 3122 West Olympic Boulevard in 1971. He poured his time and energy into this venture, and in six years he grew his business twentyfold. The proud owner of a new black Mercedes, Lee was in the process of opening his second business, a restaurant.

Lee's immigrant saga—and those of hundreds of thousands of others—began in the turbulence of South Korean society following two major wars.

Between 1961 and 1979 President Park Chung Hee set the nation on a path of rapid industrialization, or "guided capitalism" rooted in the development of a manufacturing sector and export economy. The nation's transformation—by the 1980s deemed a "miracle" similar to Japan's a decade earlier—entailed significant shifts in the socioeconomic order. An echelon of wealthy industrialists sat atop a new urban class, their rise facilitated by a symbiotic relationship between government and business. The conglomerates they led, called *chaebol*, gave political and financial support in exchange for state favors such as foreign loans, tax evasion, price-fixing, and preferential rents.

The South Korean "miracle" had its downsides, stemming from the country's dependence on more powerful and developed nations. Its quasi-colonial relations with the United States subjected it to arrangements such as being a dumping ground for surplus US products. Such was the case during the 1950s and 1960s when US grain poured into South Korea, depressing Korean grain prices and triggering the calamities of rural depopulation and "over-urbanization."[69] And while the development of an export economy created opportunities in cities, it intensified the rural to urban migration that strained infrastructures and outstripped available jobs.[70] Further compounding population pressures were a post–World War II return migration of Koreans from places like Japan and Manchuria; a post–Korean War baby boom; and otherwise welcome developments from better medical care, such as reduced mortality and improved fertility.[71] Agricultural crisis and urban overpopulation would be challenging anywhere, but they were particularly dislocating in a country mired in the shadows of colonialism, division, and war. As Won Moon Hurh observed, an "acute sense of normlessness" enveloped Korean society, helping to set the groundwork for a wave of emigration.[72]

State actions—and inaction—added to the incentives to leave. Development and governance under Park Chung-hee revolved tightly around the interests of the military elite and large businesses "without a corresponding sense of social responsibility" toward the needy.[73] Believing political democracy was antithetical to social and economic stability—he had arisen to power through a military coup—Park curbed personal liberties, freedom of the press, and labor activity, and revised the constitution to allow for his lifetime rule. The Korean Central Intelligence Agency (KCIA) struck fear in the population for its secret information gathering, manipulation of public opinion, and suppression of opponents.[74] Few were spared from the uncertainty of the Park Chung-hee years; the economically displaced, intellectuals, political dissidents, North Korean refugees, white-collar workers facing immobility, and even wealthy businessmen had reasons to worry about their security and futures.[75]

In 1962, the South Korean government began encouraging selective emigration to relieve population pressures while also drawing monetary remittances and building international prestige.[76] This included arrangements for some 17,000 emigrants to West Germany to work in occupations like mining and nursing; about 15,000 to Brazil and Argentina to develop agricultural colonies; and about 25,000 to South Vietnam to work for US companies.[77] These emigration schemes fell short, as South Korea's population continued to climb, from 24.9 million in 1960 to 34.6 million in 1975, making it the second densest country after Bangladesh.[78]

Meanwhile, prospective emigrants increasingly set their sights on the United States. Decades of US troop presence, diplomacy, missionary work, commerce, and broadcasting ensured a steady flow of positive information into Korea about the United States. When some of the earliest post-1965ers returned to Korea with enticing stories, they "advertised and exaggerated the prosperity and well-being that an emigrant could hope to find."[79] In 1970, the per capita income was $251, and although by 1980 it had risen to $1,355, this was still far below what one could earn in the United States.[80] The expansion of education and training in fields as varied as cosmetology, auto repair, computer programming, and medicine facilitated emigration by giving people relevant and qualifying skills. As South Korea became integrated into the global economy, knowing English and understanding US customs afforded professional and social advantages that inclined more people to travel to the United States.

The United States would ultimately be the destination of three-quarters of Korean emigrants, and under the framework of the Hart-Celler Act, they utilized all avenues for admission. Family and occupational preferences were both heavily used, the latter peaking in 1972 at 45.1 percent.[81] From there, family-based immigration started to pull away and rose to 77 percent by 1975. Once immigrants gained permanent residency or citizenship, they could sponsor other family members. Those family members later qualified to bring relatives, and so on, creating a multiplier effect and diversifying the socioeconomic profile of the Korean immigrant community. Nonimmigrants and undocumented immigrants represented two other significant groups within Korean America. Nonimmigrants were legal temporary residents, primarily students and tourists. Most Korean undocumented immigrants were nonimmigrants who had overstayed their visas. Between 1950 and 1976, nonimmigrants composed about 15 percent of entering Koreans.[82]

If the archetypal pre-1965 Korean immigrants to Hawaii and the United States were poor, unskilled, and uneducated male laborers, their counterparts in the 1970s were a sharp contrast. There were thousands arriving each year, and the typical newcomers were college-educated, urban, and middle class. Such a profile reflected the preference categories of the immigration system and the likelihood that these groups had access to information and resources. This was also a young and "economically active" group, with the majority under the age of thirty-nine.[83] Many came via a third country, such as Hi Duk Lee, who gained entry through his wife, a nurse who had qualified under employment preferences.[84]

Koreans' presence was all the more striking due to their concentration on the West Coast and big cities, and no destination stood out more than Los Angeles, the largest port of entry for Koreans, and by 1982 home to the largest Korean community in the United States.[85] The 1970 Census counted 8,900 Koreans in Los Angeles County, and in 1980 the number climbed to 60,618. Unofficial numbers veered significantly from these official figures. In *Westways Magazine*, the writer Jack Smith estimated in 1976 there were 70,000 Koreans just in the City of Los Angeles, the majority of them recently arrived. "It is as if the entire population of a city the size of Santa Barbara, speaking and reading an alien language, had moved into the Los Angeles metropolis almost overnight," he wrote.[86] Eui-Young Yu believed the 1970 census figure of 69,130 was an undercount and that it was closer to 113,000.[87] Augmenting this presence were Koreans in the suburbs of Hawthorne, Monterey Park, and Gardena, and to the southeast in Orange County, who "come to Korea Town at least once a week to shop, mostly for food."[88]

Koreans immigrants distinguished themselves through their "extremely high" rate of self-employment as business owners. Korean American Cooke Sunoo observed of Los Angeles in the late 1970s, "Hardly a week goes by without the 'grand opening' of a new storefront with han'gul signs proclaiming grocery stores, restaurants, barbershops, hamburger stands, gas stations, or some other small business."[89] According to a study published in 1977, an estimated 15 percent of the Korean labor force in Los Angeles was self-employed, 50 percent higher than in the overall US population.

Between 1975 and 1977, the number of Korean-owned businesses grew from 1,142 to 2,268, making up 1.5 percent of all establishments in Los Angeles County, nearly twice their proportion in the population.[90] Eighty percent of their businesses were in retail or service industries, most commonly food stores, gas and auto service stations, clothing stores, women's accessory and specialty stores, and repair services. Other kinds of enterprise included manufacturing, wholesale, finance, and construction firms.

A common path that immigrants followed started with the purchase of a business with low capital requirements and high commodity turnover. Wig shops and gas stations were two examples. The businesses usually required intensive labor and the work of unpaid family members, typically spouses and children, which helped keep costs low and assured a reliable labor supply. If the venture prospered, the merchant could acquire and operate a larger, less labor-intensive establishment, such as a grocery store. Selling real estate was considered the pinnacle of ethnic entrepreneurial success among Koreans. It was also the most difficult arena to crack.

Explanations for Koreans' unusual "success" ranged from sociological theories about "opportunity structures," to reductive generalizations and group mythologies. Social science research delved into how factors like education, Westernization, and familiarity with modern life, as well as access to resources through personal savings, bank loans, and rotating credit systems called *kye* facilitated their entry into business ownership.[91] Paul Ong, Edna Bonacich, and Lucie Cheng wondered whether people willing to take the leap of migrating to another country were freer from the hold of nationalism or collective identity compared to others and therefore could pursue individual and family survival with an unburdened and singular focus.[92] South Korea's process of rapid industrialization and capitalist development and conflict with the Communist North may have also instilled in many a strong commitment to the values of capitalism and individualism. "The only things that really count are adaptability and willingness to work hard," observed one journalist covering the community.[93] Others—often Koreans themselves—offered their own explanations about a collective and innate ambitiousness that they tapped into to as entrepreneurs.[94] Chun Y. Lee, a Korean American who served on the city's Board of Zoning, said that Koreans formed many organizations because they were drawn to titles.[95] Randy Hagihara expanded on this, saying "I joked that if you put seven Koreans in a room together they come out with seven different organizations and each one of them wants to be president."[96] Sonia Suk, who achieved entrepreneurial success as one of Koreatown's earliest real estate developers, credited her people's work ethic to their history as survivors of colonialism and war. "The idea is to work hard, save money and educate the children . . . We enjoy life later after security because we've mostly had a hard life. And we are a very independent people."[97]

Stories about Koreans frequently invoked historical suffering to provide context for their image as hardworking, noncomplaining immigrants in the United States. This then set up the next stage of their narrative, chasing and achieving success in their adopted home country. Key to their exceptionalism was their participation in entrepreneurship at a time when running a small business was becoming exceedingly difficult. *Westways* lauded Koreans' purportedly "remarkable grasp of American-style private enterprise," and commitment "to work hard and live the good capitalist life."[98] It was this mastery of and allegiance to US values, then, that could explain their success as immigrants. "We Koreans," Young Cho boasted, "are the second Puritans in this country." Hyung Ki Jin, a professor of finance at Cal Poly Pomona, said despite whatever difficulties, Koreans endured whatever hardships and disadvantages because they "have a tremendous respect for the United States. They believe in everything the United States is doing."[99]

On the other hand, these remarks about hard work, due rewards, and extraordinary sacrifice underscored an insidious aspect of the valorization of self-made success in US culture. Young Cho, a forty-nine-year-old former engineering professor, got a job inspecting aircraft engines because of his aviation experience. He saved enough to buy a gas station, which he said he operated every day from 7 a.m. to 10 p.m.[100] Byung Min's tale of overwork was even more extreme. He ascended from a grocery store clerk to a manager and finally a supermarket owner. Describing his journey, Min said he worked seventeen-hour days and "was just like a machine. . . . At night when I came home, I would fix myself a sandwich and fall into the chair. I was too tired to take my clothes off. Sometimes I would fall asleep and wake up with the sandwich still in my mouth."[101] These travails, presented as examples of heroic sacrifice rather than harrowing exploitation, were worthwhile because of the eventual material payoffs that awaited. Young Cho lived in a $250,000 house in the affluent suburb of Woodland Hills and earned $50,000 per year. Byung Min and Sonia Suk drove Cadillacs, and Hi Duk Lee, as noted above, drove a Mercedes.

Korean immigrants' outstanding willingness to work under extreme hardships seemed to explain why so many of them ran businesses in predominantly Black and Latino neighborhoods. One study found that of the 1,580 Korean-owned businesses in and around Koreatown, about half were in the "peripheral" neighborhoods of Watts, South Central, and East Los Angeles, where opening a business required low capital investment and faced few competitors. The "average Korean firm," observed Edna Bonacich and Tae Hwang Jung, "is in a location whose characteristics are 'worse' than the county average."[102] During the mid-1980s, there were about five hundred Korean-owned businesses in South Central alone, which was noteworthy because it was a "ghetto . . . where many others have failed."[103]

Stories about Koreans in "peripheral" areas "bear[ing] the costs of dealing with a poorer, more crime-ridden population" played into ideas about Black neighborhoods as dangerous and positioned immigrants either as saviors of the urban wasteland or its collateral damage. In an article about Koreans in Baltimore from 1978, the *Pacific Citizen* described families "under the threat of robbery, assault and, at times, even murder in the slum ridden ghettos outlining the city."[104] It told the tragic story of Soon Ye O, a thirty-eight-year-old mother of six who was shot and killed while working at her grocery store. Her grieving husband felt betrayed by the promise of a better life in the United States.[105]

Korean immigration to Los Angeles during the 1970s and 1980s reveals much about how the world was changing in the late twentieth century. Their experience sheds light on the mutually constitutive relationship between migration, urban development, and economic restructuring amid globalization, and the ways that immigrants moved through and cohered the layers of the postindustrial order. Koreans who came to the United States after 1965 were responding to dislocating effects of rapid industrialization in South Korea and opportunities that the reorganization of production and labor created in the United States. Their presence as consumers and merchants enhanced the transnational structure and resources that then helped to expand South Korea's export markets. US-based business owners drew an edge in local markets from their connections to Korean producers to ensure their success. Korean-owned retail businesses in Los Angeles thus served many functions and clientele, from nail salons patronized by the professional and managerial class to swap meets in the retail desert of Compton.

Their ability to live and work in harrowing conditions without asking for or turning to public resources validated ascendant neoliberal values. Celebrating small entrepreneurs' sacrifices, hard work, and material rewards underscored the system still worked and needed no fixing. To be sure, some observers pointed out the insidiousness of lauding Koreans for overwork, but their voices were few and mostly limited to the confines of academia. David Kim and Charles Choy Wong argued perceptively that "the reasons for Korean entry into entrepreneurship ironically belie the idealistic precepts of American equality," and Edna Bonacich and Mike Davis, among others, suggested that immigrant entrepreneurship was a modern form of "cheap labor" fueled by "family self-exploitation."[106] Was their story a vindication of US opportunity or a sobering statement about the intractability of systemic social and economic inequality?

Meanwhile, as observers tried to relate them to a larger understanding of the nation and world, Koreans and Korean Americans embarked on an intraethnic journey of their own. They struggled to explain to themselves and others what it meant to be Korean in a diverse nation with a great deal of racial baggage. The US-born and longer established Koreans expressed both solidarity and puzzlement toward the newcomers. As they navigated American life as racial and ethnic minorities, they found that they shared little in common with the Chinese and Japanese Americans to whom they were most often compared. These communities, by way of their greater numbers and longer historical presence, had footprints in Los Angeles that the Koreans lacked. There was no historic downtown Koreatown to revitalize and identify with. Instead, they saw themselves as building from scratch, trying to stake a claim on an area where they had no previous presence or claim. As Koreans in Los Angeles adapted to American life and developed a sense of group identity and purpose, they confronted uncharted territory and would redefine ethnic identity, racial politics, and minority relations.

CHAPTER 2

A Little Seoul Sprang Up

Place Entrepreneurs and the Koreatown Concept

SONIA SUK'S 1984 MEMOIR, *Life on Two Continents*, tells a familiar story of a penniless but plucky immigrant who makes good in the United States, though her life was anything but ordinary.[1] When the memoir was published, she was in her sixties and still active as one the most powerful and well-connected Koreans in Los Angeles. One journalist called her the "Dean of Koreatown Real Estate."[2] Not one to play down her accomplishments, Suk had an ostentatious personal style to match. The cover photo on *Life on Two Continents* shows Suk standing in front of an iron gate, grinning slightly and wearing a white fedora, large rimless glasses, several strings of pearls, and a bright blue double-breasted blazer. Inside the book are numerous images, including one of her in a Hawaiian print ensemble and crocheted hat, posed next to her 1973 Cadillac Coupe deVille whose license plate said KOREAN. Other pictures captured aspects of her professional accomplishments: one conveys gravitas as Suk sits in a cluttered office and holds a phone receiver to her ear, while another shows her standing like a conquering hero in front of a Koreatown commercial building.

Suk was born Suk Soon-Hee in Pyongyang, Korea, around 1917. Though her family was middle class, they experienced repeated uprooting and uncertainty due to colonization and war. Suk remembered being a rebellious and unconventional youth with a strong interest in machines, especially motorcycles and automobiles. In 1934 at the age of seventeen, she claimed, she became the first woman taxi driver in northern Korea. By her early twenties, Suk was married with two children, but she had grown restless

FIGURES I AND 2
(OPPOSITE) Pictures
of Sonia S. Suk from her
1984 memoir, Life on Two
Continents (Seoul: Dong A.
Printing, 1984), 18, 81.

with her domestic life. She followed an itinerant path for much of the 1940s, spending time between Japan, Korea, and China while her children were under her mother's care in Seoul.

In her retelling, Suk's journey from war-torn Korea to sunny Los Angeles was unlikely and circuitous, fueled by her independent spirit and entrepreneurial instincts. Living in Tokyo sometime before World War II opened her eyes to the possibilities of international trade, and while in Seoul during the war, she ran businesses importing and selling everything from scrap metal to squid. Japan's withdrawal from Korea set the stage for an inspired opportunity that became her entree into real estate; in late 1945 she seized dozens of homes vacated by the departing occupiers. The events of Suk's life from the end of World War II through the 1950s were a whirlwind and include her immigration to the United States in 1948; a stint at Montreat College, a Christian school in North Carolina; a move to Monterey, California, to attend junior college; and her relocation to San Francisco. In San Francisco she completed a degree in international trade at San Francisco State University in 1955, started a kimchi factory, and worked at the American Korean Association. She briefly returned to South Korea to connect with her trading company before settling in Los Angeles in the early 1960s.[3] Unsure if her future lay in an unstable postwar Korea or an equally uncertain life in the United States, she made a fateful decision in October 1962. Suk saw an ad in a newspaper by a development company called California City seeking agents and offering free training in real estate transactions, law, contracts, loans, investment, sales, and ethics. She answered and soon found her calling.

Suk said she first tried to sell the "Korea Town concept" in San Francisco during the mid-1950s, but "there weren't enough Koreans at the time to make it work."[4] Los Angeles, with its Korean population of about two thousand in the early 1960s, looked more promising. After completing her training, she worked as an agent for the Saito Real Estate Company before starting her own firm in 1964. Suk said that she saw potential just south of downtown around Olympic Boulevard and 7th Avenue and convinced co-ethnics in an older Korean cluster near the University of Southern California to sell their property to the university and relocate. In the 1960s to 1980s, she negotiated the sales for what became some of the most important establishments and community spaces in Koreatown, including the VIP Palace, Kang-suh building, Olympic Dduk House, and Korean Airlines office. Her real estate knowledge and social capital facilitated the completion of nascent Koreatown projects like the Korean Community Center on Western Avenue and an eighteen-story home for senior residents.[5] Suk was a major property owner as well, with a portfolio encompassing apartment buildings, coffee shops, and other establishments.

Property was also at the core of Suk's politics. She identified as a Republican, she explained, because she credited Republican politicians for allowing Koreans to become property owners in the United States.[6] Yet, she was a pragmatist and cultivated ties and working relationships with whomever was in power. This included Tom Bradley, Los Angeles's long-serving mayor (1973–1993), for whom Suk served in different posts over the years thanks to her standing in the Korean community and connections in South Korea. She appeared to have forged a genuine and lasting friendship with Bradley's wife Ethel.

Eager to seal her legacy as a pioneer and role model, Suk also included in her memoir copies of certificates, letters, and ephemera that demonstrated her involvement in civic, church-based, business, and other causes. Prominent among these were letters of appreciation from Tom Bradley for her contributions to the city and President Ronald Reagan for supporting the Republican Party and his election.

In writing her story, Suk might have hoped that her life and career could inspire fellow Koreans chasing their American dream, which for her revolved around acquiring commercial or income-generating property. She was not so singular in this regard. Thousands of immigrants from South Korea who had experienced war and division in the 1940s and then received US tutelage about the virtues of capitalism in the 1950s and 1960s arrived in the United States ready to apply those lessons. In turn, Suk and other real estate promoters sold Koreatown on the gambit that Koreans were good property owners who improved neighborhoods and raised values. According to Hank Yim, the owner of the Olympic Realty and Investment Company, between 1973 and 1978 Koreans at least doubled the value of property in the Olympic Boulevard area, from $5 per square foot to between $10 and $20.[7]

Suk's career in real estate is striking in light of the history of anti-Asian discrimination in California. For much of the first half of the twentieth century, Asian immigrants could not own property—due to their status as "aliens ineligible to citizenship"—and the neighborhoods they occupied tended to be segregated and derided as dangerous, diseased, and foreign. Times had changed, however, and by the time Suk enrolled in real estate classes, Koreans faced no legal barriers to citizenship or property ownership. And since the 1960s, cities that once disdained, contained, or destroyed their ethnic places now embraced them—San Francisco's Chinatown and Miami's Little Havana, for example—as "purveyors of transnational commerce as well as culture" that could spur economic growth while signaling their enlightened and inclusive multiculturalism.[8]

This chapter explores the development of Koreatown during the 1970s and 1980s, focusing especially on the role of immigrant place entrepreneurs like Suk, who carved out a piece of Los Angeles for Koreans—where fellow co-ethnics could live, work, and enjoy community—while they built their own fortunes. They promoted Koreatown as a vehicle for ethnic representation, shrine to property ownership, and emotional beacon for Korean Americans. In turn, a narrative emerged that credited the Korean "influx" for saving and rejuvenating a "deteriorating area" that had been "forgotten by the rest of the city."[9] However, the description of Koreatown as "one of L.A.'s newest neighborhoods" elided the presence of non-Korean residents and misleadingly suggested Koreans filled a blank space with only blight to be erased.[10] Such perceptions gave business leaders, developers, and architects the freedom to envision and build Koreatown how it suited them, and they did so with the guiding principles of improving property values and "selling Korean culture to Los Angeles."[11] But the disconnect between dreamy aspirations and on-the-ground obstacles complicated these efforts and, thus, shed light on the unlikely and fraught origins of urban ethnic neighborhoods that emerged in the late twentieth century.

Dreams and Visions

Koreatown's popular origin story usually begins in October 1971 when Hi Duk Lee opened the Olympic Market on West Olympic Boulevard, on a block also occupied by a Korean-owned bookstore and photo shop. With personal savings and a loan from Crocker Bank, he paid $12,000 to the Korean owners who had largely maintained the same establishment of its original Japanese owners. Lee decided to cater to co-ethnics by replacing the Japanese sign with one in English and Korean and restocking the store with fruits, vegetables, cuts of meat, and other products that would appeal to Koreans.[12] According to Lee, this made Olympic Market the first true Korean grocery store that was not a wholesaler. Before long, customers came, turning the store into a go-to place for Koreans in Southern California. Lee said 1976 was an especially good year, as business was profitable and his story even drew attention in the *Los Angeles Times, Newsweek*, and several television channels. Olympic Market's success encouraged further migration and establishments nearby, including additional supermarkets, restaurants, housing, schools, churches, temples, newspapers, clinics, and a community center. A once modest block with a few Korean-owned businesses had expanded to a two-square-mile area that people started to call Koreatown.[13]

The sociologist Ivan Light has discussed how the origins and rise of contemporary ethnic places tend to be portrayed as organic and leaderless processes, which obscures the critical role of "immigrant place entrepreneurs."[14] In Koreatown's case, this group included Sonia Suk and Hi Duk Lee, and the Korea Town Development Association (to which both belonged), formed in 1973. They envisioned the mid-Wilshire district, with its inexpensive real estate and location near downtown, as the site of a booming enclave and emotional home for Korean immigrants. To make those visions a reality, they networked with city officials, reached out to prospective Korean emigrants, and raised money on both sides of the Pacific.

These efforts were also possible because of a broad shift in US culture and attitudes during the mid-twentieth century in which the nation's multiculturalism was not just acknowledged but actively embraced. This would have effects in many arenas of public life, including city politics and urban planning. Ethnic places were no longer reviled as dangerous and threatening and instead were highlighted in official tourist guides as must-see attractions. In large, diverse cities like Los Angeles, government offices responded with commissions, initiatives, and staff positions to represent and respond to the needs of particular minority communities. Tom Bradley hired his first Korean American staffer, Jun Kim, in the mid-1970s after a Japanese American aide convinced him that the community's rapid growth and unique challenges called for a dedicated liaison. Kim's hiring was a symbolic form of recognition and inclusion, and it also gave leaders from the community, including the place entrepreneurs, built-in access to the halls of power.[15]

The 1970s and 1980s were a busy time of real estate transactions, construction, promotion, and new immigration. In 1974, amid Olympic Market's brisk business, Hi Duk Lee dreamt bigger. He wrote in his memoir that he wanted to help grow and shape Koreatown into an enclave that would reflect the immigrants' culture, express their pride in postindependence South Korea, and "promote Koreans in this multiracial society."[16] He purchased a block on Olympic and Normandie for his next project, a restaurant and a night club. As Koreans were growing their footprint in the mid-Wilshire district, developers hoped to guide this growth and make Koreatown a cultural "two-way street" that "introduces Koreans to America," and "can also introduce Americans to Korea." They believed that attracting non-Koreans required upscale and aesthetically appealing establishments. "So far it has gone largely ignored by tourists, and the business community would like to see that changed," remarked journalist William Overend in 1978. "Some would like to dress the area up a bit, perhaps adding ornamental gales like those that greet tourists and the restaurant clientele who flock to Chinatown."[17] Though he would later wonder if it had been a wasteful and foolish endeavor, Hi Duk Lee spent enormous resources, labor, and international travel to import blue tiles for his nightclub. The opening of Young Bin Kwan, or VIP Palace, in May 1975 marked another high point in his career. Determined to draw "American" customers who fit his vision of a high-spending, swanky, fashionable clientele, Lee wrote, "I needed American customers. Korean customers complain and complain and cannot wait five minutes. Americans can wait even thirty minutes in the lounge with a cocktail and wine and they order higher priced items."[18] He hired a general manager, named Nick Medvid, who helped turn VIP Palace into a go-to event space, hosting everyone from the Korean Secretary of State to Republicans working on President Ronald Reagan's 1984 reelection.

By the mid-1970s, people were noticing and remarking that Olympic and 8th and other blocks west of downtown had a distinctive ethnic Korean feel, though Koreatown in these early years was more of an idea than a cohesive spatial reality. *Westways Magazine* praised the immigrants settling in the area because they did not seek "concealment in the multitude. Instead they have concentrated, planted their cultural flag."[19] Descriptions of Koreatown's anchors and borders varied widely, but generally it sat somewhere in the vicinity of Washington, Wilshire, Western, and Hoover. The 90005 and 90006 zip codes were also used to locate Koreatown. To Boyle Heights resident Randy Hagihara, a third-generation Japanese American, Koreatown had emerged south of Wilshire and then "started spanning into Hollywood."[20] He associated it with the sudden transformation of spaces, including his beloved Toho theater on Wilshire near La Brea, where he watched movies from Japan, "especially Samurai movies. I remember going there frequently as a kid." Later as an adult, he was in the area, hoping to glimpse the theater that held such fond childhood memories. "One day I was driving by, I looked at the Toho La Brea. I almost crashed. They turned it into a Korean church!"²¹ The clusters of small businesses provided an array of services and enhanced transnational commerce through the sale of imported clothing, wigs, electronics, shoes, canned goods, soy sauce, and dried food.

Compared to the denser Chinatown and Little Tokyo sections of downtown, Koreatown was sprawling and uncontained, so a constant challenge for place entrepreneurs concerned harnessing and showcasing the area as a unified entity. By the 1980s, newly established Korean development firms were trying to take Koreatown to the next level. As mom-and-pop businesses continued to proliferate, construction on major, multimillion-dollar shopping centers and other projects also started to become commonplace. Though these projects were not always completed, simply announcing them or breaking ground was news in and of itself and added to the hype around Koreatown as an emerging destination for commerce and shopping.²² The largest and most expensive of these projects was Koreatown Plaza, a $25 million, three-level, 430,000-square-foot shopping center occupying the block on Western, Oxford, 9th, and San Marino. Construction began in early 1985 and was completed in mid-1987.²³ It was at the time Koreatown's largest enclosed retail center, featuring an international food court, specialty stores, restaurants, a supermarket, and a bank. Architect Ki Suh Park of Gruen Associates said it would "give a new, colorful dimension to Koreatown, resulting in a pedestrian-activity pattern similar to commercial developments in Chinatown and Little Tokyo."²⁴

Though heartened by the number of big and small businesses to the area, developers still worried that Koreatown's expansion was proceeding in too scattershot a manner and needed tighter, more intentional growth if it were to achieve its potential. Hi Duk Lee assessed in the early 1980s that it still lacked a distinct visual and aesthetic Korean imprint and had followed a pattern of growth that sacrificed quality for quantity. He and architect David Hyun were among those advocating for large-scale, comprehensive developments in the belief that this would give Koreatown the community "focal point" it needed while also alleviating mounting problems such as inadequate parking, traffic congestion, and dangerous driving conditions. More intentional planning, said Hyun, would secure a prosperous future for Koreatown and save it from its current trajectory of crime, physical deterioration, and inaccessibility. "[Unless] it is directed with sufficient force it cannot be contained," he urged, "It's going to run all over the place, which is what it's doing now."

Korean placemakers had the early support and encouragement of City Council member David Cunningham, whose district included Koreatown. At a December 1979 community event presided over by Gene Kim and David Hyun, Cunningham talked up the "exciting possibilities" for Koreatown and how it would eventually be "one of the top attractions in Los Angeles, a place tourists feel they 'must see.'"[25] He praised Koreans for making "a definite mark on . . . the Olympic Boulevard area" in a span of five years, and especially because "real estate values have soared." Cunningham shared the place entrepreneurs' desire for a "commercial strip with strong identification ties to the Korean culture; a street of stores, shops, and offices which will be a pleasure to the eye, as well as the pocketbook."[26] Toward this end, he asked for community support for and involvement in developing a "specific plan" for Koreatown that would contain suggested building and zoning regulations and other guidelines and would eventually be incorporated into the city's Wilshire Area Master Plan. This step, Cunningham assured, would put Koreatown on the path to being "the most beautiful area in all of Los Angeles."

In conjunction with the work on a specific plan, Cunningham asked Hi Duk Lee and David Hyun to envision and develop a project similar to Little Tokyo's Japanese Village Plaza, which had opened in 1978. The Japanese Village Plaza, of course, held particular significance for Hyun, its chief architect. He believed it was the linchpin for Little Tokyo's reinvention from a run-down neighborhood and source of embarrassment for Japanese Americans to a model of successful revitalization and "showcase of Japanese capability."[27] Hyun wanted to outdo his accomplishment in Little Tokyo to help Koreatown not just achieve its potential but also outshine Los Angeles's other Asian communities.[28] He and other immigrant place entrepreneurs spoke of their desire to harness Koreatown's unique attributes, including its nebulous borders and unwieldy size.[29] "Unlike Little Tokyo or Chinatown, Korean Town has room to grow," said one broker in 1985, about the fact that Koreatown, depending on the borders, was up to five times larger than the other areas.[30] Also, although mid-Wilshire had a legible history that preceded the arrival of Koreans, the story of Koreatown was unwritten, a fact that gave placemakers the conceptual freedom to forge ahead without the constraints that came with acknowledging the past, honoring memories, or preserving sites.

Hyun had already been envisioning a bigger, better version of Japanese Village Plaza for Koreans. In 1979, he unveiled his plans for "Korea City," which would be the first comprehensive and large-scale Koreatown project. It does not appear to have been a part of an official city master or specific plan and was largely a vehicle for Hyun and the Korea Town Development Association (KTDA) to rally support for development. Hyun described it as a mixed residential development with retail, cultural, housing, educational, medical, and recreational facilities that would serve local and international clientele. As far as the location, it would occupy the area bordered by Vermont, 8th, Western, and Olympic. Korea City generated considerable initial excitement and attention, garnering coverage in the *Los Angeles Times*. Reporter Sam Kaplan explained, "[Koreans] yearned for a development that would give the community an identity similar to what Little Tokyo does for the Japanese and Chinatown for the Chinese."[31]

Hyun promised that Korea City would deliver in these ways. For promoters, Korea City was a vehicle for making their mark as an ethnic community in Los Angeles and the United States and a means to continue Koreans' story as a people. As such, a great deal of emotional rhetoric about history and the future informed how they talked about Korea City and other development plans. Hyun repeatedly invoked the pride, yearning, and dreams of Korean people as he tried to sell the idea of Korea City. Koreans, "both here and in Korea," he said, "deserved" a development "to spotlight the Korean people's near-unparalleled growth in the world's economic and cultural cycles."[32] It was not enough for immigrants to have done well in the United States; they needed a spatial stronghold in the city, a place that could be a stage for and reflection of their belonging in and contributions to Los Angeles. Koreatown, continued Hyun, "can become a national symbol for the United States of how a new immigrant people have succeeded in a relatively short period of time. . . . For Korean-Americans to achieve such a dream in 25 years is without historical precedent. This achievement by a new immigrant people can show to the world at large that America is for all people." Hank Yi of the KTDA said Korea City would be "a legacy to our children, and the second and third-generation Korean Americans."[33] A visible and dynamic Koreatown, he said, would signify that Koreans had "overcome all barriers to our dream, not only for our children, but also for the city of Los Angeles."[34]

Signs, Streets, and Parades

While boosters touted Korea City as a potentially game-changing development that would bring to fruition people's hopes and dreams for a strong, visible community, commercial profitability, and a space to call their own, Koreans had been engaged in small, modest, yet equally powerful, actions through which they marked and staked claims to the area. While engaging in public relations and outreach with city officials to spread awareness about Koreatown, immigrant place entrepreneurs also worked to systematically remake the sights and sounds of Olympic Boulevard. The KTDA acted early and quickly, with a sign giveaway, annual festival, and community cleanup campaign. In doing so, it placed Koreans figuratively and literally in the streets, supplanting earlier or competing claims to the area and asserting a new ethnic and moral geography for Koreans in Los Angeles.

Cooke Sunoo's impression of the early 1970s was that visibility for Asian American communities "was just starting to emerge . . . there was not really a defined Koreatown at all."[35] The brainchild of the first KTDA president Gene Kim, installing Korean language (hangul) was an economical and effective way to disrupt the area's existing landscape and imprint Koreans upon it. In 1973 he approached business owners in and around Olympic-Vermont and offered them free Korean-language signs for their storefronts. They were simple and hand-painted—Sonia Suk said she made some of them—but they were remarkably effective. Businesses and immigrant shoppers could more easily find one another, and the signs—despite their low cost and homemade quality—effectively branded their buildings and blocks as Korean and announced that "suddenly Korea Town existed."[36] Without signage in hangul, said Sunoo, even Koreans might have assumed the presence of Korean businesses was limited to "two restaurants and a grocery store." The signs, thus, gave an "almost overnight" visibility to the array of Korean businesses in the area and would be "one of the things that really started to make K-town blossom."[37]

If business signs were a quiet-yet-potent way for Koreans to place themselves on the visual and cultural landscape, the annual Korean Town Festival, which started in 1974, made a bold, multisensory statement to all of Los Angeles. The message was that Koreans were *here* and a part of the city's multicultural fabric and that their presence would only grow. As the *Los Angeles Times* noted on the occasion of the 1979 festival, "More than

170,000 Koreans have come to Southern California since 1971. . . . Fifty thousand of them have settled in Olympic Blvd's Korea Town, and an additional 15,000 migrate here each year."[38] A parade down Olympic Boulevard representing different facets of the Korean American community was the event's highlight, drawing tens of thousands of spectators. In 1975, its second year, the parade drew about forty-five thousand visitors of different racial backgrounds and featured dozens of floats, martial arts demonstrations, equestrians, bands, and some 120 different clubs and civic groups.[39] In 1979, the attendees numbered an estimated seventy thousand.[40]

The festival offered visitors the kind of superficially exotic and dubiously foreign experiences that immigrant and ethnic communities were expected to provide as a condition of their membership in the multicultural mosaic of Los Angeles and the United States. Moreover, the characterization that the Korean Town Festival captured, "the perfect blend of the old world and the new" with "traditional dance costumes . . . and pretty girls," could have described any festival in the city that was branded as ethnic.[41] When framed by such language, the event limited the Korean American community to a role of fulfilling outsiders' consumption and entertainment desires and encapsulated a paradox facing immigrants and ethnic minorities in the late twentieth century. Following the sixth annual festival in 1979, a reporter said that Koreans "proved . . . they have mastered one US tradition—the art of the parade."[42] Notwithstanding the flip and breezy tone of the remark, it called attention to the balancing act often demanded of ethnic minorities to adapt culturally while remaining sufficiently—or superficially—foreign.

Jan Lin has explained that public ethnic celebrations like the Korean Town Festival represent the "collective effervescence" of a community, which has made them something of a double-edged sword. On the one hand, they can reduce ethnic communities in the ways discussed above. On the other, they have played a crucial role in ethnic placemaking, as powerful vehicles for community leaders and stakeholders in consolidating their power and advancing their interests. For their part, city officials and boosters took an interest in the celebration, in realizing Koreatown might help shore up Los Angeles's status as a cosmopolitan and multicultural metropolis. Elected officials also recognized that outreach with the local Korean American community could confer political benefits, so supporting an annual event that drew media attention made good sense. Mayor Tom Bradley regularly attended and even served as the parade's grand marshal in 1980.[43]

It was a natural occasion for correspondences, the exchange of well wishes, and building of goodwill between the Mayor's Office and Korean American community. For instance, in 1975, Bradley sent a letter of congratulations to the committee for its "very successful and beautiful cultural event." In August 1977, he expressed to the committee and leaders in the community his excitement for the upcoming festival, while also reflecting on its significance for the city and nation.[44] "The City of Los Angeles," Bradley wrote, "has the distinction of having a populace composed of ethnic backgrounds from around the world reflecting the very principles upon which this Country was founded."[45] In this respect, the local Korean population was an asset to the city. "We are proud the Korean people have selected the City of Los Angeles for their home. While exerting efforts to become an integral part of our society," he said to the Reverend Song Cha Kim, pastor of the Wilshire Christian Church, "The Korean people have retained their beautiful customs, cultures, and traditions, sharing them with us each year."[46] For their part, people from the community reaped what recognition and rewards they could from their association with the festival. Staff member Jun Kim helped to raise the event's prominence and political capital of the organizers. In a memo from September 25, 1975, for instance, Kim recommended that Bradley award city commendations to four KTDA officers, citing their "untiring efforts" to showcase the "biggest event in this community."[47]

As with the free business signs, the Korean Town Festival inscribed Korean-ness on the geography of Los Angeles. The latter, being a festive and celebratory affair that messaged to Los Angeles Koreans' positive contributions to the city, additionally made a statement of their ownership of Koreatown, literally and symbolically. Another event coordinated by the KTDA put an especially fine point on the statement. On Wednesday, August 15, 1979, it launched the first of what it called its monthly cleanups. At approximately 7 a.m., about sixty "broom-toting" adults and children converged at a corner of Olympic and Irolo and started sweeping, fanning out several blocks to the east and west.[48] Like the KTDA's other campaigns, the cleanup sought and garnered local media attention. The *Los Angeles Times* published an article that was accompanied with photographs of people diligently sweeping the sidewalks. One man wore his taekwondo uniform while doing so. The campaign was a master stroke of image crafting that supplanted any notion that Koreans were unruly immigrants who degraded their surroundings with a picture of grateful newcomers dutifully and happily cleaning the streets. Min Soo Park, the consul general of South Korea said, "We do all this sweeping in our own country. . . . We might as well do it here, too."[49] The KTDA further claimed that the cleanups signified Korean immigrants' assimilation in and valuable contributions to the United States. "We Koreans . . . are reviving the tradition of hardy Europeans who brushed and washed cobblestone streets, as well as the custom of Asians sweeping their front yards before they left for work."

With the signs, street festivals, and cleanups Koreans placed themselves onto the physical and cognitive map of Los Angeles and made a case for their belonging that was both self-orientalizing and assimilative. In this process, they also created a moral geography of Koreatown, illustrated in one observer's remark that Koreans had turned a deteriorated area with growing numbers of poor Blacks and Latinos into a bustling Asian commercial zone with a "look of affluence." Ki Sung Kim of the Korean Association of Southern California echoed this in a 1978 letter to Tom Bradley in which he stated, "We, as newly formed residents, have developed the area" from a run-down street" to "one of the brightest spots in the City."[50] Koreatown's rise was indexed not merely by the appearance of Korean people and businesses but also the accompanying story that their arrival and settlement had made life better. The flip side of this—as in any stories of settlement—was that the erasure of people and communities that stood in the way could be easily brushed aside as inconsequential. Besides, Koreans throughout the greater Los Angeles area "need a place to identify with," insisted University of Southern California ethnic studies professor Yong Mok in 1979.[51] The reverence for property they demonstrated in the cleanups and through rising real estate values powerfully attested to their deservingness.

A culminating event in this period of placemaking was the installation of the Koreatown sign on the Santa Monica freeway in January 1982. Two years earlier, developers had successfully lobbied the city to formally redesignate the mid-Wilshire district as Koreatown. Prominent English-language signs subsequently appeared at major stretches and intersections. A freeway sign fell under the purview of the California Department of Transportation, and after some waiting and negotiating, Koreatown leaders learned the sign was in the works and would be located at the Normandie off-ramp. For the immigrant place entrepreneurs, this was as a major accomplishment. A sign outside of Koreatown on a heavily utilized highway represented public validation and promised heightened awareness of the neighborhood. It would also hopefully spur further growth. "The sign identified the neighborhood by its new name, attracted custom, and encouraged Korean settlement," explains Ivan Light.[52] The KTDA wanted to turn the sign's installation into a ceremony conferring historical weightiness to the occasion. On January 12 at around noon, it assembled a group of esteemed Koreans and government officials, including Tom Bradley, California Department of Transportation director Peter Oswald, the Korean consul general in Los Angeles Min Soo Park, and Hi Duk Lee (then president of the KTDA), at the Normandie off-ramp as a crew from the California Department of Transportation put the sign in place. A photographer from the *Korea Times* captured the scene, a curious gathering of workers and people in suits on the shoulder of a busy highway, that was nonetheless deemed a historic moment for posterity.[53]

The official recognition of Koreatown—of which the Santa Monica freeway sign was one instance—was on the one hand a culmination and logical outcome of efforts years in the making and on the other a departure from and a papering over of local conditions, and it widened the space between the area's image and daily life. When the city designated Koreatown in 1980, Koreans made up about 7 percent of residents in the area.[54] They were, however, dominant by metrics relating to momentum business and finance, and also had on their side a determined public relations strategy of asserting their claims to space. As a consequence, Koreatown's trajectory could obscure as much as it revealed. For example, the establishment of the Oriental Mission Church at a former Ralph's grocery store on North Western Avenue, just north of Beverly Boulevard, became an appealing piece of Koreatown lore because it illustrated Koreans' inventiveness and spiritual dedication. Lost in the retellings was the impact of another grocery store closure and with it the reduced services for local residents. And while the installation of Korean-language signs added a new and striking element to the visual landscape, they had always stood alongside and intermixed with signs in Spanish, English, and other languages. In other words, Koreatown had never been anything but a multilingual and multiethnic neighborhood, even as its invention as a monoethnic space insisted otherwise.

Self-Sufficiency

More than a staging ground for building wealth, Koreatown would itself be a source of political and social capital. Immigrant place entrepreneurs banked on *what* Koreatown was and could be, and just as crucially, *how* it was coming to be. As discussed in chapter 1, local and national newspapers found in Koreans a reliable source of harrowing yet heartwarming stories of immigrant grit and American opportunity during the 1970s and 1980s, with such unsubtle headlines as "The American Dream is alive in Koreatown."[55] That story introduced readers to T. Young Suhr, who immigrated in 1969 with hopes of applying his Korean master's degree to work as a teacher. Unable to secure a teaching job, he started selling auto parts out of a Korean-owned gas station, the profitability of which allowed him and his wife to expand the business in a brick-and-mortar storefront they purchased in a "deteriorating Los Angeles neighborhood." Suhr's American dream did not end there. He and a Korean partner eventually bought a warehouse and saw sales for their auto parts business grow to $500,000 per year.[56] Like Hi Duk Lee, Suhr was thinking ambitiously for Koreatown, specifically about how increased activity in the area would raise demands for hotels and other services for visiting Korean businessmen. Determined to grab a share of this potential market, he tore down his store to build the Western Inn at a cost of $2.1 million.

Such stories complemented the efforts of immigrant place entrepreneurs. The author of the article discussed above, Earl Gottschalk, concluded that thanks to Suhr and the thousands of other tenacious Korean immigrants, a once run-down portion of Los Angeles was now a "thriving center of Korean small businesses" and "one of the fastest-growing ethnic business areas in the country."[57] Not only were they "making it," but they were also doing so under difficult conditions and without help, underscored by recurring descriptions of run-down blocks and shabby buildings where they worked. Koreatown leaders shrewdly deployed this rhetoric to shape and control the development of the mid-Wilshire area and bolster their standing with government officials and mainstream institutions, including the media. For instance, in a November 1978 letter to Tom Bradley about projects on Olympic Boulevard near Western and Vermont, KTDA president Sea O. Choi reminded him that Koreatown "has become a model case of a town rehabilitation without government funds."[58] The following year, the Korean Association of Southern California president Ki Sung Kim sought Bradley's support for a shopping center, stressing that Korean immigrants just wanted "to build a better future for the town," and had already "beau-

tified" Olympic Boulevard with new construction.[59] "Koreans have taken
run-down structures, weedy vacant lots and neglected streets in the previously declining area and turned them into thriving businesses, interspersed
with clean, landscaped areas."[60]

The combination of favorable media coverage, success of people like
Sonia Suk and Hi Duk Lee, and correspondences between the city and immigrant business leaders and developers solidified a public-facing identity
for Koreans that valorized property and self-sufficiency. The textures of
this identity were fleshed out when publications like *Westways* proclaimed
that Koreatown proved Korean immigrants possessed "such old-fashioned
American virtues as industry, thrift, dependability, and enterprise."[61] Or
similarly when the *Wall Street Journal* detailed Koreans' purportedly disci-
plined approach to money. It reported that they did not like to borrow it,
only doing so to expand already profitable operations, and would routinely
pay 30 to 50 percent down for a loan. Won H. Chung, president of the California Korean American Hanmi Bank, said Koreans looked at bankruptcy
as a "great shame."[62] As reporter Earl Gottschalk concluded, "Korea Town
is largely self-sufficient," because the immigrants making up its business
community were self-sufficient. And lest he had not made the point em-
phatically enough, he continued, "the Koreans' success in the United States
demonstrates that the nation's ladder of upward mobility still works. Even
in low-tech, unglamorous, small retail and service businesses, the Koreans
have proven that hard work, attention to detail and the entrepreneurial
spirit can still pay off."[63]

At What Price?

The immigrant place entrepreneurs saw little difference or tension between
ethnic politics on the one hand and the development of Koreatown on the
other. Thus, insisting on the self-sufficiency of Korean people went hand
in hand with promoting the area as a monoethnic bastion of consumerism
and private property. While this was a shrewd and effective tactic, it also
came with trade-offs. Affordable housing, for instance, lagged behind the
development of offices and retail, and it was not until October 1983 that
the first housing project by a Korean investment company was announced,
a twenty-unit development called the Country Club Townhomes.[64] Further, most of the residents of Koreatown—non-Korean, working class, or
poor—were consistently ignored or symbolically erased. Making Koreatown

a community of business and profits followed neoliberal, supply-side principles and resulted in a set of glaring contradictions. And while following
these principles yielded rewards for the immigrant place entrepreneurs, it
did not materialize the large-scale developments of their dreams.

The struggles over Ardmore Recreation Park illustrated the priorities of
private commercial development and the Koreanization of space, as well as
the unequal outcomes the processes maintained. Ardmore was in the heart
of the burgeoning Koreatown, near the VIP Palace, and was overseen by the
city's Parks and Recreation Department. Many locals saw it as a neighborhood sore spot due to its inadequate facilities. In 1978, on learning that the
city was planning to extend the park to Olympic Boulevard, a group of Korean residents and business owners petitioned Mayor Tom Bradley and the
Parks and Recreation Department to either halt or redirect the expansion.
Though not yet officially designated as such, they stressed that the plans
would affect the heart of "Koreatown" and threaten construction of a new
shopping center on Irolo and Olympic. They emphasized how the retail and
commerce they brought was taking the "run down" area into a "progressive"
and "right direction" and bringing much needed income.[65] Jung Su Lee, the
president of the Korean Chamber of Commerce of Southern California, also
touted the "outstanding" character and citizenship of the investors, George
and Young Hwang, and the KTDA president Sea O. Choi expressed his
"hope that the City of Los Angeles encourage the more and better town development such as the Hwang's shopping center."[66] Arguing against the park's
expansion, Choi reiterated the promise of profitability and how "in the next
five years, Olympic Blvd. will be one of the most prosperous areas in town."[67]

Korean business leaders were not just concerned about Ardmore preventing commercial expansion. The park also represented an obstacle to the
cultural and social Koreanization of the area. In this regard, the priority
was less about stopping Ardmore's expansion than about controlling it. Its
location made it a natural outdoor gathering space for the Korean American
community, but it was underused due to the inadequate facilities. Hi Duk
Lee complained the park drew drug dealers, litter, and other unsavory factors.[68] He later tried, unsuccessfully, to change Ardmore's name to Pagoda
Park and transform it into a symbol of Korean pride, complete with a museum and amenities for the community such as a senior center.

The concerns about Ardmore Park also highlighted a disjuncture between
Koreatown's development as a monoethnic neighborhood and the area's de-

mographics and social conditions. The owner of Nasung Gift Store, Jong Whan Cha, estimated that 70 percent of customers in Koreatown were Korean though they made up less than a quarter of its residents.[69] According to the 1980 Census there were 31,410 residents in the area bordered by Pico, Wilshire, Vermont, and Western, of whom about 50 percent were Latino and 12 percent were Korean.[70] The percentage of the county's Koreans living in Koreatown had actually dropped, from 37 percent in 1977 to 29 percent in 1981. Just 11 percent of Koreans living there in 1972 remained five years later.

The pursuit of profits combined with existing residential patterns shaped Koreatown businesses' prioritizing of white customers, Koreans from the suburbs, and tourists, as opposed to developing ways to better serve the area's local residents. John Han of the KTDA worried that Korean customers by themselves were "too limited to support an endlessly increasing number of businesses. Korean business owners need to go beyond the Korean market and sell to Caucasians as well." He also lamented the lack of a cultural center, civic auditorium, and other attractions that would show the public that Koreatown was more than "a community of small businesses."[71] Promoters walked a fine line between being accessible to white customers and providing the exotic experiences those very customers desired. It was one thing to pull this off with the annual Korean Town festival but a different challenge convincing people to visit Koreatown year round.

Including Koreatown's residents in development plans would have meant giving weight to issues of economic justice and the desires of non-Korean people. Residents suffered from chronic and high unemployment, which affected 10 percent of Asian men, 15 percent of Latino men, and 20 percent of Black men.[72] A scarcity of affordable and decent housing also strained daily life. Between 1970 and 1980, the Koreatown corridor saw a more than 12 percent decline in the housing stock while the residential population actually grew by nearly 10 percent and median housing values jumped from $23,240 to $82,334. Korean immigrants were no less affected by these and other problems. By the mid-1970s, as the public and government agencies became more aware of this population, they realized the dire state of social services. A January 1975 County Department of Community Services report cited unemployment, crime, domestic strife, juvenile delinquency, undocumented status, and language barriers as problems affecting Korean immigrants and impeding their successful transition to life in the United States.[73] A hotline service was set up in 1973 to help integrate them and connect them to services, and in the first year alone, it received 283 calls for help on everything from car accidents and legal trouble to job searching and business assistance.

It was never clear how such problems would be addressed by commercial development that prioritized retail and upscale establishments.[74] Nor did place entrepreneurs seem particularly interested in incorporating Latinos and Blacks as stakeholders in Koreatown's future. When these communities did come up, it was more as inconveniences or obstacles to be circumvented than rightful stakeholders. For instance, the street cleanups discussed above gave Koreans an outsize visibility and image as saviors of a neighborhood that they actually shared with Blacks and Latinos. Meanwhile, the presence of the latter two groups was at best implied and assumed to be responsible for harm—be it the "hardcore graffiti," crime, or disarray that Koreans were dutifully cleaning and fixing.

The boosters of Korea City acknowledged that affordable housing was low on their list of concerns and that the project "would force the relocation of some Korean and non-Korean commercial and residential properties."[75] Another large-scale project, called Korea Village, which may have been an offshoot of Korea City, proposed the inclusion of housing units that would have been subject to federal guidelines. Richard Rosenthal of the City Planning Department warned that this meant any apartments would first have to be offered to those being relocated. "That means the Latinos and blacks, not the Koreans," he clarified.[76] In part because of this, Korea Village had been planned and discussed quietly and only among Koreans. One of its spokespersons, Gene Kim, explained this "privacy" was necessary in order "to gain support for the project from the city and the Latino and Black communities that might be affected, as well as from among the Koreans themselves." This was a disingenuous position, and excluding the groups was more likely a tactic to evade collaboration and prevent other parties from influencing or challenging the plans. Reflecting developers' singular focus on their interests and inattention to the broader community, Kim added, "Some will be very envious of what we'll be doing."

Even as they were clear on whom Koreatown was and was not for, immigrant place entrepreneurs still struggled with the area's disorganization, unsightliness, and lack of spatial cohesiveness. Complaints emerged, for instance, about the "explosion" of mini malls in Koreatown and Los Angeles more generally. Derisively characterized by one community activist as "examples of the

FIGURE 3   Article from Koreatown Weekly, December 1982, p. 17, touting the Korea City project, led by David Hyun. https://cdn.calisphere.org/data/13030/6h/hbod5nbo6h/files/hbod5nbo6h-FID161.jpg.

fast food mentality in architecture," the malls often had design features that exacerbated traffic and other problems. Those in Koreatown usually had parking lots in the front, which "[broke] the strips of buildings that line most major commercial avenues," as well as curb cuts that disrupted pedestrian traffic.[77] Furthermore, as Olympic became a busier shopping area and motorists used the street as an alternative to the Santa Monica freeway, an increase in accidents involving cars and pedestrians resulted.[78] Traffic officer Steve Hillman warned that crossing Olympic Boulevard was perilous and that "this is primarily Asian people we're losing here."[79] The noise, litter, and traffic associated with Koreatown's growth led City Council members Hal Bernson and Mike Woo to call for new limits on commercial development near residential areas and measures such as adding lighting and banning early morning trash collection.

Resistance to Koreatown's expansion did not turn into a full-blown nativist movement but did take the form of xenophobia-laced, us-versus-them rhetoric. As discussed earlier, remarks about Koreans' habits concerning money and what one Korean broker called their "dynamic, aggressive, and ruthless" nature were offered to explain their entrepreneurship, but such ideas also animated worries about a whether there was a nefarious side to their activities and plans for Koreatown.[80] Reporter Diana Sherman described a purchase by a Korean doctor and his wife of a thirteen-thousand square-foot site with a dilapidated building for the exorbitant price of $300,000. "What amazes and disturbs some brokers," she wrote, "is that the Koreans don't negotiate over the price of property. They often pay the first price the seller asks and often in cash." Sherman explained that this would drive up the value and cost of land and buildings in the area and price out other would-be buyers. As Koreatown's prices rose, immigrant developers moved on to eye the nearby Wilshire corridor between Hoover and Western as the next area to conquer.

The images of Koreans as unskilled or unsavvy commercial developers and Koreatown as an unruly ever-expanding entity was as frustrating for immigrant place entrepreneurs as it was useful for associations trying to stop them. In 1985, the Country Club Park Neighborhood Association fought a Korean restaurant's rezoning request to turn an adjacent residence into a parking lot. The association's secretary Katherine Miller vowed to the Board of Zoning Appeals that it would "unalterably oppose any commercialism attempting to creep into our residentially zoned neighborhood of stately, graceful, historic homes." Though the area in question was outside the boundaries of Koreatown, Miller said she was "very concerned about the rights of the people who do live in what's designated Koreatown."[81]

David Hyun conveyed the exasperation of Koreans who had to contend with strict limits on development and construction but then shouldered blame for Koreatown's shortcomings. "When one shopping center is put on Vermont Avenue . . . they say, 'Oh wonderful! Two or three is maybe OK,'" he said in 1985. But when you see five or six, you say, 'Why don't these Koreans know how to build well? That's not the case at all! They're building under the city regulations that existed before they came. They're revitalizing under a handicap—under existing zoning and parking codes and they're inadequate."[82] Developers were constrained by a maze of zoning codes, general plans, and new proposals, which inhibited large-scale mixed-use developments. The cultural and community center in the Korea City plan, for example, would have required the rezoning of residential property for commercial and community use. In February 1984, a group of Korean businessmen and activists pressed the Planning Commission to allow structures taller than three stories and give Koreatown the same leeway it proposed for developers downtown and in the Wilshire corridor.[83] Hyun reminded the commission of Koreans' feats in urban development and urged it to lower the barriers to further construction and growth, so they could accomplish even more. "Since 10 years ago, the Olympic Blvd. corridor has been the site of amazing self-renewal, from urban decay to urban revitalization," he said. "This has been achieved almost exclusively by private financial means." Hyun claimed that rising property values led to a 500 percent increase in taxes the city was able to collect and that limiting Koreatown development would discourage continued "self-revitalization."

Claims of self-sufficiency notwithstanding, no large-scale project could go it alone as a wholly private enterprise, and zoning and building restrictions were just the tip of the iceberg. A project like Korea City or Korea Village required more money, coordination, and labor than the Korean community—with leadership from the KTDA, Hyun, Lee, and others—could muster on its own. This was where otherwise supportive City agencies and officials drew the line. The CRA made clear it lacked funds for Koreatown projects and, along with City Council member David Cunningham, encouraged them to raise their own funds. Cunningham said private financing would also ease the bureaucratic red tape and blunt potential lawsuits, thus facilitating speedier completion. Otherwise, he warned, it could be twenty years before Korea City was a reality. Simply initiating work on a Koreatown Specific Plan under the Department of City Planning required an initial outlay of $200,000 to hire a consultant, rent a project office, and conduct surveys and research. This was unusual because the creation of specific plans was usually undertaken and funded by the city, but "in the case of Koreatown, all of the initiative was community based."[84] David Hyun expressed confidence that through his Korea City, Inc. corporation he could raise the money.

Little happened from there. A citizens advisory committee with community members was formed to assist the City Planning Department, but there are no official records of meetings until 1985. By the time stakeholders inquired about being designated a CRA redevelopment area, they were told Koreatown would likely be ineligible because "it is not a blighted area."[85] Ironically, their self-driven, privately financed improvements, though modest in scale, had effectively disqualified them from receiving public funding and support for larger scale projects. "The planning department did not feel that Koreatown was blighted enough to warrant a redevelopment project," said senior city planner Peter Broy in 1982. They continued to receive encouragement and sympathy but little else. Another city planner, Ruby Ann Justis, remarked three years later in 1985 that Koreans "really want this" but they "are going to have to muster up a tremendous amount of political support."[86]

Hi Duk Lee chalked up the lost momentum to a sluggish economy as well as Koreans' inability to work together on long-term goals. After the initial enthusiasm he and David Hyun drummed up, no one took the "next step." "From my experience," Lee wrote, "many Koreans are smart but do not work for the long run. They can start something, but have trouble growing it and getting past their greed."[87] The president of the Koreatown Chamber of Commerce, Barney Moon, blamed internal fissures in the Korean community, particularly the perception that the KTDA and Gene Kim "were not working for the whole community."[88] Worried that the large-scale plan would never materialize, Lee tried to go it alone with his plans to expand the VIP Palace site into a plaza with offices and a hotel. In 1982, high interest rates and a still lagging economy forced him to scale down the cost of the project from $10 million to $4 million and delay the anticipated completion from August 1983 to March 1984. Meanwhile, the lot sat vacant and overgrown with weeds.[89]

After repeated delays and deadlocks, revitalization plans for Koreatown came under the direction of a non-Korean development and employment agency called the Pacific-Asian Consortium in Employment (PACE) in 1984. Its director Glenn Sanada said, "I think the only way was to work together. . . . The program lent the opportunity for that to happen."[90] PACE worked with Koreatown businesses and in partnership with the Korean Chamber of Commerce, KTDA, Koreatown Federation, Korean Building Contractors Association, Korean American Institute of Architects, and Korean American Coalition.[91] In August 1984, it submitted an application to the Commercial Area Revitalization Program Effort (CARE), a federal grant program that assisted local businesses that was administered by the city's Community Development Department (CDD).[92] PACE hoped to promote Koreatown's economy by offering business seminars for merchants, improving safety and security, making public improvements, enhancing tourism, developing real estate, and "geographically centraliz[ing] Koreatown both on the map and in the minds of people outside the community."[93] Though the workmanlike rhetoric and approach of PACE lacked the flair of his Korea City campaign, David Hyun nonetheless expressed hope in 1984 that it would allow Koreans to finally show they were an "important force" in the city and be given their "long-awaited recognition."[94]

Into its second year, after receiving about $300,000 from the city and federal government, the Koreatown revitalization program under PACE and with CARE funds was headed for "collapse." This was due to changes in federal funding guidelines and the community not meeting the benchmarks the program required.[95] The fizzling of this effort also spoke to intractable contradictions of trying to develop "Koreatown" as a monoethnic space in a multiethnic community. PACE never had complete buy-in from the Korean business community.[96] The assistance and integration the CARE program and CDD provided, however, was also contingent on serving the area, not just its Korean stakeholders. The CDD, for instance, replaced *Korean* with *minority* in its recommendations because federal funds could not be reserved for one group. "The director told those attending that the city wants the community to understand that the program benefits are not just for Koreatown merchants who are Korean, but all minority businessmen within the designated area."

Immigrant place entrepreneurs built Koreatown and made their mark through entrepreneurship, capital accumulation, property development, and claims to self-sufficiency. Such a conditional and transactional form of belonging reflected the diminished opportunity and scarcity of the times. Thus, they organized street cleanups to message to the city that Korean immigrants were earning their keep, which obscured the reality of capital and government divestment in poor neighborhoods with large numbers of immigrants and non-whites. A starker example of this paradox was the opening of a sheriff substation in Koreatown in 1981. Prompted by high crime in the area, which impeded development and hurt the neighborhood's image, the station was entirely privately financed. While this enabled the city's continued neglect, Koreatown leaders like Gene Kim and Hi Duk Lee touted the substation as yet another example of Koreans' remarkable tenacity and self-sufficiency.

Having immigrated from Korea to the United States in the 1950s, the journalist K. W. Lee was overwhelmed upon encountering Koreatown. "A little Seoul sprang up," he wrote in 1979, "and this BK Korean has much to get used to—the flavor, the texture and the smell of Korea Town." To see and stand inside Koreatown caused him to reflect on his earlier years and opened the emotional floodgates. Unlike the post-1965 immigrants, Lee "had no Korea Town to turn to for solace." Instead, he wrote, he was part of "a generation of rootless sojourners who carried a secret Korea Town in our desolate hearts between fleeting encounters and inevitable departures." He continued further, "We had holes in our soul—welling pain inside, but nowhere to hide our feelings of somewhereness. Korea Town was nowhere."

K. W. Lee's wistful writings and his self-description as a BK underscored how Koreatown was an idea and aspiration as much as it was a place. More than just a setting or a backdrop, it was a symbol that they *did* belong somewhere. It was also a vehicle for the dreams of entrepreneurial immigrants and locals eager for their city to make a comeback. Perhaps because those dreams were such an appealing contrast to the messy and intractable realities on the ground—whether the non-Korean residents, the concentrated poverty, the disorderly spatial layout of the ethnic community—it was easier to elide those factors and focus on the Koreatown that people wanted to see. "There is no question that the Koreans intend to make the Olympic Blvd. area their own," said Richard Rosenthal of the Department of Planning in 1979. By the mid-1980s, they had, but in other ways, they never could.

CHAPTER 3

Searching for Koreatown

Generational Divides and Cultural
Bridges in Korean America

IN 1979, K. W. Lee started the *Koreatown Weekly*, the first all-English newspaper for Korean Americans. Belying its name, the paper's reporters worked mostly in Southern California, its printer was in Sacramento, and its stories covered communities and concerns across the country. *Koreatown* strove to be a news source as well as a virtual gathering place for Korean Americans across place, generation, and time. Editors also hoped to reach non-Korean readers who were curious about the rapidly growing immigrant community. In its inaugural issue, they explained that their mission would be to inform readers of "the remarkable saga of a hardy and brave people from the Land of the Morning Calm," while giving Korean Americans "a mirror and forum for self-discovery and identity" and "a bridge to our homeland and heritage." *Koreatown's* contents ranged widely, from in-depth reporting on the movement to free the imprisoned immigrant and accused murderer Chol Soo Lee to ruminative essays by young adults about being Korean American in the 1970s and 1980s.

Shortly after its launch, *Koreatown* changed the life of Sophia Kim, a 1.5 (immigrated as a child) Korean American, self-identified member of the "knee-high generation," and recent college graduate.[1] She was working at a women's shelter, which reporter Randy Hagihara visited while he was working on a story about Asian Americans and domestic violence. Learning that an all-English language Korean American weekly existed was a revelation that "sparked my imagination," Kim said.[2] She proceeded to lobby K. W. Lee for a job, first being hired for office work and then moving up as a writer. She recalled writing about "a little bit of everything," from human interest articles to stories about Korean American youth and politics. "[We] wanted the politicians and people who spoke only English, people in the mainstream community to know what was going on in the Korean community as small as it may have seemed."[3] Kim's time at *Koreatown* eventually launched her into a fruitful career in journalism that included interning at the *Los Angeles Times* and writing for the *Korea Times Los Angeles*, the *Los Angeles Herald*, and other newspapers in Southern and Northern California.[4]

Though separated by a large age gap, Sophia Kim and K. W. Lee belonged to a small, diverse cohort of Koreans in America who preceded the much larger wave of post-1965 arrivals. As such, they often felt alienated from yet drawn to the newcomers, seeing them as both kinfolk and strangers. As journalists, Kim and Lee wanted to cover the growth of Korean immigration and its implications for the Korean American community and US society writ large. They felt called on to guide readers through newly urgent conversations about ethnic solidarity and politics, and as Korean Americans themselves, often participated in them as well.

This chapter explores how, against the backdrop of increasing immigration, Korean Americans grappled with their identities, assessed their relationship to Korean-ness, and formulated new conceptions of belonging as ethnic minorities in the United States. It foregrounds the perspectives of 1.5-, second-, and third-generation Korean Americans, who on the one hand distinguished themselves from the newcomers but on the other were drawn to them, in order to connect with their own lost or unformed sense of Korean-ness. They wrote copiously and dedicated themselves to organizing, doing so with great urgency to meet and make sense of the historic moment of change, both in their ethnic community and in the nation due to the transformative forces of immigration.

An important context for this process was the rise of hyphenated nationalism in the larger culture, which extolled the idea of the United States as a nation of immigrants and a collection of ethnic cultures. A tenet of the ascendant ethos of liberal multiculturalism, hyphenated nationalism appealed to people for its broad inclusiveness; nearly every American, save indigenous people, could claim migrant roots of some kind. During the late 1960s and 1970s, as grandchildren of immigrants from the late 1800s to early 1900s entered adulthood, many embraced an ethos of hyphenated nationalism, enacting a phenomenon the sociologist Marcus Lee Hansen called the "third-generation dilemma" in 1938. According to Hansen, immigrants—the first generation—were cultural outsiders who experienced rejection in US society. Their children—the second generation—achieved mainstream belonging but often discarded their ethnic cultures in the process. Their children—the third generation—lamented the choices of their parents that robbed them of their heritage and left them—in their perception—culturally bland or empty.[5] As historian Matthew Jacobson notes, this generation, "who had known nothing but 'American' culture," became determined to "quit the melting pot" and zealously engaged in pursuits like studying immigration history and old-world languages, learning folk dancing, tracing genealogies, and going on homeland tours.[6] Non-white Americans, however, faced more complicated and limited choices than simply learning Italian or going to a Saint Patrick's Day parade. For instance, African Americans' loss of their ancestral cultures under slavery was not the result of choices made by earlier generations eager to assimilate. And Asians and Latinos two or three generations removed from their immigrant roots had a knotty relationship with hyphenated nationalism due to the surge of newcomers from their countries of ancestry who represented living reminders of the heritage they had lost.

The influx of immigrants from Korea reconfigured the social terrain and jolted US-born and longtime Korean Americans. Previously, all they had known was being part of a tiny, barely visible minority. They had grown accustomed to being mistaken for or lumped with other Asians, or as David Hyun remarked, being seen as "second rate Japanese." Perhaps, some pondered, the enhanced visibility of Korean people by way of immigration opened a door for Korean Americans to join the more established Asian Americans. Such hopes, however, gave way to sobering realizations about the tenuousness of ethnicity, community, and personal identity. Aware that they were becoming vastly outnumbered by the newcomers, Korean Americans reckoned with their poor grasp of hangul and other aspects of Korean culture while wondering what held them together as a group. K. W. Lee, for instance, felt a strong affinity with all Koreans in America, but he also believed that unity and solidarity should not be taken for granted. "If we take a good look at ourselves," he wrote in 1982, "we are far from being alike. We are . . . a mosaic of people from different times and different places seemingly thrown together in a new land by a time warp."[7] A legacy of colonization, exclusion, and war had produced this "time warp" and shaped

Koreans' fitful, lopsided immigration patterns. From the late 1970s and 1980s, Lee, Kim, and many others, as the chapter will show, tried to build bridges across these temporal and cultural divides to forge and articulate a new Korean America.[8] This journey brought equal shares of exhilaration and bewilderment and shed light on the ongoing, always changing, and ever unpredictable process of finding oneself and one's community vis-à-vis ethnicity.

Other Kindred People

The rise of Korean migration after 1965, which accelerated in the 1970s and 1980s, occurred as many second- and third-generation Korean Americans came of age, and these two demographic forces would profoundly impact one another. Providing much insight on this were writings from the perspectives of young adults in their teens and twenties, many of these published in the *Koreatown Weekly*. They included the stories of Carolyn Ayon, Julie Suhr, and Dennis Chang. Suhr recalled a childhood spent wishing she looked like the white American curly-haired child actor Shirley Temple and separating herself from other Asians. Ayon, meanwhile, described growing up in a predominantly white community in Worcester, Massachusetts, and Chang had a relatively insular middle-class life, which he assumed was the case for other Korean Americans. When Ayon learned there was a growing Korean community in Boston, she was excited and hoped to finally "meet other kindred people, people who would accept me for what I am."[9] In college, Suhr befriended Korean immigrants her age for the first time and subsequently came to embrace her "love of the culture and appetite for its food" and identity as a "100 percent hankook-salam [Korean person]."[10] Chang worked at the Korean Cultural Center in Los Angeles, where his eyes were opened to the diversity of the Korean American experience, especially regarding poverty and delinquency in Koreatown. He recalled one youth who lived with his parents, a sibling, and an aunt in a two-bedroom apartment. "All of a sudden," he said, "four other people from Korea come and now there are nine people living in the apartment. The kid ends up sleeping on the ground. He got into a conflict with his family, and he got thrown out. As soon as he left, he went right into a gang."[11]

Ayon, Suhr, and Chang's reflections glimpsed some of the ways that post-1965 immigration impacted the lives and self-perceptions of 1.5-, second-, and third-generation Korean Americans. The growing numbers of and public attention to Korean immigrants raised intriguing possibilities and inescapable questions they wanted to explore. Would they finally resolve their conflicts of identity, embrace an ethnic consciousness, and advance themselves in solidarity with co-ethnics? Would the preponderance of recent immigrants assist or impede the status of Korean Americans in the US social and political order? Moreover, who should step up as the leaders of the community in this era? A palpable urgency to understand what was occurring, rise to the moment, and shape a promising future informed the pages of Korean American publications, new organizations, and numerous gatherings. In addition to writings by members of the second and third generation, these included events such as a historic "reunion" of about two hundred Koreans and Korean Americans at the Ambassador Hotel in August 1980. They also included the organizations Korean-American Students Conference (KASCON) and Korean American Youth Foundation (KAYF), which aimed to develop the consciousness and leadership of young Korean Americans.[12]

A recurring theme in Korean Americans' writings and gatherings around this time was finding common ground with recent immigrants and across the generations. Acknowledging that this would be difficult work, third-generation Korean American Cooke Sunoo was confident that Koreans would rise to the challenge, citing past experience. "Their [immigrants'] children will be sharing the same experience and the same types of feeling my (second generation) parents went through," he said.[13] Others were similarly optimistic. At the first KASCON retreat in 1981, held at Camp Conifer in Angelus Oaks (about two hours west of Los Angeles), thirty young Korean Americans—representing immigrants and the US-born—gathered to discuss a range of topics. As *Koreatown Weekly* reported, attendees had "notable and emotional discussion . . . around the differences between the first- and second-generation Korean-Americans at camp. The first generation shared their past experiences and hardships when they immigrated to the United States. Their stories touched the hearts of all." Dennis Chang and Julie Suhr described their own breakthroughs after interacting with immigrants. Working at the Korean Cultural Center gave Chang insights about his identity and responsibilities as a Korean American. "It gives you a perception of who you are and what you are doing here," he said. Suhr shared her relief at finding peace with her ethnic identity, crediting her friendships with Korean immigrants: "It is not easy being a Korean American, but it's a characteristic I wouldn't trade for the world."

That said, for every heartwarming story of interpersonal connection or psychic epiphany, there was a tale of disappointment and bewilderment, which underscored that simply sharing a country of origin was not a magical force that effortlessly enjoined people in mutual affinity and solidarity. People also had encounters fraught with misaligned and uncommunicated expectations. Such was the case for Caroline Ayon when she went to Boston to meet other Koreans. "Most of the people had been born in Korea," she said, "and although they may have lived in the United States for several years, they considered themselves Korean, not Korean-American." Ayon lamented how "a world of difference" separated her from the new immigrants and the language barrier proved insurmountable, so "[disappointment] and sadness were in my heart as I began the one-hour drive back to Worcester."[14] Jai Lee, an immigrant who had come to the United States as a high school student, found herself the object of expectations like Ayon's. At her new school, second- and third-generation Korean Americans "were excited to meet me because they didn't know too many immigrants." To get around the language barrier, she recalled doing "a lot of nodding and smiling." Lee's social life with her new friends included attending gatherings addressing topics that were salient to them but could be puzzling to her. The second and third generation, she related, were fixated on "trying to figure out who they were . . . there were full panels, like 'Who Am I?' 'Am I Korean or am I American?'"

The awkward politeness, resigned disappointment, and unexpressed confusion over the interactions between immigrants and Korean Americans likely stemmed from realizations that they had little in common in terms of life experiences. The fitful patterns of immigration had created a large social, cultural, and temporal divide in Korean America. K. W. Lee channeled this when he named the BK, the "before Koreatown" generations, the cohort with whom he identified. The BK were the predecessors of the post-1965ers. As such they were a small but varied lot, including labor migrants who went to Hawaii as early as 1903, students arriving in the 1950s, and their descendants. The BK came to the United States before Korea's modernization, when it was under Japanese colonialism or devastated by war, and so tended to have poorer and less educated backgrounds than those arriving after 1965. The BK Koreans experienced the anti-Asian movements of the early twentieth century and lived in America at a time when exclusion was the policy. By contrast, the post-1965ers were a "new breed" who arrived with notable advantages, observed journalist K. Connie Kang. They were more likely to be college graduates and possess professional backgrounds, they left a modernized Korea, and settled in a nation that was much more inclusive than it had been for the BKs. They also transplanted themselves at a time of accelerating global inter-connectedness. As a result, argued Kang, they "don't suffer the pangs of dual loyalties and dual identities," "nor were they constantly reminded of their own inadequate command of the language and culture of the majority."[15]

Such statements shed light on how BK Koreans understood themselves as a unique group in the rapidly growing and diversifying US Korean popu-lation. But they did not just see themselves as worse off or less advantaged. Because they were assimilated and knowledgeable about American life and had social capital and access to key publications and organizations, the BK Koreans believed they were distinctly qualified to intellectually frame and explain the significance of immigration while also helping the newcomers through their hard-earned wisdom. This was a variation on the traditional cultural mediator role that the children of immigrants often play between immigrant communities and mainstream society. But through their efforts, the BK Koreans also revealed their own long-simmering anxieties about fit-ting in or "making it" in the United States as racial minorities, which the presence of newcomers—or the pejorative "FOBs"—brought clarity to.

As BK Korean American writers sought to break down who the recent immigrants were, they often did so by using themselves as points of refer-ence. The subjects of money and status provoked especially charged com-mentaries. "When we look soberly at the Korean landscape we are building in America," wrote K. Connie Kang, "we can't help but notice how much time and energy we devote to making money." Kang judged this devotion as a moral deficiency and the result of mixed-up priorities, and worried this would reflect poorly on all Korean Americans. K. W. Lee called immigrants who went into business "Cadillac Koreans," similarly suggesting that their singular pursuit of wealth entailed costly personal trade-offs, including not having interesting lives outside of work. "Fact is," Lee wrote, "often as I eat out and frequent restaurants where Koreans dine, I have never heard someone ask, 'What book are you reading now?' or 'Have you ever seen that play?'" Kang remarked more pointedly, "I'd like to suggest to those Koreans who flaunt their wealth [and] titles . . . to take a look at themselves in their mirrors. It is just possible that they may not like what they see."

Such remarks about the newcomers echoed intraethnic debates occurring in all communities upended by immigration. As discussed above, awareness of Korean migration activated a vague hope for communion among some of the BKs, but an equally common reaction was to express anxiety and practice disidentification. At the 1980 Ambassador Hotel reunion, Charles Yoon, a Beverly Hills oral surgeon and older member of the second generation, derided and shamed those young Korean Americans trying to retain or recuperate their Korean-ness vis-à-vis their social affiliations, criticizing mainstream society, and insisting on calling themselves "Korean American." To Yoon, this was a form of self-foreignization that made no sense. "I am thinking . . . after being here for this many years that this is our country and that we are real Americans," he said.[16] They were lucky to live in a place and time where racism no longer affected Koreans, and they could be "totally accepted" if they "spread out" and stopped "trying to be Korean." His daughter Lisa agreed and credited herself as a model for other third-generation Korean Americans. She seemed proud to have never had any Korean friends as a child, and claimed she never experienced racism. Too many of her peers, she bemoaned, fixated on difference, and "the more it separates you from the mainstream . . . you can't do that if you want to get ahead."[17] Yoon worried that the presence of so many unassimilated newcomers who did not speak English, congregated among themselves, and brought attention to Koreans as foreigners could make life more difficult for all Koreans.[18] And it was not just their own fate that worried them; the children of the new immigrants could suffer as well. Journalist Holim Kim rebuked immigrant parents who failed to culturally adapt and raise their children as 100 percent American. "[The] parents . . . are the ones who made the choice to come to a country where the majority is white, the language is foreign, and the customs and culture different." By making this choice, Kim wrote, they had an obligation to embrace their new country fully and "push our young into the American mainstream as far and high as they are able to go—into politics, business and other professions." To do otherwise was a grave failure that would hurt families and all Korean Americans.

Others rejected the conceit that the BKs were in any position to judge and advise other Korean people. Tai Bong Chung, who immigrated in the mid-1960s and lived in Northern California, said it was actually the Korean Americans who should be learning lessons from the immigrants. He thought it was ironic and misguided to suggest there was something wrong with simply working hard. Besides, the immigrants tended to be better educated than the longer rooted and more Americanized Koreans. "Not even five percent of the Korean business people can read the *San Francisco Chron-*

icle. They don't know English, but they can do small business. Sheer blood and guts," he said admiringly.[19] Instead of giving condescending advice, Korean Americans, Chung implored, should offer their compassion and assistance. Korean immigrants are a "lonely lot," he said. "Just be a friend to them. You help them buy an apartment, find a house or job for them."[20] In a slightly different vein, an attendee at the 1980 Ambassador Hotel reunion questioned the very notion that the immigrants were a separate group to be kept at a distance by co-ethnics. "These (immigrant) people are you," the attendee stressed. "I don't see how you can make such a distinction. We should be sympathetic to them. They are just you."[21]

Such dialogues revealed BK Koreans' preoccupations about the newcomers and whether they would be assets or liabilities for Koreans in American society. It also revealed how, in the face of momentous and disorienting change, people often lean on conceptions of time to get their bearings and escape their worries, whether by constructing a past or projecting a reassuring future. A reader of *Koreatown* tried to assuage others with a long-term outlook, saying that "Koreans, generally, are a recent immigrant group to the United States and are too busy 'making it' to be concerned about their brothers and sisters at this stage in their assimilation." The reader called for patience from others and to take comfort in the future. "Remember, it's not going to happen overnight," they said. "Bear in mind the Japanese and Chinese have been in America over 100 years." Others saw the differences between BKs and newcomers as mere accidents of time and history, and therefore entirely surmountable barriers between compatriots. "They came here forty years later," said an attendee at the Ambassador reunion about the post-1965ers. "Therefore they are not quite what we are because we came here on the Original Boat. Does that sound familiar?"[22]

Kimchi and Hangul

A tried-and-true supposition about cultural change in immigrant communities, summed up by Tong Soo Chung in 1982, was that "the old generation continually looks back to the culture they came from, while the youths eagerly accept the new and exciting culture, sometimes even at the cost of total renunciation of their roots." This idea was undergoing a reassessment by the time he made the remark, as many young Korean Americans voiced their regrets over the "loss" of their culture due to assimilation, and asserted their desire to discover and reclaim their ethnic heritage.[23] They recognized this was a tall order, and as Cooke Sunoo expressed, "None of us seems to know how we're going to do this great feat."[24] As tangible—and with new immigration, pervasive—facets of their heritage, food and language figured especially prominently in Korean Americans' process of exploring and understanding their ethnic identities.

Young Korean Americans grappled with the social and psychological baggage resulting from the stigmatization of their heritage. They had grown up bombarded by messages that their ancestral food and language were strange and should be renounced and excised if they wanted to fully belong in the United States. Having immigrated as a child, Veronica Chang remembered a time when she spoke more Korean than English, but after enduring painful rejection by her peers, she "followed and imitated Caucasians so that they would look at me as if I was one of them." She continued, "I didn't want to be a Korean" and was "ashamed to speak the language in front of my friends." Eventually, Chang forgot how to speak Korean. Shunning the Korean language went hand in hand with avoiding Korean food, which was burdened by a legacy of being reviled by outsiders. Kimchi, the spicy fermented cabbage dish, drew particular attention and revulsion due to its smell, which a *Los Angeles Times* reader described in 1975 as the most "putrefying" and "devastating" odor they had ever encountered. "I would rather breathe cigarette smoke, be accosted hourly by unwashed and unscented underarms, or suffer the indignity of emptying bedpans than enter a Korean bus at rush hour," they elaborated. Such attitudes conditioned Koreans not only to modify what they ate around non-Koreans but also to internalize the stigma associated with their food. An article in *Koreatown* from 1980, for instance, warned readers, "Some Anglos Can Smell Kimchi a Mile Away," and related light anecdotes with dispiriting lessons. One interviewee, who worked as a saleswoman with mostly non-Korean colleagues, explained that she ate kimchi during coffee breaks, "But my colleagues started sniffing and looking in my direction. . . . I would pretend I didn't smell anything. But this went on for weeks, and I just gave up [bringing kimchi]."

Coming to terms with the legacy of cultural renunciation, whether due to outside pressure and intolerance or decisions made by parents and ancestors, could be painful. *Koreatown* youth editor Alice Yang lamented that her inability to speak Korean had robbed her of a close relationship with her grandmother. As Veronica Chang tried to become friends with Korean students while in college at the University of Washington, she faced the sad truth that "I had abused my homeland and its language" and came to "re-gret . . . forgetting my native language by being ashamed of it." Such realiza-tions also provoked anger toward parents, elders, and the larger society. As Elaine Kim remarked, "If we as parents push our children into being Ameri-can, it's not fair to badger them when they don't want to learn the language or marry Koreans."[25] Common in the memories of young Korean Ameri-cans was being told, on the one hand, to be monolingual English speakers so that they would "make it" in the United States while, on the other hand, being scolded for not knowing Korean. As Alice Yang explained, it was her parents, after all, who pushed her to be Americanized but did not prioritize her learning Korean. Growing up with contradictory messages about lan-guage and culture caused young Korean Americans much personal anguish and "total alienation," described Elaine Kim.

Kim elaborated that decades of trying to assimilate on the belief that they would eventually overcome all barriers of race and ethnicity had failed Ko-rean Americans and left them disconnected from their heritage. "The only thing we have left is our face and coloring," she lamented mournfully, "which will disappear through intermarriage. We'll also lose our language and all the tradition it conveys."[26] Such revelations channeled early twentieth-century sociological theories about the "Oriental problem" or "marginal man," which held that Asians in the United States were a uniquely alienated minority, un-able to fully integrate into the mainstream despite their multigenerational presence. This was still the case in the 1970s and 1980s when second- and even third-generation Korean Americans, said Alice Yang, concluded they would "never feel completely American as they look Korean." One difference was that they could now do something about their dilemma. They could reject the shame they and their forbears once felt and embrace their language and culture. In a 1980 forum in *Koreatown Weekly* called "Is There a Need for the Korean Language?" a respondent affirmed, "I should know the language of my background" because "I will always be considered Korean no matter how Americanized I am." While Alice Yang believed her ship had sailed be-cause "I simply do not have enough time to dedicate to learning the language effectively" and she would never be "fully comfortable with Korean culture," she hoped that younger Korean Americans would grow up less conflicted and, thus, "fully comfortable" in ways that eluded her.

The revelatory and prideful sentiments of young Korean Americans about language also extended to food. David Kim was a second-generation Korean American and the youth editor for *Koreatown* whose search for identity eventually brought him to the subject. He fixated on his dislike of kimchi, or "what hamburgers are to America," speculating that, "I felt a need deep in my mind to revolt against [my parents]. Maybe it was the subconscious desire not to be Koreanized completely." He wondered if overcoming his dislike of kimchi was his "last hurdle to being a complete Korean." Kim's musings resonated with reader Philip Syung Sik Park, who identified himself as an older member of the second generation. "I can recall, as a child, my own distaste, not only for kimchee, but for nearly everything else Korean," which he attributed to growing up in the intolerant times the 1940s. "I understand and sympathize with my friend David and his concern," Park wrote. He found inner peace in his later years and saw his embrace of kimchi as a function of this. Park was confident that in the more inclusive era of the 1980s, David Kim would soon find similar peace regardless of his taste for kimchi. "To be American," Park expounded, "is not to ignore or dislike kimchee, but to attempt to guarantee that everyone's identity is affirmed and uplifted."

Koreatown Weekly's stories about food, whether reprints of restaurant reviews from mainstream publications, reports of the opening of new establishments, explorations of traditions, or personal essays, suggested a close link between culinary habits and authentic Korean-ness. College students Richard Kim and Elaine Kim told *Koreatown* that kimchi reflected the "Korean character," which was "peppery and salty" as well as "extremist." For Sophia Kim, the more time she spent in the United States, the stronger her fondness for Korean food became. She thought this revealed not just the incompleteness of her assimilation but also her hardwired preference for her native cuisine, especially the "hotter, more pungent, and more esoteric" dishes. "I must be the only Korean-American who finds hamburgers boring," she wrote. "The American food only seemed to fill up my stomach, yet never satisfy my appetite. It was as though I had only a Korean stomach." Christine Lee described a childhood tormented by an "identity crisis" until experiencing a breakthrough in college. In the genre of personal writings by Korean American young adults, college was a consistently common turning point. "By the time I graduated," Lee wrote, "I resolved my conflict by saying to myself 'you are Korean-American.' The Korean in me still prefers kimchee-chi-ghe over [American] meat stew."

Korean Americans negotiated their relationships with food and language against a fluid social and cultural backdrop in American life. Foodways and restaurants were the vanguard of the public's growing awareness of Koreans as an American ethnic group, and hangul was becoming a familiar and stable fixture in the linguistic milieu of Los Angeles. "Back in the fall of 1973," stated *Koreatown* in 1980, "the mother tongue for the burgeoning Korean Americans was about to become an extinct language among their children."[27] At the time, one Korean-language school in Koreatown served about fifty students in Southern California, but by 1980 there were 54 Korean-language schools with 3,000 students and 250 teachers, and the once-struggling Koreatown school enrolled 450 students. To the Koreatown school's principal Kil-sang Kwon, this indicated that Koreans were on their way to "[catching] up with Japanese Americans in ethnic identity."[28] To young adults, especially erstwhile alienated members of the second and third generations, the heightened presence of the Korean language offered opportunities to practice or learn the language and help newly arrived coethnics. Lisa Yu, a young bilingual Korean American, was gratified that she could use her abilities to make some difference for other Koreans. "[You] can help other Korean people who haven't learned English yet," she said, "or help Korean-American people who haven't learned Korean yet."

As they expanded their awareness of immigrant life, language also launched Korean Americans into civic engagement and political activism. The need for resources to help these immigrants was acute, as language barriers and the lack of interpreters hindered them in school, finding jobs, and other aspects of daily life.[29] *Koreatown* reported that from 1978 to 1980 the number of Korean students in California public schools classified as limited English or non-English speaking (LES/NES) rose by 42 percent. Teachers were insufficiently prepared to work with these students who then fell through the cracks and into juvenile delinquency. Language, then, was a matter of justice and survival. As the California State University, Los Angeles, sociologist Eui-Young Yu argued, bilingual support for the Korean American community was essential to help people in daily life and to create an inclusive society where newcomers could live with an "attitude of self-respect and confidence."[30]

Language support was a centerpiece of Asian American activism by the 1970s. In 1971, the Asian-American Education Commission (AAEC) was formed in response to the needs of Asian American and Pacific Islander (AAPI) students with limited English proficiency in the Los Angeles Unified School District. It was made up of thirty mostly volunteer members and provided the district with recommendations, material development, supplemental service, and information on the concerns of AAPI students.[31] In 1982, the district proposed shutting down the AAEC along with several other commissions dedicated to minorities and protected groups, at a time when its services were especially pressing.[32] From 1971 to 1981, the number of AAPI students in the district had increased by over 150 percent, from twenty-eight thousand to forty thousand.[33] In late 1982, Asian Americans spoke out against the proposed closing. Chang Kyu Shin of the Korean American Voters Alliance (KAVA) said if the closure occurred, "the LAUSC will return to the Dark Ages," and stressed that Asians had unique cultural challenges as immigrants compared to other minorities.[34]

As state-supported bilingualism emerged as a high-profile policy issue in California, it raised the political consciousness of many Korean Americans. People across society debated contentiously over everything from whether immigrant students in public schools should receive bilingual support to if election boards should provide materials in languages other than English. Despite the dominant presence of recent immigrants in their ranks, Korean Americans were divided. Byounghye Chang, the director of the Asian Bilingual Curriculum Development Center at Seton Hall University, rebuked President Ronald Reagan for his alleged remarks to US mayors that bilingualism was a "misguided attempt to preserve immigrants' native languages instead of helping them learn English." He also lambasted measures by Reagan officials that appeared to intentionally limit or scale back bilingual education programs and invoked the precedent of the Supreme Court's decision in *Lau v. Nichols* (1974) as a safeguard that must be upheld. Others opposed state-supported bilingualism, believing it ultimately disincentivized immigrants from assimilating to American life. Jong H. Lee, an immigrant and accountant in the Bay Area, blamed those who failed to learn English as responsible for their struggles and own lack of success. He boasted that in ten years he had learned English and achieved prosperity running an accounting firm that he expanded to two offices. Rather than rely on or demand bilingual support, Lee told other immigrants to "go learn English and the American culture and then you can be part of the society here." Pressing this view in the grimmest terms was the terrifying headline, "Lack of English Costs Life," the title of a *New York Post* article reprinted in *Koreatown Weekly*. It reported on the death of Noh Soon Kook, an immigrant in New York who worked as an armed night watchman for a store. After it was robbed, police arriving at the store mistook Noh for the robber, and when he did not heed their call to drop his gun, they shot and killed him.

The Korean American Story

While *Koreatown Weekly* provided a platform for Korean Americans' ruminations on their relationship to Korean culture, the paper also sought to facilitate the documentation and preservation of Korean American history. Having a tangible history was a pillar of social identity and legitimacy; it was not enough for Korean Americans to make peace with their issues over language and food. They needed a collective story. Toward this end, in February 1980, the editors asked readers to help identify influential Korean Americans to be featured in upcoming issues. It announced in grand fashion:

> For the first time in the history of Korean immigration, we are embarking on the task of searching for distinguished Korean Americans whose achievements in different fields of endeavor have made a mark on American life, so that we as well as upcoming generations can proudly claim our own models in America. The qualifications are that the candidates must be of Korean ancestry and live in the U.S. and must have made some impact on "American life."[35]

This endeavor, explained the editors, was "long overdue," and it was "never too late for our emerging Korean-American community to establish and foster such tradition."[36]

Korean Americans were not the only ones who yearned for heroes and histories with which to align. Against the "nation of immigrants" paradigm, being connected with a social or community history that situated one's group in the American mosaic became something of a requisite aspect of cultural citizenship. A people with their own pantheon of heroes and pioneers are a people with historical roots and contemporary relevance. Korean Americans, thus, often expressed envy, especially toward other Asians whom they perceived as having richer and more legible histories—like interned Japanese Americans—because it gave them tangible legacies to invoke and mobilize collective unity around. "Our older Asian ethnic groups—Japanese Americans, Chinese Americans, and Filipino Americans—have been honoring their outstanding leaders in one way or another on a regular basis," said the editors of *Koreatown* in 1980.[37] "Japanese Americans had Fred Korematsu, Filipinos Carlos Bulosan, Chinese Wong Kim Ark," but "Who did the Koreans have?"[38]

Writing scholarship, collecting oral histories, teaching the past, and building community archives were acts of reclamation and recuperation of histories that had been forgotten, suppressed, or untapped. This resonated powerfully for Korean Americans paying attention to the major demographic shifts in their community. That their history was largely unwritten and unknown to scholars and the wider public gave them the freedom to craft a story that mirrored their distinct goals and visions. "Our parents' generation was dying off," said Gloria Hahn, which was also why she co-organized the "reunion" of Koreans and Korean Americans at the Ambassador Hotel in August 1980. The pioneer generation, the first Koreans who went to Hawaii and the US mainland as laborers and political exiles during the early 1900s, were in their seventies and eighties. Unless somebody recorded or documented their lives, their stories would be lost, to the detriment of their children and grandchildren, who "felt no ties to the early Korean community" or to "Korean values, culture, history, or language."[39] Adding to the urgency to preserve the past was new immigrants' even more tenuous connection to the pre-1965 Korean American experience.

About Americans' thirst to connect with their roots during the 1970s, historian Matthew Jacobson said, "in their loving recovery of an immigrant past, white Americans reinvented the 'America' to which their ancestors had journeyed."[40] As they undertook to tell their story, Korean Americans located their roots in the sweeping saga of US immigration and the fight for Korean independence from Japan. They identified 1903 as a landmark year, when the first cohort of Korean immigrants arrived in Hawaii. The pioneers of this wave were a small group of about seven thousand people and included picture brides, multigenerational families, students, contract laborers, and political exiles. In the 1970s and 1980s, some of them were still living. Their stories would be part of the Korean American archive, and while they were alive, they served as community treasures to honor regularly. At the 1980 Ambassador Hotel reunion, twelve of these "founding members of the Korean community" were presented with certificates of appreciation on behalf of the second and third generations. One of these was eighty-year-old Crenshaw resident James Kim, who immigrated in 1916 to San Francisco and whose life experience contrasted greatly with those in the audience. His original plan had been to study abroad and return to Korea, but he remained in the United States for the rest of his life, working as a fruit picker and then grocer before retiring.[41]

Commemorating the pioneer phase of history around people like James Kim solidified an interpretation of these years as a time of extraordinary hardship and sacrifice as well as tenacity and solidarity. Accounts emphasized the intense social hostility Korean immigrants faced in the early twentieth century. In a 1979 interview published in *Koreatown Weekly*, 101-year-old Choo Eun Yang described his migration in 1906 and stressed how different life was compared to the present. "White children looked down on Orientals as if they were animals and threw rocks at them." James Kim also acknowledged the "swirl of cultural shock, bigotry from some whites, and the aftermath of federal and state laws that curbed Asian immigration and ownership of land."[42] Against these hardships Korean immigrants were remarkably resilient and organized. Their high level of ethnic solidarity and mutual support struck many as a marked contrast to contemporary lamentations about divided and adrift Korean Americans. As historian Bong Youn Choy explained in 1980, "almost every one of them belonged to several different community groups, in addition to being a member of a church."[43] Besides churches, the groups included law enforcement agencies, fraternal societies, and political groups. Among the most celebrated were Hanin-Hopsung Hyop-Hee, or the United States Korean Society, formed in 1907, the Korean National Association, formed in 1909, and the Women's Patriotic League, formed in 1919.

Korean independence and US nationalism were also key themes of the pioneer phase. The most lauded heroes of this era were immigrants who worked for Korean independence from Japan, so their veneration as historical figures entwined Korean nationalism with the Korean diaspora. These figures included Philip Jaisohn, Soon Hyun, and Ahn Chang Ho, whose biographies emphasized their service to Korea and the United States while situating them in relation to US history tropes. For instance, Bong Youn Choy explained that these "Korean leaders came to America in search of political freedom and a democratic ideology like the early British Puritans who crossed the Atlantic Ocean to find freedom."[44] Described by K. W. Lee as "our George Washington," Philip Jaisohn came to the United States in 1885 at age nineteen, making him one of the first Korean immigrants. He was also one of the first American-educated Korean physicians and the first Korean naturalized citizen. His extraordinary biography included serving in the US military during the Spanish-American War and advising General John Hodge after World War II.[45] Soo Hyun was another of the first immigrants, arriving on the second shipload of Koreans to Hawaii in 1903. In 1975, thirteen years after his death, his daughter-in-law memorialized him as "the apostle of freedom for his homeland" and credited him with safeguarding the Korean Declaration of Independence during the March 1 Movement of 1919. The March 1 movement was also commonly known as "Korea's Fourth of July" and marked the beginning of the Korean resistance against Japan.[46]

The second major stage of Korean American history was the mid-twentieth century (1940s–1960s), when the first US-born cohort came of age and a new, albeit relatively small, wave of immigrants entered. In 1947, the Korean population in LA was about five hundred. This era brought "new awakenings and opportunities to many Korean Americans," said Gloria Hahn, and it was characterized by progress and extreme challenges. The notables of the era were primarily distinguished by their mainstream achievements in their professions or service to the nation. For instance, K. W. Lee was an accomplished journalist, Sonia Suk a successful real estate broker, David Hyun a respected architect, Young Oak Kim a second-generation Korean American who served in the Japanese American 442nd combat unit during World War II, and Arthur Song the first Korean elected to the California State Senate.[47] They were also defined by living through war and division in Korea, having "undergone experiences we in the United States can't imagine: division of the country, civil war, poverty, personal upheavals, followed by intense economic development with all its disruptions."[48] Life had improved compared to the world of the pioneers, thanks to the dismantling of Asian exclusion and the achievements of the civil rights movement, but it could still be difficult and isolating. K. W. Lee reminisced about life in the US South and Midwest during the 1950s. After boarding a bus near Memphis, he tried to sit in the back but was forced by the driver to the front because he was not Black. "Aren't I colored, I thought?"[49] He went to Chicago while heading to school in Tennessee and found a much-needed respite at the Oakdale Korean Church and with the Yi family, who were like a beacon to "the lonely and weary Koreans."[50]

The lives of these second-stage immigrants illustrated progress and opportunity for Koreans during the mid-twentieth century, and this cohort included pathbreakers for subsequent generations. A *Koreatown Weekly* feature in December 1979 celebrated some of these luminaries, among them real estate broker Sonia Suk, activist Jay Yoo, and doctor Jooh Roh. They were touted as "first-generation pathfinders" who achieved professional success, created a "comfortable niche in the American mainstream," and helped "build the foundation for the continuing waves of newcomers who number 20,000 a year."[51] Unlike the heroes of the pioneer period, the midcentury role models were still active in the community during the 1970s and 1980s, so they could participate in writing their legacies, mentor young Korean Americans, and hold formal leadership roles. Young Oak Kim served on various boards and organizations, including the United Way of Los Angeles Board of Directors; Visual Communications; the Japanese American National Museum (JANM); and the Korean Health, Education, Information, and Research Center (KHEIR). David Hyun was the first board president for the KAC. They could also speak directly to and try to guide younger Korean Americans. At a 1986 voter registration event at the Ambassador Hotel, where he was honored along with several others as "outstanding members of the Korean community," Arthur Song reminded people that a few decades ago Asians faced rampant racism and immigrants from Korea could not vote or become citizens. Because conditions had improved to allow Koreans to be fully engaged in American life, they were obligated to do so.

Excavating and documenting the Korean American past helped make Korean Americans legible as an ethnic group—alongside Chinese, Japanese, and other more familiar Asian American groups—in contemporary society. It was also urgent in the 1970s and 1980s because this was a time of momentous change. The next significant phase of immigration coincided with a socioeconomic shift in Korean America. Or, as Gloria Hahn said, "just as we broke into new areas, residential and professional," a new wave began. She wondered, would the new immigrants "disperse the way we have and fade into the gray mass of Americans?" Hahn embraced the possibility that the newcomers would allow Korean Americans to participate as integral members of the pluralistic society. Not only were new immigrants arriving in unprecedented numbers but also the community was struggling with "alienation and affliction" and Koreans in general were fragmented and leaderless. In the face of the unsettling "social and psychological gap between the American-educated early immigrants and the oncoming arrivals who make up the majority of Koreans in this country," Hahn hoped these pioneers would "[show] us the way."[52]

Stepping into Politics and Leadership

In an April 1983 newsletter for the newly formed Korean American Coalition (KAC), David Hyun, the first chair of its board, looked back on Korean American history and accomplishments. He then speculated on how the future might appear, in light of the rising second and third generations and new immigrants who were gathering "by the hundreds of thousands."[53] "The story of early Korean immigrants," he said, "is a saga of endurance, humor and slowly evolving success. It describes the Korean character which enabled individuals to rise despite an extremely small society and numerous difficulties." Against the demographic changes underway, Hyun predicted that old and new patterns would play out, in that some would succeed, others would fail, and there would arise "brilliant and enduring" people among the newcomers. "The difference," however, Hyun noted, "in the advance of today's Koreans is the increased breadth of their participation in American life."[54]

No mission or charge was more emphasized for Korean Americans in the next era than participation in mainstream culture and institutions. The time was approaching not only for elders to hand off the torch in terms of ethnic leadership but also for unprecedented expansion in the number of Koreans in Los Angeles that the rising leaders could harness. Tong Soo Chung, the 1.5 immigrant and law student at UCLA introduced at the start of the book, was a prominent voice of the cohort of Korean American youth vying to lead the community as it entered this new era. He observed that young Korean Americans were excelling in school, work, and other areas of life, but "these bright and sometimes even brilliant youths are often unsure of their identity as Korean-Americans and entirely lacking in their concern for the community of fellow Korean-Americans."[55] If people from this talented yet untethered cohort could be brought into the fold of ethnic life and seize the reins of leadership, they could help advance all Koreans in the United States. "It is my hope," Chung continued, "that those generations will take the rest of the Korean community into the mainstream of American life, including politics."

People like Chung and the organization he was most identified with, the KAC, said the old guard of Korean American leaders in Los Angeles—immigrant business leaders who understood Korean American interests primarily in terms of commerce and the development of Koreatown—were under-equipped to advocate for the community as the twentieth century came to a close. In one of its newsletters, the KAC cited 1976 as a turning point when the need for a new and different style of leadership became clear. At a City Council hearing on zoning, immigrant leaders from the Los Angeles Korean Chamber of Commerce appeared to express their objections to regulations on expansion that they believed would hurt the Korean business community. When it came to light that they had read speeches written by a white American realtor, people realized "that the Korean American community . . . had no English-speaking advocacy group that could effectively represent the community's interests to the mainstream American institutions."

The KAC, formed in 1983, created a tall order for itself, as it wanted to create unity in the fragmented Korean American population, harness the power of the immigrants' numbers, and elevate the leadership of second- and third-generation Korean Americans. The latter had mainstream capital but had also been "isolated from the community like lost tribes." As Korean Americans often looked to Japanese Americans as something akin to older, more accomplished siblings whom they resented yet wanted to emulate, Chung cited the Japanese American Citizens League (JACL) as a model for the KAC. Established in 1929 and led by assimilated Asian Americans with credibility and standing both inside and outside the ethnic community, the JACL had become the most influential Japanese American organization in the country. It cultivated relationships with powerful allies in government, launched the careers of influential Nikkei politicians, and spearheaded the successful campaign for redress for internment.[56] While the JACL served as an aspirational example for the KAC, it was not a tenable blueprint because the two communities by the 1980s had little in common. The surge of post-1965 immigration gave rise to a demographically lopsided Korean American population, with new immigrants far outnumbering others. And yet, the relatively small cohort of young Korean Americans, pre- and post-1965, believed it was up to them to "[parent] their parents' generation" through groups like the KAC.[57]

The rising Korean American leaders set their sights on electoral politics, believing the forces were aligning in their favor. Tong Soo Chung lamented in 1983 that despite their accomplishments in education, entrepreneurship, and other fields, "politically . . . the Korean immigrants have done nothing."[58] He thought Koreans could take a cue from Jewish Americans, another small group whose members had achieved remarkable influence and visibility in many areas of life. "No other ethnic group comes even close to them," Chung said. He believed Jewish Americans ascended in part because of their "extraordinarily high rate of registration and voting participation," so Koreans should follow.[59] Art Song implored co-ethnics to not just vote but also seek office, because it is the "only way for Koreans or for any ethnic minority to progress socially in this country."[60] By the early 1980s, Korean Americans were lamenting that whatever economic and symbolic power Koreatown had built up had not translated to substantive political power. As the KAC vice president Duncan Lee said in 1984, "we pay a lot in taxes and give so much in donations to the outside, but we don't take in too much."[61]

With the idea that through voting Koreans would "demonstrate their power" and gain entry to the mainstream, groups like the Korean American Voters Alliance (KAVA) and KAC sprang to action. KAVA was a short-lived organization that spearheaded efforts as early as 1982 to register voters by sending volunteers to Olympic Market, East West Food Center, the Korean Parade, and other gathering places to canvass, register new voters, and hold signs reading "Korean Power!" and "Vote! It's the Only Way." They also tried to instill what for many immigrants was a novel approach to civic participation, namely that they should engage with their identities as Korean Americans at the forefront. They and other Asian Americans saw 1984 as a key opportunity, as it was a presidential election year when a critical mass of naturalized post-1965 immigrants could flex their power at the polls. That year, Koreans received unprecedented national attention as a political constituency. Ronald Reagan invited forty Korean Republican leaders to the White House to help his reelection. Asian American voter registration drives in Southern California intensified that summer, and the Asian Pacific American Voters Council (APAVC) reported that sixty community agencies representing the Japanese, Chinese, Korean, and Filipino communities had by November 1 registered over 4,300 new voters in Southern California, the largest increase the APAVC had ever seen. Regarding its own outreach, the KAC estimated there were up to 50,000 eligible Korean voters in Southern California. To Tong Soo Chung, this meant they could be a decisive swing vote in close elections. "Think what 30,000, 50,000 votes (Korean voters) could mean," he said, "The community will see benefits from this electoral clout."[62] In June 1984, the KAC announced its goal to register 5,000 people before the election. Volunteers hit the streets on weekends at churches, grocery stores, and events at large venues such as the Shrine Auditorium and Anaheim Convention Center. By October it reported signing up 1,600 new voters, short of its goal, but between this effort and that of several other groups involved in voter registration, Korean American organizations in Southern California claimed registering 8,000 new voters for the November 1984 election.[63]

The "Korean American vote" was neither large nor unified enough to decisively impact any races in 1984. Though registration drives in the first half of the 1980s reported a preference for the Democratic Party, their affiliation between the two major parties split nearly down the middle. An ethnic vote is largely illusory because people must balance many considerations and allegiances, but it remains a powerful catalyst and organizing concept in politics. Where a Korean American vote or bloc could be consequential was at the local level in districts where they were a plurality or majority. In the mid-1980s, Koreatown was perhaps the only locality that could be channeled into Korean American political power, but as discussed earlier, they never made up a dominant or unified majority of its residents. Los Angeles's ethnic and racial politics had a strong spatial dimension, whereby minority power depended in part on ethnic geographic concentrations and district lines. For instance, Latino political power and issues were intertwined with the East Side, whereas for African Americans, advocating for South Central went hand in hand with advocating for the Black community. This could exacerbate intergroup rivalry and entrench zero-sum thinking about minority representation. As Mike Davis observed, "Eastside politicians blame Latino under-representation in government upon Black 'over-representation.' Latinos, in other words, have come to see themselves as political 'have-nots', and Blacks as political 'haves.'"[64]

Such a terrain limited the options for Asian Americans, who were dispersed in Los Angeles County, and made it impossible for Korean Americans seeking to break through as players in minority and electoral politics. This became clear in a 1986 controversy over redistricting. Latino voter groups had filed a lawsuit in 1982 charging that a redistricting plan violated the Voting Rights Act by splitting the Latino vote into several neighborhoods and depriving them of political influence. Eventually the Justice Department ordered the city to create a district that was majority Hispanic in order to strengthen Latino representation, but the reconfiguration (called the Alatorre Plan) unleashed another set of controversies over Asian American representation. Mike Woo, the only Asian American council member, would have had to run for reelection in a newly proposed majority Latino district, thus potentially pitting Asian Americans against Latino voters.[65] An equally intense objection came from Korean Americans because the plan also impacted Koreatown. Koreatown had never been unified in a single district, and leaders from the community were angered that the Alatorre plan would divide the area among three districts, the fourth, eighth, and tenth. Four hundred Koreans marched on City Hall waving "Save Koreatown" signs and demanded that Koreatown be placed in a single district. Unlike the Latino challenge, however, Koreans were quickly rebuffed; the city acknowledged that while they represented a rapidly growing community with a notable geographic concentration, they were too small in number to warrant the same protection extended to Latinos under the Voting Rights Act.[66] In other words, "a minority cannot complain about vote dilution where its numbers are too few or too dispersed to be an effective majority." Even though Koreatown had forty thousand residents, Korean Americans made up, at best, 20 percent of a single district's total population of two-hundred thousand residents. The city's position was upheld by a US district judge who threw out the claim in September 1986, saying there were too few Korean American residents in Koreatown to constitute an "effective majority" under the Voting Rights Act.

The BKs, the "knee-highs," second- and third-generation, and other Americanized Koreans searched for meaning and balance amid the post-1965 surge. They set themselves apart from the new immigrants, while also recognizing it would be difficult, indeed impossible, to escape association with them. They, thus, calibrated different strategies in their approach to ethnic and identity politics and in the process remade what it meant to be Korean American in multicultural Los Angeles. As Korean Americans worked to understand, explain, and meet the historic moment, they glimpsed both exciting possibilities and daunting challenges. For one, coalescing a powerful ethnic bloc and social force was anything but a foregone conclusion. In the 1982 voter registration drives, for instance, volunteers, "most of whom are college students [experienced] the reality of Korean immigrants' attitude toward participation in government in their adopted country."[67] They reported a "cool reception" from people they approached, based on distrust and fear as well as sheer indifference about political participation, even among naturalized Koreans. The voter registration drives revealed Korean Americans neither possessed nor forged the intergenerational or cultural unity they needed to be a force in politics. "They realize they need to work out more effective and realistic methods of reaching people who are unaccustomed to democratic procedures in this country."[68]

The struggles of *Koreatown Weekly* were also illustrative of the gap between vision and reality that Korean Americans struggled mightily to bridge. The paper had always been a shoestring operation, and relying on a core of English-reading Korean Americans had been a gamble in the late 1970s and early 1980s. To K. Connie Kang, the paper's financial struggles underscored a deeper problem among Korean Americans. As she asked in a 1981 column "Why can't Koreans work together?" Kang believed disunity among Korean Americans made it impossible for ventures like *Koreatown Weekly* to succeed. "Try grabbing a fistful of sand and see what happens," she wrote. "It has become a habit with us to tell ourselves we are a people incapable of unifying and working together toward a common goal. Individually we have been blessed with stamina, talent, and perseverance. Yet put us in a room to work out a problem, and the worst in us will surface and we'll fight forever." As others often did while lamenting Korean Americans' shortcomings, Kang wondered why they could not be more like Japanese Americans, whose strong community spirit and ability to work together "[makes] them shine all over us." The paper continued along, though with less frequent issues over the years, until it folded in 1984.

Years later, Randy Hagihara remarked that the paper was "probably ten or twelve years ahead of its time."[69] Timing often factored into how Korean Americans explained their successes and failures and projected about their destiny, whether it related to Koreatown's promise, Korean Americans' rise as a force in Los Angeles politics, or people's hopes to be free of inner torment over their ethnic identity. As a result, public discussion about Korean Americans often fixated on whether it was their time, whether their time was coming, and when. As the 1980s ended, they were still casting about. The KAC was at a crossroads, with its membership plateauing and the organization unable to expand into Orange County and shed its yuppie image.[70] The divide between parents and children, immigrants and nonimmigrants in Korean America remained as concerning as ever. But as the 1990s began, they wondered if this would in fact be their decade. In terms of politics, even more Korean Americans were reaching voting age than in the previous decade. The state assemblyman Paul Horcher remarked that with a strong ethnic bloc, Korean Americans could elect one of their own to represent Koreatown.[71] Tong Soo Chung, now in his thirties and working as a lawyer at the firm Kim & Andrews, threw his hat in the ring for an assembly seat covering Koreatown after Speaker Mike Roos announced his resignation. A special election was scheduled for June 4, 1991, to fill the seat, and fourteen people announced their candidacies.[72] Chung said it was scandalous that the state legislature had no Asian members, and he believed he had a good chance of winning because the district was 22 percent Asian and covered most of Koreatown.

In an interview with *KoreAm Journal*, two months before the special election—which he would lose—Chung assessed his chances of success, pressed the urgency for a Korean American elected representative, and ruminated on all the ways his victory would be historic. He mostly articulated his prospects in terms of how his election would be meaningful for Korean Americans as a minority and the United States as an inclusive society, but then he turned his attention across the Pacific. "Can you imagine the excitement people in Korea will have over this? It will be great but let's not jump too far."[73] Whether Korean Americans were cognizant or embracing of it, the politics of Korean American-ness in Los Angeles were also inextricable from the forces of globalization, US-Korea relations, and South Korean nationalism.

CHAPTER 4

A Small World

Korean Americans and Global Los Angeles

WITH HER INSTINCTS for Korean placemaking in Los Angeles and talents for networking with powerful officials, Sonia Suk set out to make a mark on one of Southern California's most famous and iconic places: Disneyland. As she said in her memoir, in reference to the park's popular "It's a Small World" attraction, "It always bothered me there was no Korean doll in it. . . . It seemed wrong."[1] For a long time, to much of the world, South Korea was just a small Asian country about which little was known, but Suk had become convinced, by the 1970s, that it deserved global recognition and respect. Southern California had one of the largest and fastest growing Korean American communities, and South Korea was a rising power in the world. To Suk, representation on a Disney ride could be enormously significant by validating and acknowledging a people and nation that had long been denied such forms of inclusion and regard.

Opening in 1955 in Anaheim, about thirty miles from Los Angeles, Disneyland became a major tourist attraction for Americans and international travelers alike and indelibly shaped the iconography of Southern California. It fulfilled a demand for play, opening at a time when the US middle class was expanding with rising incomes, growing families, and recreation time. Disneyland also offered distinctly escapist entertainment. With its location in suburban Anaheim, Orange County, it was conceived as a playground away from the disorder of urban life and appealed to visitors with its promise of contained and sanitized vision of the United States and the world. At Disneyland, people could indulge in a cultural and temporal experience

87

washed of social and political complexity, from the nostalgically violent Frontierland to the benignly colonialist Adventureland. Main Street, the park's entry and focal point, longingly evoked a quaint, orderly, and homogeneous model of small-town America, while Tomorrowland projected a utopian technological future.

It's a Small World was located in Tomorrowland, and while it was not futuristic in concept, it promoted a geopolitical utopia steeped in messages of world peace and friendship. It was not original to Disneyland; it first appeared at the 1964–65 World's Fair in New York where it was called Children of the World and had been developed by the Disney Company subsidiary WED Enterprises as a tribute to the United Nations International Children's Emergency Fund (UNICEF). After the fair, it was shipped to Disneyland, where it opened in May 1966, renamed with the title of the ubiquitous Robert and Richard Sherman song that played on the ride. Promoted by Walt Disney as a tribute to the "enchanting world of childhood," It's a Small World took spectators on a slow-moving water ride through various scenes with dolls representing different nations, offering a cheerful and inclusive celebration of global harmony.[2] One need not scratch too far below the surface, however, to grasp how the attraction also valorized US power, hegemony, and whiteness. For example, rather than being merely an innocuous representation of the world, It's a Small World reflected a midcentury US fantasy of life overseas, where people in other nations were flat ethnic caricatures (e.g., Scotland's "wee bagpipers") trapped in a premodern past (with folk costumes instead of modern dress) or racist cliché (e.g., an audio promotion voiced by Walt Disney describing Africa as the "mysterious dark continent").[3] Despite its nod to global diversity, the dolls in the exhibit were identical besides their costumes, skin color, and hair style. Together, the elements of the ride communicated the core message that while the children of the world are basically the same, the United States is the only modernizing nation in a world where others are frozen in the past.

These critiques aside, Disneyland's power as a cultural institution was undeniable, and Sonia Suk wanted to see South Korea represented with the addition of a Korean doll in It's a Small World. To her this would underscore her country's seat at the geopolitical table, the importance of US-Korea friendship, and Korean Americans' presence in Southern California. Suk first pursued the matter with officials in South Korea's Ministry of Culture and Information but made little progress, so then she approached

Tom Bradley, who was much more receptive in light of his own interest in enhancing LA's global profile. Though Disneyland was outside the city and county, the park was still widely associated with Los Angeles. Suk's doll campaign gained momentum with a 1977 trip to South Korea by members of the Los Angeles Pusan Sister Committee, after which Bradley and the committee endorsed the goal and put Suk in charge of the effort.[4]

From there Suk worked through a lengthy process, which included meetings with Disney officials and the procurement of prototype dolls. She had hoped Disneyland would use the dolls she found in Korean and Los Angeles department stores for the exhibit, but they were ultimately rejected for falling outside the company's stringent guidelines, though it did use them as models.[5] Another point of contention that Suk remembered had to do with the language in which the Korean dolls would sing "It's a Small World." When she learned they would be singing in English, she objected, pointing out that other dolls, including those from Japan, sang in their native languages. Suk was unconvinced by the explanation that while many Japanese tourists came to Disneyland, not enough Koreans did to warrant presenting the song in Korean. However, to Suk, hearing the Korean language was not just for Korean tourists; it would bring Korea and Korean culture to the attention of everyone. Besides, she wondered, how did Disney know the visitors presumed to be Japanese were not Korean? These complaints aside, Suk was proud of the effort she led and credited it for opening subsequent doors for her, including appointments to the city Human Relations Commission, the Los Angeles Olympic organization, and the Republican delegation for the 1980 presidential election.

This chapter further explores Los Angeles's reinvention as a global city during the 1970s and 1980s and the interrelated roles of South Korea and Korean immigrants in this process. Not only did Koreans symbolize the city's increasingly diverse population, but they were also positioned as linchpins for LA's developing links across the Pacific. While the push to brand LA as a global metropolis was economically driven and, thus, outward looking, it also entailed highlighting the city's socially and culturally diverse population and progressive ethos regarding racial and ethnic relations. This marriage of globalization and multiculturalism was a key pillar of the mayorship of Tom Bradley. Throughout his terms he touted urban and economic development, global free markets, international friendship, and multicultural inclusion, and saw his efforts to build relations with South Korea and the local Korean

American community as related pieces in the reinvention of Los Angeles as a global city. And few leveraged their intersecting positions as immigrant entrepreneur, racial minority, and informal Korean emissary more skillfully than his friend and associate Sonia Suk, whose work both advanced herself and further integrated Korean Americans into global Los Angeles.

The experience of Koreans in Los Angeles sheds light on the social and political contradictions of being Asian in a global city during the late twentieth century. Champions of this idea deployed lofty rhetoric invoking equality, friendship, and mutual interests that bound the people across the world and within their municipality. They conjured an imaginary that foregrounded Asian Americans as symbols of global community and local inclusiveness and thus represented a racial and ethnic hierarchy in Los Angeles that positioned groups based on their affiliation with valued international partners and on their contributions as a community. In this configuration, African Americans and Latinos fell into the background; they were neither conduits nor symbols of modern globalization in ways that lent themselves to celebration (their experiences invoked histories of enslavement, imperialism, and disfranchisement). Nor had they distinguished themselves as poster children for capitalist enterprise in the ways that some Asian immigrants, particularly Koreans, had. However, Koreans in Los Angeles also faced a dilemma. They represented and helped to facilitate LA's globalization vis-à-vis their position as newcomers from a nation valued as an international partner. If signaling Korea was a condition of their inclusion in US society, then they would be conditional Americans and Angelenos, always somewhat foreign.

Pacific Region, State, City

"Just consider," wrote Jay Matthews for the *Washington Post* in 1984, "that 60 percent of humanity lives in the Pacific region; the fastest growing economies are there, as well as the two most advanced economies."[6] The quote came from one in a swirl of articles published around this time about the rise of the Pacific region as the global economy's emerging center of gravity. In this order, the United States and Japan were the dominant nations, and California was a key site. Not only was the state located at one edge of the Pacific Rim—an advantageous position from which to be a global transportation and knowledge hub—but it was also a large producer and exporter of goods ranging from grains to computer chips. At the same time, for the wallets of American consumers, Asian goods had been competing with or edging out US companies in everything from wigs from Korea to electronics from Japan. In 1984, foreign imports made up nearly half of all cars sold in California, a marked departure from the decades-long dominance of the American auto industry.[7] As far as international commerce, US trade across the Pacific overtook that in the Atlantic in 1984, reaching a record $121.2 billion in value compared to $115.8 billion. This was enormously lucrative for California, whose economy that year generated $10.5 billion in wages and salaries, $3.5 billion in taxes, and $35 billion in business revenue.[8] And while West Coast ports saw an increase in its customs revenues, those in New York were on the decline.

California's advantages amid the unfolding Pacific era were greater than location and what was produced there; the state also modeled an ideological and cultural disposition about business that explained its rising position in the global economy. As Jay Matthews wrote, the state was attracting a "new breed of entrepreneurs and politicians who reject the notion that US markets must be protected from Japan and instead look for ways to invade Japanese and other Asian markets." Either way, California "has much to teach would-be policy-makers of both parties who want to know where this part of the country is going."[9] Prominent among the "new breed" of politicians were Mayors Tom Bradley and Dianne Feinstein of San Francisco. Bradley, for instance, had opposed legislation that would have required the use of US parts in foreign cars sold in the domestic market on the grounds that it would impede Pacific Rim trade. He and others also assured US companies that they could expand their markets into Asia without losing their advantages against international competitors.

According to the "new breed" of politicians and businesspeople, maximizing the rewards of "invading" Asian markets meant Americans had to reexamine and change many of their assumptions about economic well-being and nationalism. In addition to keeping trade barriers low, Americans needed to diligently study and understand their potential consumers across the Pacific. They also had to view their Asian trade partners as potential collaborators rather than adversaries. The appointment of Richard King, a businessman and Korean War veteran, as California's first director of international trade in 1978 signaled the state's embrace of these principles. King projected that the state's involvement in Pacific trade would double over the 1980s and urged Californians to develop close relations with potential trade partners and familiarize themselves with Asian countries. After two terms in his position, he reentered the private sector, consulting with a range of producers in the state, including winemakers wishing to tap the Japanese market. King also promoted international trade using the language of intercultural understanding and cooperation.[10] This emphasis on cooperative rather than adversarial trade spawned organizational innovations in labor, management, and production. For instance, in 1984, the auto maker Toyota rescued a struggling General Motors plant in Fremont, California, and reopened it as a Japan-America venture.[11] Toyota, whose popular cars were surpassing American companies in the US market, now had the power to lead such innovations in multinational reorganizing, which then helped cement California and the Pacific's commanding positions and countered the rhetoric of "international trade wars."

In the globally interconnected Pacific world coalescing before people's eyes, Los Angeles stood out as a ground zero where international forces were remaking local conditions and city politics. As discussed earlier, the 1980s are replete with references to Los Angeles as *the* quintessential Pacific metropolis and the world's "gateway to America."[12] The teeming activity in the Port of Los Angeles was a prime illustration of its vitality, with shipping containers scurrying in cars, video recorders, and running shoes while exporting oranges, cotton, and canned goods. Local politicians and business leaders who recognized the potential payoffs of globalization argued that lowering trade barriers and welcoming foreign investment would fuel Los Angeles's renaissance in the closing decades of the twentieth century. As discussed in chapter 1, they were encouraged by the inflow of Asian capital into downtown redevelopment projects, which had improved the condition of streets, raised the quality of cultural life, and drew back middle- and upper-class residents and shoppers. A 1984 *Los Angeles Times* article, for instance, reported encouragingly that affluent people were returning to live downtown, and moreover, "growing numbers of the people on Bunker Hill are involved in trade with Japan, South Korea, Taiwan, China, and other countries in the Pacific." Additionally, Asia-based companies were establishing branch offices in Los Angeles and its suburbs as a further sign of the interlinked fortunes of Asian investment and Los Angeles's future.[13]

A significant share of new immigration from Asia to Los Angeles and California was also a function of globalization. It rose as a response not simply to the Immigration Act of 1965 but also to intensifying political instability in South Korea, the Philippines, Taiwan, and Hong Kong. People uprooted themselves as well as—or sometimes just—their money, which took the form of Asian capital surges into California real estate, small businesses, and banks. Such circumstances put a new frame on migration, in which "technology and means" allowed people to improve their lives or protect their fortunes without making "a total commitment to their new society."[14] This contrasted with the long-standing trope of US immigration as a phenomenon of its role as a "promised land" for the world's dispossessed and most desperate people.

The migration of Asians and investment of Asian capital underscored the growing interconnections around the world vis-à-vis the mobility of capital and possibilities of travel. But whatever the underlying stories of post-1965 Asian immigrants in Los Angeles, their presence would have implications for the images as well as substance of racial and ethnic relations in Los Angeles and the nation. The figure of the immigrant had always been potent in this regard. Still, in late twentieth-century Los Angeles, Asian immigrants embodied and projected the interlinking of US domestic ethnic relations and economic globalization in local and tangible ways that people could find unsettling. For example, in a relatively short time, Asians became overrepresented relative to their share of the US population in colleges and universities. In 1984, they made up 5.3 percent of California's population and 20 percent of the student bodies in the state's most prestigious public universities. This signaled not just a demographic shift but also a coming socioeconomic one in which people of Asian descent were projected to fill a large share of the ranks of educated white-collar professionals. If this possibility materialized simultaneously with the rapid industrialization of several East Asian countries, Asians and Asian Americans could command untold economic and political power, locally and globally.

On the one hand, this was precisely what leaders and elders in the Korean American community had in mind when they touted their goal of mainstream participation, though they also recognized it could stir mixed feelings and outright alarm among outsiders. In a 1983 *Los Angeles Times* op-ed, David Hyun assured readers that people should welcome and not fear the unfolding era of Los Angeles–Asia collaboration in which Asians and Asian Americans would become increasingly visible and powerful local players.[15] He stressed that new immigrants from Asia tended to be of a higher caliber compared to those of the past as well as contemporary migrants from elsewhere in the world because they were educated, skilled, and "share attitudes of industry and dedication to the American way of democracy." They have already, he said, "[proven themselves] immediately and immensely capable despite language barriers," by way of their "[revitalization of] local capital," which was "helping to overcome the problems of deterioration and inertia" in Los Angeles. Thus, what was unfolding in LA, Hyun proclaimed, was an "East-West Miracle," in which Asian Americans were integral "among its creators."[16] For centuries, the "East" and "West," which over time came to describe distinct geographic, cultural, and racial categories, were locked in antagonism and oppositionality, but this was no longer the case by the 1980s. Thanks to "American political and business leadership," an era of "compatibility and cooperation" had arrived. As an especially powerful showcase of the triumph of East-West cooperation, Hyun cited Los Angeles's recently developed Little Tokyo, which, as discussed earlier, he played a major role in. The "miracle" of the project, Hyun explained, also owed to the public-private partnerships behind the revitalization and the participation of Japanese corporations, recent immigrants, Japanese American businesses, and grassroots organizations.[17]

If a similar alliance with longtime Asian Americans, foreign investors, and new immigrants could be mobilized to support development in the Korean community, especially in Koreatown, then Korean Americans could play a critical role in the "East-West miracle" equal to that of Japanese Americans. This was one of Hyun's most fervent wishes. Among Asian nations, Japan might have received most of the attention and hype for its role in Los Angeles's globalization, but as early as the late 1960s South Korea was not far behind. Los Angeles was a crucial coordinating point for South Korea's rebuilding and modernization, especially with regard to growing its international commerce. In 1966, the South Korean government opened a Korean Trade Center in Los Angeles, and the following year, the Seoul-based Foreign Exchange Bank of Korea established an LA office to promote commerce between South Korea and the United States.[18] Laying this groundwork facilitated international economic and business transactions, which in the process, built connections between Los Angeles and South Korea. In 1968, for example, the architectural firm PA&E International, an affiliate of the LA-based multinational Pacific Architects & Engineers, Inc., received a contract from the Korean Ministry of Government Legislation to construct a building in Seoul.[19] The $15 million nineteen-story building, scheduled for completion in December 1969, was the largest office building constructed in Korea since the Korean War.[20] Further deepening South Korea's presence in Los Angeles was the Korean Cultural Service, which opened in 1980 on Wilshire Boulevard. An institution whose functions sat somewhere between an embassy and ethnic organization, it offered lectures, held classes to inform the public about Korea, hosted visitors, and served as a contact point for local officials.[21]

Let's Be Friends (and Sisters): The Local Politics of Globalization

The language of international friendship proved to be appealing and useful for advancing Los Angeles's interests by way of networking with South Korea. It allowed leaders to position the city as the vanguard of the Pacific Rim economy and a peaceful, cooperative world order. Moreover, Los Angeles embodied how globalization could transform US society from the inside out. Its friendship with South Korea illustrated this in a variety of ways, from generating wealth through foreign investment to the diversity and worldliness of its residents. As powerful and pragmatic as the theme of friendship could be, it could also be risky, particularly with Angelenos who might be wary about being *friends* with South Korea and its people.

Mayor Tom Bradley, on the other hand, was an enthusiastic proponent of Los Angeles's internationalism, and he adeptly deployed the language of global friendship. He championed programs such as Sister Cities as part of his mission to extend a warm hand to the world and its people and, in turn, revitalize Los Angeles. Sister Cities was established by the federal government during the 1950s as part of its Cold War strategy of using soft diplomacy to win the hearts and minds of people around the world. By linking municipalities through cultural exchanges and gestures of friendship, the program aimed to foster intimate and localized understandings between people separated by long distances while promoting the position of the United States as the leader of the free world. By participating in Sister Cities, mayors and local officials whose work and concerns had little to do with foreign relations could participate in world affairs as they also explored new avenues for local revitalization and growth.[22]

Los Angeles gained its first sister city during Mayor Sam Yorty's administration when, in 1959, it paired with Nagoya, Japan. In 1971, it formally named its sixth sister city, Pusan, South Korea. With this development, the *Los Angeles Times* said that Los Angeles now had "more 'sister cities' than any other metropolis, anywhere," and it quipped that LA should have its own foreign policy.[23] A sister city relationship was mostly symbolic, but it created a built-in line between cities allowing mayors and other local officials to stay in touch and collaborate with one another on interests big and small, from promoting commercial relations to exchanging gifts. An illustration of how cities expressed and solidified their friendship under the aegis of Sister Cities was a 1974 visit to Los Angeles by a Korean children's taekwondo group. Pusan mayor, Park Young Su, hoped this showcase—receiving local organizing support from the Korean Cultural Service—of the Korean martial art to a mostly unfamiliar US audience would "promote goodwill and close relationships between our two nations and reassure the everlasting friendship between our two sister cities."[24]

Sister Cities fostered two-way, albeit asymmetrical, exchanges, so the counterpart to a Korean taekwondo group exhibition was not a visit to Busan by a drill team from Los Angeles. Instead, traveling Americans tended to be figures of authority, such as professors or officially appointed delegations sent to teach Koreans something (and occasionally learn). And while the trips certainly enriched their education, their underlying purpose was to deepen their understanding of South Korea vis-à-vis the interests of the United States and Los Angeles, and to assert their dominant position in this unequal friendship.

One striking aspect of the maintenance of US hegemony by way of the language and symbols of friendship during the Bradley era was its diverse and racially progressive face. This was on display, for example, during a November 1977 visit to South Korea by a delegation of twenty-seven representatives from the Los Angeles Human Relations Commission, Pusan Sister City committee, and local business community for an official Sister City mission.[25] The two-week goodwill tour included stops at Pusan, the Demilitarized Zone (DMZ) at the North-South border, a visit to the grave of an unknown soldier, and tea with the last Korean princess. A delegation with significant African American and Asian American representation on a global mission made for powerful optics supporting the idea that Los Angeles employed an inclusive and racially progressive approach to international relations. It also underscored that even local stakeholders in the city, whether Black community leaders, Korean immigrant entrepreneurs, or white financiers, should care about South Korea and its stewardship by the United States. Black delegate Jessie Mae Brown explained that the trip reminded her and others of the long-standing commitment by the United

F I G U R E 4   This photo was taken during a 1980 visit to Los Angeles by the mayor of Busan, Choi Suk-won, at a reception hosted by Tom Bradley. From Sonia S. Suk, Life on Two Continents (Seoul: Dong A. Printing, 1984), 114.

States to defend South Korea against Communism and assist in its postwar recovery. "[Each] year," she wrote, "thousands of American fighting men and women join their compatriots in Korea for the mutual purpose of maintaining peace and security on the Korean peninsula." South Korea's transformation "from a war-torn, underdeveloped country to a . . . rapidly developing industrial and trading nation" that was "on the threshold of self-sufficiency" was a credit to the "unselfish dedication of the United States."[26]

Korean immigration was a key factor shaping relations between Los Angeles and South Korea. As has often been the case historically with other nations that sent large numbers of immigrants, South Korean government officials were mindful of and interested in the treatment and standing of its nationals in the United States. They, thus, often invoked the Korean immigrant community in their correspondences with Tom Bradley's office. This made Korean residents of Los Angeles—figuratively and substantively—linchpins in the discourse of friendship and mutual concern between Los Angeles and South Korea. For instance, in June 1977 Hyon Hwack Shin of Korea's Ministry of Health and Social Affairs sent Bradley a letter of gratitude following a visit to Korea by a group of Korean senior citizen residents of Los Angeles, which his office helped to coordinate. Shin expressed his belief that the assistance would "result in a more solid relationship between the two countries." He also hoped that his office "would continue to extend a helping hand to the Koreans, our people, in Los Angeles."[27] Seoul Mayor Koo Ja Choon echoed many of these sentiments and also conveyed his gratitude to Bradley for the assistance, which he understood as showing "your interest in and concern about Korean residents living in your city."[28] A few days earlier, Bradley had sent Koo a letter thanking him for holding a reception for the visiting senior citizens and said they returned "overjoyed from their visit to your beautiful city."[29] He also thanked Koo for gifting him a gold medallion, which he said he would treasure as an "expression of friendship" between Seoul and Los Angeles.

When they took the form of landmarks in the city's symbolic landscape, expressions of friendship became tangible, enduring, and public. And while immigrant placemaking in Koreatown—whether through signs or parades— aimed to assert Koreans' belonging in multicultural Los Angeles, South Korean placemaking in the city imparted something different. It conveyed and paid tribute to South Korea's rising power and global presence while signaling the importance of LA in that process. In 1976, the Republic of Korea gifted the city a seventeen-ton friendship bell in commemoration of the US bicentennial. The bell was placed in a pavilion built in a traditional Korean architectural style and was located in Angels Gate Park in San Pedro.[30] The Korean Cultural Service explained the significance of the pavilion's location, saying it would "[overlook] the Pacific Ocean on San Pedro bluff," and, thus, serve as "a prominent landmark to all sea vessels entering the harbors of San Pedro and Long Beach."[31] The bell also served as a focal point for different historical and ceremonial occasions concerning US relations with Korea. For example, it was renovated and rededicated in 1982 to mark the hundred-year anniversary of the US-Korea Treaty of Amity, which had become widely recognized as formally beginning modern US-Korea diplomatic relations.

Discontents of Globalization

The upsides of globalization and US-Korea relations were enormous, whether they had to do with wealth from international investment, nurturing relationships between people and communities around the world, or animatronic children of various nationalities singing about the smallness of the world. The insistent and sanguine refrains about global harmony and synergy might have distracted from but did not dislodge the ever-present elements of xenophobia. White supremacy and national chauvinism run deep in US history and have always accompanied or lurked under the surface as the nation has extended its power around the world and opened its borders to newcomers. And in a time of accelerated globalization, conditions emerged for gestures of international connection and friendship on the one hand but backlash and racialized resentment on the other. Asians found themselves at the center of both.

As discussed earlier, the idea that Americans should embrace globalization and their international partners had detractors who saw many downsides. Indeed, close and sustained relations with Asia since the mid-twentieth century also set the stage for a resurgence of anti-Asian racism in American life. The US involvement in the Korean and Vietnam Wars gave it a chance to shape the post–World War II order as a leader of the non-Communist world, but these engagements also cemented and brought home racist ideas about Asian people as faceless enemies, weak and dependent "others," and subhuman "gooks." Americans previously unfamiliar with countries like South Korea, Vietnam, and Thailand could now situate them as part of the undeveloped world; as places to destroy, subdue, and modernize; and as nations whose wretched populations were desperate to flee and enter the United States as orphans, refugees, and military brides. Moreover, when Asian countries began to modernize economically, US racism and chauvinism adapted. Japan's rapid industrialization, for instance, gave rise to so-called trade wars, prompted by the desire to protect US producers and workers, but they took very disturbing forms. For instance, in the midst of the crisis facing domestic automakers during the 1970s and 1980s, "Buy American" rallies were held where people gleefully took sledgehammers to Japan-made vehicles while slipping back and forth between expressing economic nationalism and virulent intolerance.

Amid heightened globalization and the rise of Asian immigration, the lines between looking out for US interests and embracing malignant racism could blur to a disturbing degree. Horror came home in an especially vivid and terrifying way as Asians became the targets of grisly high-profile attacks. To discuss two examples, in 1982 Vincent Chin, a Chinese American resident of Detroit was savagely beaten to death by two unemployed white men, one of whom had worked at an auto plant. Before an altercation broke out between Chin and the assailants, a witness heard one of the white men tell Chin it was because of "you motherfuckers" that they were out of work. In 1989 a white gunman who had spoken openly of his hatred of immigrants shot and killed five children—all Cambodian and Vietnamese—at Cleveland Elementary School in Stockton, California. It was at that time the worst school mass shooting in US history. Such tragedies threw cold water on the idea that immigration and other developments drawing the United States and Asia more closely together would bring forth an era of inclusiveness, harmony, and friendship. The world might have been getting smaller, but not everyone was singing happily about it.

Developing and promoting Los Angeles-Korea friendship entailed fundamentally remaking US-Korea relations and Korea's image in the US imagination. While the United States and South Korea were allies throughout its postindependence years, the relations between the countries were bumpy and often tense. From the 1940s, when Korea was liberated from Japanese rule and divided into North and South, South Korea was something of a junior partner to the United States, seen as a bulwark against global Communism and a partner in Asia-Pacific diplomacy. However, trust between the nations could be shaky, as South Korea depended on the United States militarily and worried in the face of changing Cold War priorities if the United States remained committed to its protection.[32] Trouble between the US and Korea also arose over Americans' criticism of the authoritarian regime of President Park Chung-hee. Tensions came to a head in the mid- to late 1970s over allegations of conspiracies on US shores in the so-called Koreagate influence-buying scandal. Tied up in the affair—which involved charges of bribery by purported Korean double agents masquerading in Washington DC's social scene—were beliefs that Koreans were innately corrupt and politically immature, and were trying to exploit the generosity of the United States for ulterior and self-interested motives.[33]

The good feelings and references to familial bonds that pervaded Los Angeles's global branding stemmed from what were likely sincere sentiments, but they also raised a smokescreen that deflected from the realities of US-Korea relations, racism against Asian people, and other troubling conditions on the ground. As discussed in chapter 1, the economy of the late twentieth century was failing to address structural inequality and racial disparities of wealth, instead often deepening them. The gap between the haves and have-nots was widening, and paths to mobility were closing. The economics of urban redevelopment, for example, left struggling communities worse off.

It was becoming clear that prosperity reliant on transpacific commerce had many downsides. A growing lament, noted in the *Washington Post*, was that entrepreneurs cared more about making money selling things to foreigners than US workers.[34]

The travails of the Korean Friendship Bell pavilion provide another illustration of the limits and blind spots of Los Angeles's brand of globalization and international friendship. The bell was a lofty statement affirming mutual interests and the commanding position of both Los Angeles and South Korea in the Pacific region. It was also repeatedly vandalized due to cutbacks in city budgets. Employees in charge of the park's security lost their jobs when a third of the city's public works security staff of 58 people were laid off. In February 1982 vandals defaced the monument, writing "No Nuke Power" in red paint on the bell and pouring more paint on the granite railings surrounding the pavilion. In the aftermath, Councilwoman Joan Milke Flores denounced the acts of vandalism as egregious because they targeted a gift from Korea to the United States. Bradley reached out to the consulate general Min Soo Park to express his outrage and assure Park that the incident should not be taken as a statement of local attitudes toward South Korea.[35] The installation of the pavilion and its subsequent neglect and vandalism illustrated the uneasy balance between urban aspirations, global ideals, and local scarcity.

Olympic Dreams

Two years after the Friendship Bell was defaced, the city was busy showcasing itself on its biggest global stage yet. The 1984 Olympic Games captured Los Angeles during a critical moment in which forces decades in the making had culminated. The timing was fortuitous, as the city could show off its glittering downtown to the world and seal its image as a prosperous international metropolis. The Olympics brought together the world's most elite athletes in a celebration of global friendship and sportsmanship while participants and audiences could root for their nations and bask in their pride. Much was at stake for whatever city hosted; not only would it hold the world's attention for sixteen days but it would also be responsible for executing an array of operations and services for the athletes, guests, tourists, and media from all over.

In addition to reaping the glory and revenue that went with hosting the Olympics, Los Angeles officials and boosters hoped the event would spur local infrastructure improvements and jumpstart economic development. This was not Los Angeles's first turn as Olympics host, but the last time was in 1932, seemingly a world away from the 1970s and 1980s. The city had come close in the competition for the 1976 games; officials secured early support from Japanese, South Korean, and Indonesian committee members and the deputy mayor Joseph Quinn traveled to Asia to tout Los Angeles's facilities as well as plans for a mass transit system connecting the Coliseum to the main Olympic village.[36] Despite these efforts, the hosting honors for 1976 went to Montreal, Canada.

Los Angeles's moment in the spotlight finally came when it was selected to host the 1984 Summer Olympics. The Los Angeles Olympic Organizing Committee (LAOOC) led the planning and was intent on pulling off an unforgettable event that showcased the city, which by the mid-1980s more fully embodied its promise as a place of modernity, globalization, and glamour than it had just a decade earlier. The year 1984 was already a big one for the city as it had hosted the Democratic National Convention in July.[37] A crisis in the months leading up to the Games occurred when the Soviet Union announced in May that it would not participate, partly as a reaction to the US decision to skip the 1980 Olympics in Moscow. This was unacceptable to Tom Bradley and the LAOOC president Peter Ueberroth, who were counting on their Olympics being the biggest and most spectacular yet, so they sought permission—ultimately unsuccessfully—to travel to Moscow in the hopes of convincing Russian officials to reconsider.[38] Without the Soviet Union, the Games carried on from late July to mid-August and came to be widely considered a great success.

The intensified national and international media attention on Los Angeles before and during the Games highlighted the city's ethnic and cultural diversity as an aspect of its unique character and as a function of its globalization. In coverage preceding the Games that gave tips and advice to potential visitors, the local ethnic communities were highlighted as features of a larger buffet of experiences. In one overview of Los Angeles, the *Washington Post* recommended downtown as an appealing and interesting destination for the traveling connoisseur of culture, its density making it especially accessible. "Within a five-mile radius of the financial district's tall glass structures and the Music Center's performing arts complex are Chinatown, Little Tokyo, Koreatown, and Olvera Street, the 200-year-old Puebla de Los Angeles."[39] Koreatown stood out as a particular curiosity, as both an integral part of global Los Angeles and as a wholly unfamiliar entity to the average American and foreign visitor. "For miles it seems you are in a suburb of Seoul. The neon signs are in Korean. The churches, the stores, the professional offices serve a Korean community that may exceed 250,000."[40]

For Korean and Korean American residents of Los Angeles, the 1984 Olympics were not just an outlet to express ethnic and national pride, they were also an opportunity to solidify their sense of local belonging and ownership. As the Olympics in Los Angeles brought back memories of when the city had been host in 1932, people were reminded that one of Koreatown's main streets, Olympic Boulevard, was named in honor of those Games. Two of the runners in the torch relay that preceded the official start of the 1984 Games inspired tremendous community excitement in Koreatown. One of the torch carriers was Korean national Sohn Key-chung, the winner of the 1936 marathon and member of the 1984 Korean Olympic Committee. As his portion of the relay went through Koreatown, Korean immigrants and Korean Americans alike cheered him on.[41] Also selected for the torch race was a sixteen-year-old student from Glendale's Hoover High School named Susan Choi. The first Korean American to participate in the relay, Choi ran down Sunset Boulevard near Echo Park and afterward took part in the 11th Annual Korean Parade.[42] The Olympics also allowed Tom Bradley's office to further cement his goodwill with South Korea and the Korean American community. Staff member Jun Kim relayed to him that the impressive performance of South Korean athletes had stirred great pride among the city's Korean and Korean American residents, and he credited Bradley for helping to make South Korea's successful showing possible. Kim also praised Bradley for connecting his promotion of the Olympics to outreach with Korean Americans by attending local events in the community, which contributed "greatly towards building and enhancing the general morale of the Korean Community."[43]

While generating positive spirits in the public about athletic competition against a backdrop of international friendship, the Olympics also gave business and government leaders the chance to put their economic and ideological ideas into practice. The large-scale spectacle of the Olympics, after all, could not be pulled off without spending a great deal of money. As the state was in the thick of the taxpayer's revolt, citizens regarded the prospect of paying for the Summer Games with public funds as a nonstarter. That Montreal was still paying off its debts from the 1976 Games suggested these might not be the best use of state resources anyway. Bradley, thus, "conceived the plan under which a group of local businessmen, not the city, would organize the Olympics, paying for them largely with revenues from television broadcasting rights and contributions from private corporations."[44] The LAOOC promised that it would not use any tax money for the Olympics.

The reliance on the private sector raised concerns and questions about whether the Olympics could be a vehicle of community and civic spirit when the LAOOC was also seeking to make profits on the order of $15 million. Hosting the Olympics could not conceal the city's challenges described above and instead magnified the contradictions of being a "world-class city." About a week before the Games opened, the former president of the Los Angeles Chamber of Commerce Ted Bruinsma said that despite the impressive economic growth of the city and its enviable downtown, "three miles in any direction from where I sit, we have major social problems that aren't being faced." He cited a struggling school system, racial conflicts, unemployment, inadequate housing, and the city and state's inability to meet the needs of its growing immigrant population. "We are not planning sufficiently for the problems they will create," he warned.[45] The downside of bringing attention to Los Angeles's wealth was it also highlighted the contrast between the haves and have-nots. To the east of the new skyscrapers were the working poor neighborhoods of East LA and Watts, and off Wilshire near MacArthur Park was a community of about a thousand Marielitos from Cuba. Then after turning off Wilshire to the south was Olympic Boulevard and Koreatown, which then changed as abruptly to Vietnamese and Cambodian refugees, and then to El Salvadoreans, Guatemalans, Hondurans, and Nicaraguans.

As a member of the Citizen's Advisory Commission and one of fifty thousand LAOOC volunteers, Tong Soo Chung followed the controversy about the Olympics being exploitative and overly capitalistic and told readers of the *Korea Times* that these accusations were a red herring. He agreed that fees to attend events were excessive and that the International Olympic Committee (IOC) and LAOOC should have subsidized poorer nations. However, he also wanted people to understand that the LAOOC was simply trying to avoid losses and be a sound, conservatively managed organization. This, it should be lauded for, he believed. Moreover, Chung said the profits would go into communities as donations to organizations, including those serving Korean Americans such the Korean Youth Council and Korean American Youth Foundation. Whether or not such promises would be kept troubled him less than the prospect of the city incurring massive debts to host the Games. "I would risk being called too 'capitalistic' rather than ending up with a debt of $1 billion and more millions in interest for years to come," said Chung. "Wouldn't you?"[46]

The selection of Seoul, South Korea, to host the next Summer Olympics in 1988 only validated and further boosted the impression of South Korea's rising position in Pacific and world affairs, while also deepening the connections between Los Angeles, Korean Americans, and South Korea. During the closing ceremony for the 1984 Los Angeles Games, an ebullient Tom Bradley declared, "The Games of the Olympiad are an important international tradition which brings people of the world together in joyous celebration of life and peace. It is the single most important worldwide event that transcends all boundaries, be they political, cultural or racial and fills the heart of the world with love for fellow men." He offered his best wishes to the people of South Korea as they prepared to host the next Summer Olympics and praised Seoul as "the jewel of Asia."[47] At the invitation of the Mayor of Seoul Kim Yong-Rae, Bradley attended the 1988 Olympic Games along with two staff members.[48]

As it had been for Los Angeles in 1984, hosting the Olympics in 1988 was a rare and momentous opportunity for Seoul and South Korea. Just twenty years earlier, the entire country was considered premodern, and in 1988 the city stood proud as one of the world's rising metropolises. Moreover, since the early 1960s, the South Korean government promoted a sporting policy as a nation-building strategy, so the 1984 Games had been pivotal for the impressive performances by its athletes, whom the state had significantly invested in and then celebrated as national heroes and "warriors." The country took an even bigger leap when it hosted the Games in 1988, considered an apex for Korean sporting nationalism.

The Olympics-fueled nationalism in South Korea spilled over to the people of Koreatown, Los Angeles. Not only were they filled with pride as they watched their home country take such a prominent place on the world stage, but they also saw striking parallels between the trajectories of South Korea and Koreatown. In any event, the Games called for community revelry and a renewed push to boost Koreatown's economy and visibility. Two weeks before the start of the 1988 Games, the annual Koreatown parade included a celebration of the Olympics. At an Olympics-themed party held at Koreatown Plaza, Senator Pete Wilson made an appearance, using the occasion to court the Korean vote. Business owners, still hoping to attract the same volume of tourists that Chinatown and Little Tokyo drew, hoped the Olympics would create new interest in Koreatown at a precarious time. "Like Korea," wrote journalist David Wilson, "Koreatown sees itself on the edge of economic change, one that could bring expansion and prosperity or recession and decline."[49]

As much as the Seoul Olympics activated the pride of Korean Americans, it was also the source of controversy due to unflattering media coverage of South Koreans. For example, in the wake of a televised boxing match during which several South Korean Olympics officials physically attacked a referee, Korean Americans worried that the spectacle would have negative repercussions for all Koreans and criticized the US media's disproportionate and unfair characterization of Koreans as irrational and violent.[50] Regarding ongoing protests against the South Korean government, K. Connie Kang bemoaned US reporting that painted the country as dangerous and chaotic, particularly with footage showing student protestors being violently suppressed. She worried such images gave a distorted impression of the country and its people and that American television viewers would be afraid to travel to and otherwise engage with Korea.

Kang blamed the arrogance of Americans and ignorance of their media. Foreign correspondents and news desk editors often lacked special preparation or training for their positions and had only superficial or second-hand knowledge of the countries on which they reported. Though the Olympics were supposed to cultivate a spirit of equality and friendship and respect for the host society, American visitors in Seoul seemed indifferent to learning Korean and instead expected Koreans to speak English. "Koreans are going to have to accept the fact that the whole country cannot be held responsible for the actions of a few hot-tempered and unthinking people among them," wrote Kang, "just as the United States ought not to be held accountable for the misbehavior of a handful of its citizens."

Back to 1984, on the eve of the Los Angeles Olympics, an article in the *Los Angeles Times* highlighted the recent "glitter" in downtown thanks to redevelopment, and also remarked on how this contrasted to parts of the city unlikely to draw the same attention. About Watts, it said, "Blacks still occupy the heart of this community, but, at the edges, Hispanic and Asian immigrants are moving in, not always peacefully."[51] Five years earlier, after the city had won its bid to host the 1984 Games, a reader for the Black newspaper the *Los Angeles Sentinel* expressed anxiety about how it would accelerate globalization at the expense of African Americans.[52] The reader implored, "If we don't start creating business, the man will come in once again and take all of the tourist and black money to his banks and communities."

CHAPTER 5

"Most of These Areas Were Formerly Black"

Interracial Conflict in South Central and the Burning of Koreatown

FOR MARLA GIBBS, the changes were in plain view, and they were jarring. In a 1983 interview with the *Los Angeles Sentinel*, she proclaimed her love for her adopted city of Los Angeles but then lamented, "You just look up and next thing you see all the writing is in oriental all down the street. Next thing you know is they have bought up the whole neighborhood. . . . I mean, we have even Korean Towns. Most of these areas were formerly Black."[1]

As an actor on what was then one of America's most popular television shows, Gibbs was hardly a typical Black Angeleno. Still, her life story resonated with those of thousands of others who had headed out West in search of better lives, and her remarks captured an ambivalence that many shared. Born in Chicago in 1931, Gibbs spent her early years in the Midwest before moving to California to pursue acting. Fame came her way in 1975 when she stepped into the role of the wry housekeeper, Florence Johnston, on *The Jeffersons*, a comedy centering on a nouveau riche Black family that had "moved on up" from working-class Queens to a plush Manhattan apartment "in the sky." *The Jeffersons* broke ground with its predominantly Black cast and would become one of television's longest-running series (1975–1985). While the family's wealth set them apart from the African American population at large, the series' tackling of issues like class, status, and race relations gave it social relevance rarely seen in network comedies of that era.

At the height of the popularity of *The Jeffersons*, Gibbs was a stalwart champion and booster of the performing arts in Los Angeles's Black community; among other activities, she opened the Vision Theater in Crenshaw in 1981. While her remarks about Koreatown registered disdain, she expressed them in the context of a larger lament about how Blacks were losing ground in the neighborhoods they struggled to make their own. In the 1980s, most Black Angelenos were a generation or two removed from their own migrations from the South and Midwest, and already a new wave of arrivals was coming from foreign countries, putting up their native language signs as if to mark their territory and communicate to Blacks that these spaces were no longer theirs.

This chapter follows key developments from the mid-1960s to the early 1990s shaping Black-Korean encounters, and how relations between the communities captured public interest as a subplot of the larger saga of the struggling inner city. While common legacies of discrimination, migration, and socioeconomic struggle might have nurtured affinity and solidarity among Koreans and Blacks, countervailing forces that engendered suspicion and ill will frustrated and derailed progress toward developing a foundation of interethnic understanding informed by the belief that their fates were linked. The dominant framing of Black-Korean relations by the 1980s was competitive and adversarial—whether in merchant-customer altercations or accusations of property encroachment—illustrating capitalism's socially divisive effects as well as its impact on identity politics and ethnic organizing. As incidents of theft, harassment, assault, or interpersonal awkwardness accumulated, the reactions of journalists, politicians, and activists eventually crystallized the idea that animus between Koreans and Blacks was intrinsic and insurmountable, which in turn shaped daily life, social interactions, and responses to subsequent incidents. It also contributed to a sense of inevitability that the other shoe would drop, as it were, and that the next offense, whether committed by a Black or Korean, would bring on pain and destruction on an untold scale. That shoe dropped in late April 1992 when the verdict in the Rodney King police brutality trial was delivered.

That a case involving a Black motorist beaten by LAPD officers was the prelude to a riot in which Koreatown burned to the ground and Korean immigrants found themselves the targets of mounting rage directs us to expand our frame for understanding this flashpoint of Black-Korean relations. As historian Brenda Stevenson has depicted, the story of Koreans and Blacks in Los Angeles, which included violent and tragic moments, are also two stories of migrant hopes and dreams that ran parallel and intertwined with each other.[2] To flesh out this story calls our geographic attention to an area that was known as South Central. In Koreatown, as discussed in chapter 2, Koreans sought to prove their worthiness, distinguish themselves, and build political capital by generating wealth as property owners, business operators, and real estate developers. In South Central, Koreans did not envision turning the area into a monoethnic bastion of commerce and tourism. They did not bring to it a placemaking vision; it was simply a place to work, make money, and invest minimally. In turn, a set of competing narratives about the dreams of Blacks and Koreans took hold. Blacks were trying to protect their neighborhood from and be treated with dignity by people they regarded as interlopers, while Koreans were trying to survive difficult circumstances and serve an area that others had abandoned.

From Black Capitalism to Foreign Takeover

By the mid-1960s, cities like Compton and neighborhoods like Watts and South Central—once emblematic of Los Angeles's dynamism and a better future for Blacks—had become reminders of the unfinished fight for racial equality and the deferred dreams of the civil rights movement. Retail establishments were shuttered. Dilapidated buildings and streets sat in disrepair. Schools languished with diminishing resources. And good jobs were fewer and farther between. The growing concentration of impoverished Blacks in these areas was a startling consequence of divestment by the state, employers, and middle-class Americans. These trends, moreover, signaled that these communities were on their own as far as future development.

One beacon of hope for Black Angelenos' economic autonomy and prosperity was the Black-owned and -controlled Bank of Finance, which opened in 1964 on South Western Avenue. Neglect of Black communities and discriminatory lending practices in the banking industry had locked them out of property owning, generational wealth, and the middle class, a problem that could be alleviated by Black-owned banks, believed the founders. One of them, real estate broker Onie B. Granville, moreover, promised that the Bank of Finance would "create a pride of ownership and do something positive for the black community." It tapped a politically powerful group of Black economic and professional elites in Los Angeles to help raise capital and serve as officers and trustees. The board included future City Council members Gilbert Lindsey and Edward Granville. The Bank of Finance prospered in its first decade, financing homes, consumer purchases, and businesses. Soon after its establishment, a second South Central office opened on

South Vermont Street.[3] The *Los Angeles Times* reported that it was one of the SBA's most active partners that lent to small business owners in Los Angeles.

Its auspicious beginnings notwithstanding, the Bank of Finance always struggled due to the built-in disadvantages of servicing an underresourced clientele. That, combined with the economic recessions of the 1970s, which pummeled community financial institutions, would eventually seal its fate. For customers during the 1960s, the low-interest mortgages they could secure were critical lifelines into homeownership. Still, the loans' correspondingly low yields translated to low profits for the bank, which then disincentivized giving similarly generous mortgages to customers in the 1970s. The decade's inflationary spiral resulted in a cash squeeze throughout the economy, raising the cost of borrowing and triggering loan defaults. By 1980, the Bank of Finance's viability was grave. Hobbled by losses, its reserves drained by $1 million, and unable to replenish its coffers, it could not ward off regulators, so in late 1979 it came under state supervision. The following spring it was put up for sale.

The drama over the Bank of Finance included suspicion about a set of shadowy figures with Asian names who in 1980 purchased enough stocks to become majority shareholders. To the public, little was known about Yong Song, Tadao Fuse, and Karl Hak Chung Chun, except that their acquisitions had resulted in the bank suddenly coming under the ownership of Asians. Bank of Finance officials had tried to keep the institution under Black ownership. For instance, when it initially went up for sale, a consortium of Black buyers presented a bid for $1.5 million, but the offer fell short of the amount needed to rescue it. In early 1981 they and other Black consortia were outbid by a group offering $2.4 million.[4]

The media described the investors and buyers as Asian and Korean and quoted sources that called the bank's fate a foreign takeover. Left out of the reporting were details such as the fact that Yong Song was from Cerritos, California, or that Karl Hak Chung represented Korean American businesspeople.[5] But these were quibbles that must have struck observers as inconsequential, whether because the outcome remained the same—a Black community lost its bank—or because Asian Americans were still Asian and, therefore, presumably foreign. For example, in *Black Enterprise* magazine, writer Liz Grant emphasized the elusiveness of "the Korean group" that took control of the Bank of Finance, how little the public knew about them, and their unspecific "substantial business interests in China." Citing unnamed banking industry sources, Grant said that Asian groups had been scouting vulnerable US banks. "Since black banks have traditionally had the least amount of capital reserves," she wrote, "they are now the most likely takeover targets."[6]

The Bank of Finance was renamed West Olympia Bank, and under its new owners became the fourth Korean-owned bank in Los Angeles. In this incarnation, it aimed to serve the growing Korean community and further develop Koreatown. The rise of West Olympia, then, was less a nefarious foreign takeover than it was a case of an immigrant community trying to establish economic roots. But while the Korean managers of the former Bank of Finance were not agents of distant overlords in Asia, to many Black residents this was a distinction without much difference; they were still losing their beloved community bank. Whatever West Olympia's vision or intention, it remained the "formerly Black-owned Bank of Finance," whose purchase signified "an increasing pattern of non-Blacks assuming control of vital interests right in Blacks' own backyard." A *Los Angeles Sentinel* reader lamented that the community was being treated as "a commodity to be bought and sold to the highest bidder."[7] The departure of several Black bank officers—according to the bank, due to long-planned resignations and in one case an ethical violation—and hiring of employees of Korean descent nonetheless confirmed people's fears that "this may be the beginning of a [purge] within the bank, and the possible replacement of Blacks by Asians."[8] West Olympia tried to dispel the impression as inaccurate, noting in February 1983 for instance that it employed Black managers and a staff that was 70 percent Black. Paul Davidson, a Black assistant vice president for business development, insisted the bank remained committed to serving the entire community and supporting Black businesses. "It is important that the community understand that West Olympia is not forsaking it," he said.[9] Despite those assurances, local sentiment remained antagonistic toward the Korean-owned establishment; stories circulated of the bank's declining quality of service and customers opening accounts elsewhere.

Confirmation of suspicions that West Olympia was always going to be a Koreatown bank came in late 1983 and early 1984. In October, West Olympia opened a predominantly Korean-staffed Koreatown branch on Western Avenue while running the former Bank of Finance at the Vermont location. Then in January, it announced it would close the South Central Branch. Karl Chun, the board chairman, explained, "The banking industry is in a period of transition, forcing institutions to pursue new strategies for growth."[10] The bank's assurance to shareholders that it would continue to support minority enterprises rang hollow when it told the existing customers to close their accounts or move them to the Koreatown branch. A group of Black bankers discussed keeping the branch open by purchasing it back, a goal ultimately deemed unworkable because it would have required the Black community to place more than $3 million in the bank, a prohibitively high amount.

The bank was gone, and bitterness remained and was directed at a variety of targets. "Not only can they attempt to hit in the Black community," wrote James Cleaver, "they have the financing of their own bank to give them that extra added financial push."[11] One Black physician and supporter of the Bank of Finance blamed members of his own community, namely those "who had no faith in what we were trying to do."[12] One resident told Cleaver that the establishment of the Koreatown branch was an ominous sign, saying "taking over the Bank of Finance and then opening a branch in the Koreatown area gave them the foothold [Koreans] need to operate a major financial institution, without being involved with the Black community."[13] The 1984 firing of Matthew Kennedy, a Wilshire employee from the Bank of Finance's early days, sparked outrage when he accused the bank of racism. It also set off a wave of consternation that the Korean management team treated the Black branch with little regard and never seriously intended to serve the community.[14]

So-Called New Americans

The saga of the Bank of Finance was one aspect of a disorienting storm that hit Black Angelenos after the 1960s. As it came under Korean American ownership, it seemed some of their worst case fears about the impact of immigration on their community were coming true. If the bank's beginnings symbolized African Americans' quest for uplift and freedom, its closure confirmed that they were losing ground while forced to compete with minorities from other countries.

Essays and letters published in the *Los Angeles Sentinel* in the late 1970s and early 1980s shed light on the evolution of attitudes about immigration among African Americans and its emergence as a wedge issue that separated them from Asians and Latinos. A pivotal issue in this regard was the racially disparate US treatment of refugees. In 1980, columnist Jim Cleaver took legislators to task for showing generosity and compassion to Southeast Asians and Cubans escaping Communism but withholding it from Black Haitians fleeing the oppressive Duvalier regimes. The following year, Stanley Robertson pondered skeptically if churches and charities urging to admit Southeast Asians from Communist regimes would have argued as passionately for Black refugees.[15] Cleaver called this "another kind of racism" that revealed the pervasiveness of anti-Black attitudes reaching even into immigration debates and policies. Discussing the recent system and politics of immigration admissions, Cleaver said, "The Vietnamese did not have to wait. The Koreans did not have to wait. The Arabs did not have to wait. All the other nations, which incidentally were not Black, did not have to wait."[16]

Otherwise abstract conversations and worries about immigration policy took concrete form in the face of developments like the Bank of Finance's change of ownership and installation of Korean-language signs over storefronts. And for many Black Americans witnessing these changes and hearing these debates, a common belief took hold that the admission of newcomers from other countries worked against their interests. In 1979, for instance, after the United States authorized the entry of thousands of people from the Soviet Union, *Los Angeles Sentinel* reader Hue Forton brought the issue home by invoking Black struggles amid the immigration of Asians and Latin Americans. "Take a good look around your community," he implored, "what to do you see? Korean, Chinese, Mexican. They have bought the old neighborhood store." Such attitudes became commonplace and more pointed in the pages of the *Sentinel*; regarding changes in their neighborhoods, another reader fumed in 1981 that Koreans and Mexicans were "taking over" Olympic Boulevard and Central Avenue, respectively, and turning "our Los Angeles" into a "foreign country." Shortly thereafter, yet another lamented, "The Mexicans have the money and the Koreans do too," but "Black people have nothing."[17] Giving further voice to the deeply intertwined anxieties about immigration and Black well-being, columnist Stanley Robertson opined, "The current immigration tide, both legal and illegal, is objected to and seen as a major threat to Black economic and civil advancement."[18] He continued, "Nobody wants to really say it, "but, because Blacks are paying taxes (many who really can't afford to do so), there are many so-called 'New Americans' who are receiving and benefiting from all types of government aid programs and services, services and programs which are not available to many Blacks!"[19]

What praise *Sentinel* writers did give to Koreans was couched in the paper's pro-business outlook and tough-love approach toward problems in the Black community. It was not a means of extending solidarity or sense of shared fate between Blacks and Koreans. It was a way to express admiration from a distance. "Whatever hang ups [Koreans] may have are not the kind which shackle their minds or ambitions," said A.S. Doc Young.[20] Young had a regular column about local happenings and often expressed his admiration for immigrants, particularly entrepreneurs. In 1977 he implored his readers, "Take a look around Los Angeles and see how the Koreans, Japanese, Filipinos, and Mexican-Americans are capitalizing on the opportunities which abound in this country. They are quietly aggressive. They are geared to be long distance winners."[21] He later wrote about a Korean cashier at a sundry shop with whom he regularly interacted. He praised her for her tenaciousness in the face of a considerable language barrier and wondered why there were so many Korean business owners. Koreans, Young said, "like to run businesses. . . . They don't like to work for anybody."[22] He hoped Blacks would be inspired by this example to uplift themselves, acquire "moral values," and get "out of the ghetto." He was concerned that too many Blacks in the community were consumed by anger and hate and had grown overly fixated on race as the cause of their disadvantages and problems. Immigrants, by contrast, "have not been conned into believing that 'this is a white world.'"[23] Young rattled off a list of other laments: "We are not a race of people who accept the fact of life that business and industry rule the world. We are not a race whose No. 1 priority is swimming in the mainstream of business and industry. We are a race of people who constantly attempt to discount the important of business and industry." With a note of resignation toward his fellow Blacks and a subtle nod to Korean entrepreneurs he concluded, "We don't want to create any millionaires."[24]

Stressful interactions also vexed residents, and in particular the "drama over the grocery store counter" became a fixture in commentaries about life in South Central over the 1980s.[25] James Cleaver conveyed the increasingly common complaint that once a store fell under Korean management, the service would go from "kind and courteous" to awkward and rude.[26] An NAACP official said in 1985 that she had heard "scores of complaints" from African Americans about Koreans, touching on everything from their curtness to tendency to overcharge customers.[27] "They don't even say thank you," said one South Central resident. "And then, if you're a penny or two short, forget it. They'll tell you to walk all the way home and bring back the exact amount of money." To add insult to injury, these store owners were allegedly taking whatever meager wealth existed in South Central outside of the community. Cleaver shared an anecdote from a reader claiming that an Asian restaurant owner charged high prices and provided poor service to a clientele that was 80 percent Black and, in the process, became wealthy in a short period of time.[28]

Observers invoked cultural difference and mutual ignorance to explain the clashes. Melanie Lomax, a vice president of the Los Angeles NAACP, observed that "both groups are not educated about the other's cultural heritage."[29] According to Charles Kim, with more education, customers would show more patience toward merchants, who were simply introverted because of their shaky command of English.[30] In turn, merchants should extend the warmth and friendliness that customers wanted. Education would also give Koreans an understanding of what Blacks in the United States had endured and fought for, for the benefit of all minorities who followed in their footsteps. Because most Korean immigrants arrived after the civil rights movement, they had no direct experience with and little knowledge about the Black struggle for freedom. They did not necessarily see their own concerns and hardships in terms of racism and, thus, perceived little in the way of a common ground or shared fate with African Americans. According to local activist Larry Aubry, Koreans "must understand why blacks resent a presence of 'outsiders' in their community," but for their part, he said Blacks must better understand Koreans, and that they were not indistinguishable from other Asians.[31]

An irony of the situation was that the West Olympia Bank under its Korean owners did not fare better than the Bank of Finance under Black ownership. In 1984, it was in trouble due to loan losses, and state regulators ordered its transfer to another institution called the Wilshire State Bank. The FDIC would protect the 1,500 mostly Korean and Black bank customers, but not the shareholders.[32] Things improved little, as in December 1985 the bank announced the Western Avenue branch, which served more of the Black clientele than the Wilshire branch, would close on January 31, 1986. According to former executive Matthew Kennedy, the Western Avenue branch—also known as the Black branch—had already effectively become little more than a place to deposit rather than borrow money, as officers turned the bank's focus to developing Koreatown and assisting Korean businesses.[33] Articles played up the perception that Koreans were "part of a long line of outsiders who have bought up chunks of their community, exploited their dependence on local merchants and then used the profits to move to safer areas."[34]

The responses from Koreans to these accusations ranged from bewildered concern to angry defensiveness. People from the immigrant business community countered that Blacks should be grateful that they were being served at all, which of course did not quell the anger.[35] "Some of these were closed stores and we went in there and opened them up," explained Tong Soo Chung, in his capacity as KAC spokesperson. "We can look at it this way and say we actually do them a favor having a store there so they don't have to travel five or 10 miles and do their shopping."[36] Chung also believed that the rancor stemmed from Koreans' and Blacks' divergent relationships to the neighborhoods where they interacted. Korean merchants regarded their businesses as investments and vehicles to make money, not as a means to join the community where they worked. "They don't look at it as a lifelong investment," he explained, and as a result they did not do neighborly things like send their children to the local schools or support Little League teams, and "that's a source of the problems."[37] If people did not not understand why or how Korean-owned stores "seem to be sprouting on every corner," the merchants were doing little to create understanding and defuse resentment.[38]

Debates over who could more rightfully claim space and the basis of those claims evoked historical themes of settlement, conflict, and displacement, albeit among marginalized minorities. Though Los Angeles's neighborhoods had undergone persistent and ongoing demographic change, African Americans' longer presence compared to Korean immigrants seemed to bolster their position that it was they who were encroached upon by outsiders. Koreans, on the other hand, saw themselves as akin to pioneers whose rightful presence was buttressed by their dedication to capitalist enterprise and improvement of the places in which they settled. As Charles Kim and David Hyun wrote in 1991 about areas where clashes between Korean business owners and Black customers occurred:

> The battleground is one of the poorest of retail environments, a poor African American neighborhood that was abandoned by white merchants, where non-resident Angelenos fear to walk alone. In this retail wasteland the opportunity to open a retail store is open to anyone. There are no takers by outside retailers, except the poorest and most disadvantaged Korean American, a recent immigrant. He is well educated with a small network of family and close friends but he cannot practice his profession or find work in Koreatown; he cannot work at jobs that require English or familiarity with American customs. He does not qualify for unemployment or welfare. This immigrant is desperate to earn a livelihood.[39]

Kim and Hyun stressed that many Korean immigrants too lived under precarious conditions and were merely trying to survive. "In this needful situation, the retail environment of an African American community offers an opportunity" because rents and purchase prices were low. "The liquor sales (and grocery) transaction requires minimal English: the numbers to 100 and the words *dollars* and *cents*."[40] And yet, emphasized Kim and Hyun, they were taking on huge risks with their "desperate investment" and they worked themselves to the bone.

Friends or Foes?

Through the 1980s and into the 1990s, with the escalating occurrence and coverage of violence involving Blacks and Koreans, a foreboding sense of anger and despondency fell over South Central Los Angeles. Events in 1986 and 1991 were especially pivotal in impressing on the public consciousness the existence of interracial conflict, which in turn ratcheted up tensions on the ground. In March and April 1986 three separate incidents occurred in which Black youths killed four Korean business owners: Jung Keun Chong and his wife Jung Ran Chong at their store on 5th and Normandie; Lee Kee Hong in his liquor store; and Tae Choi at his hamburger stand. Then in 1991 the killings of two African Americans in Korean-owned liquor stores— Latasha Harlins by Soon Ja Du at Empire Liquor Market in March and Arthur Lee Mitchell at St. John's Liquor Store by Tae Sam Park in June— attracted nationwide attention. Though South Central was a focal point of the troubles between Koreans and Blacks, the issue transcended any one neighborhood. For African Americans, the violence was just the latest manifestation of a historical pattern of racism and neglect affecting their community. To Koreans, it illustrated the dangers they faced and lack of protection they received as minority business owners. In 1991, Koreatown was the scene of 48 murders and 2,500 robberies, and Koreans had been the number one target of anti-Asian hate crimes in the area. As incidents of deadly violence supplanted quotidian encounters of awkwardness or rudeness as the backdrop of Black-Korean relations, a cloud of stress and terror loomed over Black residents and Korean business owners alike.

Between 1986 and 1991, public officials, civil rights groups, neighborhood organizations, and churches tried to defuse conflicts and reframe the events involving Blacks and Koreans, while urging people to summon their better angels and seek common ground. A key voice in this effort was the Black-Korean Alliance (BKA), formed in April 1986 in the wake of the string of Korean merchant killings. Affiliated with the City and County Human Relations Commissions, the BKA described its members as "dedicated civic, religious, political, and business leaders committed to eliminating cultural misunderstandings and improving existing relations between the two communities."[41] Its mission was a daunting one that included combating simplistic media depictions and working to transcend people's narrow prejudices so they could understand how inner-city violence concerned everybody, was not limited to Black-on-Korean crime, and affected business owners of all races.[42] The BKA also refuted the impression that Blacks and Koreans related to each other only as antagonists, and it urged people from the communities to see each other as potential allies, friends, and fellow travelers. One of its leaders, Larry Aubry, explained that the BKA's goal was to "reduce the tensions so that [Blacks and Koreans in South Central] could relate to each other in more a humane way, a more civil way," and to make "the whole environment safer for economic development." Toward fostering these more humane and civil relations, members put much stock in person-to-person connections and created opportunities for Blacks and Koreans to be in the same spaces to recognize their shared interests and common humanity. Using churches in this way could be especially powerful.[43] The BKA also elevated members like Chung Lee as an exemplar of how to be a good Korean merchant in a Black community. As the owner of a market near the Jordan Downs public housing project in Watts, Lee prided himself in his positive relationships with neighborhood children and teens, which included sponsoring sports teams and hiring students from Jordan High School.[44] For Chung, the formula was simple: take an interest in the people and community one serves and invest in their well-being.

Though made up of skilled, thoughtful, and dedicated members, the BKA had disadvantages that impeded its mission. It was a low-budget operation that came together in an ad hoc manner, largely on the initiative of concerned public servants in the Human Relations Commission. It, thus, never received the support and resources it needed to effect major and lasting changes in areas such as Black youth unemployment and neighborhood capital divestment, instead relying on playing advisory or facilitator roles to existing offices and organizations. The BKA was also limited in the effectiveness of its community outreach due to its officers tending to be civil servants from city and county government who relied on their political leverage rather than local standing. Because it was not well known to the communities it sought to represent and advocate for, its community events suffered, such as a poorly attended Korean-Black picnic in Compton. Its difficulties also exposed some of the challenges of pan-Asian unity and the inadequacies of what Helen Zia described as an "old style multiracial coalition" by the 1980s.[45] The root problems the BKA was trying to fix were intransigent and required much more than dialogue. As Marcia Choo of the Asian Pacific American Dispute Resolution Center reflected, "In our zeal to do the right things, we sometimes tried to fix things without consulting with the community."

Because the BKA included a range of actors representing the public and private sectors, church-based and secular organizations, and Black and Korean interests, its initiatives were broad, and those with a business focus tried to exert their influence. This did not always make for a happy and harmonious synergy, as one Korean BKA member described the Korean American Grocers Association (KAGRO) officers with whom they worked as "aristocrats of Koreatown" without a meaningful stake in places like South Central.[46] But businesses could not be ignored in the Black-Korean efforts because they were after all the settings of the interethnic tensions and conflicts that people were paying the most attention to. Moreover, City Hall was disposed to heed and prioritize the concerns of the business community. Tom Bradley and other officials believed it made good sense to give business owners and bankers a central role in the work of repairing relations between Koreans and Blacks, both because of the specific circumstances of disturbances but also their abiding belief that businesses would lift communities out of the hardships fueling the conflicts in the first place. Thus, the BKA had little choice but to work with merchant groups on initiatives like developing business codes of ethics, raising Black youth employment, and promoting joint merchant-community programs.[47] For their part, Korean merchants seemed motivated to implement changes. In response to the 1985 uproar over the *Los Angeles Sentinel*'s stories about Asian merchants, over one hundred Korean shop owners formed a business association aimed at improving relations with the Black community on the rationale that this was a good business strategy.[48] If Black customers felt respected and received good service, the reasoning went, community relations would improve, people and their property would be safer, and the bottom line would benefit.

The specter of interracial conflict was certainly worrying for those invested in Los Angeles's brand as a prosperous and cosmopolitan city on the economic cutting edge. Tom Bradley had staked his mayorship on this idea. He had come to power as LA's first Black mayor in part on his banking background and pro-business views, and so believed that championing business and racial equality could go hand in hand. As turmoil over Black-Korean relations intensified in 1991, he looked to the business community to collaborate on solutions and took pains to ensure it did not feel attacked.[49] In April, his office and the Korean Chamber of Commerce of Los Angeles worked together to organize a trip to South Korea by a delegation of Black and Korean business leaders, both a bonding mission and a chance to explore potential joint economic ventures for Koreans and Blacks in Los Angeles. In September, hoping to defuse anger arising from the killing of Arthur Lee Mitchell and subsequent boycott of St. John's Liquor Store, Bradley hosted a conference for South Central merchants at Kinsey Auditorium. Panels informed aspiring business owners about obtaining loans and government contracts. They also urged merchants to use crime prevention and city police rather than take matters into their own hands, and to utilize dispute resolution services and customer service representatives to deescalate problems. The conference also encouraged the formation of a South Central Merchants Association to strengthen business owners' ties to the neighborhood and bring together merchants across race and ethnicity.[50] Getting buy-in from Korean American banks, which financed many of the Korean-owned businesses in Black neighborhoods, was critical. Worried they were becoming skittish about lending and investing to business owners in this atmosphere of interracial strife, Bradley convened a meeting in November at the Hyatt Wilshire with Ben Hong of Hanmi Bank, in which officers from the six local Korean American banks discussed how to improve merchant-customer relations.[51]

Given the central and authoritative role assigned to the business community in improving Black-Korean affairs, the goals of city-led efforts were modest, ultimately limited to seeking friendly and peaceful social relations and overall maintaining the economic status quo. Businesses were advised to be kinder, banks were asked to keep lending, and Blacks and Koreans were encouraged to explore joint business ventures. Little was done on entrenched structural problems such as discrimination in lending or the entanglement of unemployment and crime, which required much more than improved customer service or adding minimum wage jobs. And despite members' deep understanding of the problems in South Central, the

BKA's work was generally limited to assisting businesses in being better, such as collaborating with KAGRO on an employment/cultural exchange program.[52] It also suggested that Korean American banks make "cultural sensitivity" courses a requirement for borrowers to receive a loan, and members worked with the Human Relations Commission to develop a training program for merchants that included role-playing exercises to dispel their misconceptions about African Americans.[53] A centerpiece of the BKA's work, especially in 1991, was developing a Code of Ethics for Merchants and Customers, in conjunction with the Martin Luther King, Jr. Dispute Resolution Center and Asian Pacific American Dispute Resolution Center. A survey it undertook in July 1991 of twenty-four business owners that included Blacks, Koreans, Chinese, Bangladeshis, and Latinos revealed an overwhelming interest in a code that would provide uniform guidelines on matters like refunds, exchanges, receipts, customer communications, and dispute resolution centers.[54]

The flurry of meetings and development of proposals were not just a reaction to a rise in complaints and violent altercations, but also a strategy to deal with store boycotts, which threatened local commerce and brought unwanted media attention. Boycotts drew a cross-section of participants from those wanting to punish store owners to others wishing to facilitate healing and lasting peace. Reverend Edgar Boyd of the Bethel AME Church saw boycotts of Korean-owned businesses as a vehicle to bring attention to the harm caused by products like alcohol, and hoped such activism would root them out of the community.[55] Rochelle Pegg, the president of the South Meadowbrook Block Association, thought boycotts could be an effective tool among many strategies for Black uplift by confronting and pressuring businesses. They were, she thought, a more productive way to channel Black anger into organizing, as opposed to people erupting in chaos and "destroying their own community," as she said had occurred in 1965 during the Watts uprising. Pegg believed that when all parties participated in calling an end to a boycott, this could be a productive approach to addressing disputes and laying groundwork for lasting peace. The ending of a boycott organized by the Organization of Mutual Neighborhood Interests (OMNI) of two Korean-owned swap meets in November and December 1989 glimpsed the potential of this hopeful vision. In a meeting with managers and OMNI representatives, the former agreed to create a customer service system, hire Black youth and Black customer representatives, post clear return policies, and provide English-language training for Korean merchants. Cooke Sunoo lauded the outcome, saying that "given the proper conditions, people have the power to resolve their own problems, rather than the police or a judge." Two years later, OMNI led a boycott after the killing of Arthur Lee Mitchell at St. John's Liquor Store by Tae Sam Park. The boycott ended after the parties agreed to a "truce," brokered by Bradley's office, in which the owners agreed to close and sell the store.

Others doubted that boycotts could be an effective strategy for change. Echoing the responses of Korean merchants to activists, Anthony Essex of the Los Angeles NAACP also pushed back on the demand that stores hire Black youths from the community. These businesses, he explained, typically relied on unpaid family labor and generated razor-thin profits; they could not possibly hire enough workers to make a dent in the rate of unemployment among Black youths.[56] If they were forced to hire more people and raise their wages, he added, businesses would go bankrupt. Also deemed unrealistic was the idea to use boycotts to elevate Blacks into business ownership and thus balance the economic power in neighborhoods. While Korean-owned stores had become symbols or reminders of Black economic disfranchisement, they were not *the* obstacles to Black entrepreneurship; the lack of access to capital was. Finally, the common demand of boycotts—for Blacks to be treated with courtesy while shopping—was so basic and modest that to make the demand could seem like a form of defeat in itself.

Such doubts about the ability of boycotts and other types of protest to foster mutual support, coexistence, and economic justice were always present and informed the activism of a key segment of Black leaders. Most prominent among them was Danny Bakewell, whose uncompromising stance toward Korean storeowners often intentionally fanned rather than quelled interethnic tensions. Bakewell believed the only business-minded strategy that made sense was to support Black businesses exclusively. Virginia Taylor Hughes, a furniture store owner and leader of a Black merchant group illustrated this position when she said she was willing to travel further and pay more "to a brother rather than go somewhere they don't even know how to talk to me."[57] Tim Riley, a thirty-eight-year-old salesman and father of two had given up on living in Los Angeles altogether. He told about an encounter with a Korean storeowner in his neighborhood in which he was accused of theft after he had returned to the store to retrieve a bag of groceries he had left behind. The incident left him so angry that he wanted to "do something violent to that guy and his property." He thought he would be better off in a city like Atlanta, where Blacks were the majority and already held power. "I don't think a multicultural place like Los Angeles is good for black people."

By late 1991, leaders in the Los Angeles Korean American community were starting to splinter over what strategy and tone they should employ. Tensions especially emerged over whether Koreans should continue to call for multiracial peace and friendship or take a more militant stance. The St. John's crisis was an especially stressful flashpoint. During a June 27, 1991 meeting of the BKA to discuss the boycott, members discussed whether Koreans should act or stay quiet for fear of a "NY situation," a reference to the Red Apple boycott that occurred after a physical altercation between a Korean store owner and a Black Haitian customer in Queens, New York. They debated whether to engage in outreach to non-Korean shoppers; one member suggested holding sales could be a way to rebuild goodwill.[58] Meanwhile, others were losing patience. During the boycotts of St. John's and Empire, David Hyun and Charles Kim published a defiant essay attacking the protestors, especially Danny Bakewell, for making excessive demands that victimized and trampled the rights of Korean merchants. The boycotts, they charged, were "an illegal and damaging interference with a private business." Accusations of racism leveled against Koreans by Blacks, moreover, were misleading and misdirected. "Boycotting, demanding and threatening, through the dominant African American community, against a small emerging Korean American community, is wasteful. Korean Americans will never submit to unfair and hostile demands. They have latched on to the American Dream. They will never let go."[59]

As the mood intensified, people both on the ground and removed from day-to-day events weighed in, trying to rise above the scapegoating and taking seriously the root causes of local strife. In 1990, Pastor Robinson Gaither of the Faith United Methodist Church reminded people that Black anger was not new, but the rage they were expressing in the boycotts of Korean-owned stores was fueled by the misguided policies of Reaganism. "The past decade," he said, "has been one where African-Americans feel left out of the national agenda, have felt that business will go on as usual regardless of their needs, that the nation needn't worry about them." He was no happier with the Democrats, who "have, for years, taken the black vote for granted." Unable to take their frustrations to the powers that be, explained Gaither, Blacks lashed out at the closest and easiest targets.[60] Loyola Marymount psychology professor Ronald Barrett agreed, saying that Blacks were "fed up with the failure of their traditional leaders and the government to remedy inequalities." He said the 1990s ushered in a "new racism" in which African Americans continued to suffer under the white power structure and became entangled in conflicts among minorities. Black rage and the conditions that gave rise to it must be taken seriously, Barrett pressed, but he did not believe boycotts or vilifying Korean merchants were the answers. Nor would Black-Asian feuds be resolved through well-intentioned but naïve appeals for people to be more polite to one another. Seeking to expand people's frame of understanding, Tong Soo Chung argued that the conflicts were symptoms of the fact that Blacks and Koreans were both outcasts in a system that exploited both groups and confused them into seeing each other as competitors for scarce resources. Such explanations, attuned as they were to the historical and structural explanations for inequality and interracial conflict, however, did little to lessen people's anger in daily life, alter the media's coverage, or soften the tone of figures like Danny Bakewell.

Black Korea and the Media

Through much of the 1980s and into the 1990s, activists and officials were bedeviled by the media. They used it, decried its power to distort and inflame, and could not escape it. By 1991 it had become one of the paramount concerns regarding Black-Korean relations. More generally, the issue of representation had become a centerpiece of Korean American activism. The reach of mass media—newspapers, television, and film—gave it enormous power to shape its consumers' innermost ideas and concepts about people and the world, and popular culture had an especially insidious history for Asian Americans. From the halting and menacing neighbor Mr. Yunioshi in *Breakfast at Tiffany's* to the alluring yet innocent prostitute in *The World of Suzy Wong*, Asian representation veered between buffoonish and degrading, if not completely erased. These realities, and the fact that well into the 1960s such characters were usually played by white actors in yellowface, spoke volumes about Asians' marginalization in the United States. The Korean American actor Soon-Tek Oh understood this problem intimately. "To be a minority and have no role models is like being a nonexistent culture," he said in 1980.[61] What few parts were available to Asian actors were "ugly," "offensive," and "degrading," forcing them to make moral compromises that perpetuated stereotypes that made everyday life difficult for themselves and future generations.[62]

By the early 1980s, Oh did think things were improving. He was grateful, for instance, to play the comparatively multifaceted role of Lee in the 1981 television miniseries *East of Eden*, but he also knew that Asian Americans could not simply wait for better roles to come along. Indeed, changing the landscape on representation called for activism, vigilance, and when necessary, protesting mainstream culture. For his part, Oh helped to found the renowned Asian American theater company East-West Players in 1965. Also, Asian American activists were increasingly organizing against unfavorable depictions. For example, in 1980 a San Francisco group called the Coalition of Asians to Nix CC (Charlie Chan) was established in protest of the popular fictional detective who had been a longtime source of embarrassment for Asian Americans. Members picketed at Golden Gate Park against filming for the latest Chan feature and successfully pressured Mayor Dianne Feinstein to scuttle a scheduled shoot in Chinatown.[63]

In 1983 the KAC led campaigns against two major targets, the television show *MASH* and *Time* magazine. *MASH* was a beloved program and cultural sensation, and for many Americans, the only source of images and information about Korea. Before the much-anticipated series finale, the KAC released a statement, covered in the *Los Angeles Times*, that credited the show's "humane and sensitive portrayal of the ravages of war" and significance of setting a major network show in Korea but then lambasted its "woefully deficient and insensitive . . . portrayal of the Korean people and culture." This included depicting "a supposedly Korean person wearing a Vietnamese-style hat wandering around in a Japanese-looking village mumbling nonsensical syllables that were supposed to be the Korean language."[64] The *Time* magazine kerfuffle stemmed from an article that misspelled numerous names and contained factual errors about businesses and residents in Koreatown, and readers alleged that it perpetuated stereotypes about Korean youths as criminals.[65] Protestors demonstrated outside the magazine's offices, sent letters, and demanded apologies and concessions. A meeting of Korean representatives, the magazine's bureau chief, and the article's author seemed to have accomplished little except for the activists to be told they were overreacting and that *Time*'s reporting was fair and balanced, yet Korean Americans declared victory because of the attention their campaign garnered and the dynamic organizing they executed.[66] *Koreatown Weekly* boasted that *Time* "unwittingly may have awakened a sense of unity among the fragmented and fractious Korean settlements in the new land"

and hoped the episode would help pave the way for a national civil rights group, like the JACL or NAACP, for Koreans.[67]

As Korean American activism turned its focus to media, leaders were sensitive about how the group depicted in stories about Black-Korean relations. The *Los Angeles Sentinel* found itself in hot water despite its limited reach compared to network television and national magazines. A series of articles by James Cleaver published in 1983 were believed to be the first to use the Black-Korean conflict framework, and it provoked outrage.[68] Tong Soo Chung denounced Cleaver's writings as "unprecedented media attacks" that dealt "a big psychological blow" to Korean immigrants who were "just beginning to feel comfortable with the way of life in Los Angeles after a decade or more of hard work and adjustment."[69] Though the columns in question did not name a specific ethnic group (Cleaver referred to "Asians" throughout) Chung said it was obvious he was referring to Koreans.[70]

Anger toward Cleaver and content published in the *Sentinel* about Korean immigrants escalated to the point that the County Human Rights Commission and UCLA Asian American Studies Center addressed it at a June 1984 "interethnic relationship workshop" to discuss relations between Korean merchants and Black customers, interracial tension more broadly, and the media. Cleaver was one of four speakers at the event, which also included Chung Lee, the Korean merchant and BKA member.[71] Now a deputy for County Supervisor Kenneth Hahn, Cleaver maintained he was merely giving voice to grievances that Blacks were expressing privately. He drew on his own experience of going to Asian-owned stores in Black communities, and "from the minute I walked in the door until the minute I went outside the door, I was followed." Right or wrong, he stated, "Black folks are angry . . . because here are a bunch of foreigners, a bunch of folks who don't speak English, who can't vote, who come here with money." Merchants, moreover, must understand that their customer is very likely someone who "does not have a job or has not worked and has got a welfare check that gives him $226 a month for a family of four."[72]

Into the 1980s, Korean Americans continued to scrutinize and protest media. As discussed in chapter 4, they were exhilarated by having the world's attention on Seoul when it played host to the 1988 Olympics but also anxious about the potential for ignorant commentary about Korean people by the US media. This was part of the backdrop for their outrage over a *Rolling Stone* magazine article titled "Seoul Brothers" by the satirist P.J. O'Rourke.

Writing about the upcoming South Korean elections, O'Rourke was mostly enthralled by the subject, but parts of the article took familiar demeaning turns.[73] For instance, his imitation of Korean language included such gibberish as "YO-YO CAMP STOVE HAM HOCK DIPSTICK DUCK SOUP HAT RACK PING-PONG LIP SYNC!!!!"[74] He proceeded to mock South Koreans for their "eyeglass-fogging kimchi breath," "throat searing kimchi burps and terrible, pants-splitting kimchi farts," and "same Blackgama hair, the same high-boned pie-plated face . . . the same sharp focused look in 1 million identical anthracite eyes." The KAC took quick action, organizing protests at the magazine's Beverly Hills office and released a four-page statement expressing dismay at once again being robbed of "their individuality and human qualities; instead the writer paints a picture of identical, non-thinking, almost subhuman masses."[75] With its audience of over one million readers, "Rolling Stone influences the opinions of many Americans," and by publishing the "Seoul Brothers" article it was "endorsing the ridicule of Koreans and helping to plant "potential seeds of prejudice by reinforcing negative stereotypes regarding Asians and Asian Americans."[76]

Korean American activism intensified with the protest against *Rolling Stone*, a campaign that drew support from a broad, diverse coalition that included the JACL, Korean American Bar Association, Asian Pacific Legal Center, Councilman Mike Woo, and the Mayor's Office.[77] In a letter to *Rolling Stone*, Tom Bradley threw his support behind the protestors stating, "I have joined with the Asian Pacific community in this multiethnic coalition" and decried the magazine's "terrible injustice to the Korean community and their culture." The uproar prompted *Rolling Stone* editor Robert Wallace to travel to Los Angeles for a meeting with Korean American leaders, where he apologized "for any insult that has been caused." He explained that the magazine meant no harm against anyone and later agreed to a set of demands, including printing some of the letters of protest, publishing more balanced features about South Korea and the Korean Americans, and creating an internship for Asian Americans.[78]

Three years later, in October 1991, race, mass media, and politics came together in an even more combustible way when the rapper Ice Cube released "Black Korea," a track from his album *Death Certificate*. The one-minute song began with an audio snippet from Spike Lee's 1989 race relations drama, *Do the Right Thing*, specifically the scene where the character Radio Raheem, who needs batteries for his boom box, angrily and comically be-rates two Korean store workers. The song invoked the turmoil in Los Angeles and illustrated how Korean storeowners had become a default target of Black rage. The lyrics "pay respect to the black fist or we'll burn your store right down to a crisp and then we'll see ya because you can't turn the ghetto into Black Korea" especially raised eyebrows and prompted outcry.

Heartened by its campaign against *Rolling Stone*, the KAC took the lead in pushing back on Ice Cube and, on November 4, issued a statement and held a press conference in which it called on retailers to stop selling *Death Certificate* due to its "violent and derogatory lyrics," "particularly against Korean-Americans."[79] The statement singled out "Black Korea," "Us," and "No Vaseline" for "actually [promoting] violence" and added that the album was also anti-Jewish. Ice Cube and Priority Records' freedom of speech did not, the KAC noted, give them license to disseminate work that "encourages an attitude of racial hate." Moreover, the track should be especially condemned in light of the ongoing efforts of Koreans and Blacks "to put aside the differences and to attack the real enemy afflicting both communities—crime, violence, and economic deprivation." As with the campaign against *Rolling Stone*, a broad coalition of organizations came together to support the protest, including the California Korean Swapmeet Sellers' Association, Wisenthal Center, KAGRO, and Korean Chamber of Commerce.

The controversy over "Black Korea" brought into focus what many Koreans had been feeling with regard to their position vis-à-vis African Americans but rarely said aloud. As Dong Suh, the son of a Korean grocer said, it showed how powerless Koreans were against African Americans in US society. "When compared to Korean Americans, African Americans are a numerical and political majority. Ice Cube does not realize that as a member of the majority he wields real power against Koreans."[80] James Bernard of the *Source* said, "Ice Cube is very angry and he expresses that anger in harsh, blunt, and unmistakable terms. But the source of his rage is very real. Many in the black community, particularly Los Angeles, Ice Cube's home, feel as if it's open season on blacks."[81]

The uproar was also a stress test for the Mayor's Office, which was already struggling to respond to and manage Black-Korean issues. Bradley's staff aide and Korean American liaison Yoon Hee Kim briefed him on the situation regarding Korean and Jewish Americans' outrage. "The lyrics in one song threatens and promotes violence against Korean American, another calls for the murder of a Jewish music industry figure, and yet another talks about 'Japs' buying everything out."[82] The KAC and other Korean American groups also pressed Bradley to denounce *Death Certificate* and state his support for their community, citing his record on making "this multi-cultural city [a] better place to live" and for taking an interest in the Korean American community.[83] "As a minority group, we do not have much to do about [prohibiting objectionable material]. Since we have trusted your fairness and reasonableness as a mayor of such great multi-cultural city, we believed that you may be the only and the best person we can send this petition."[84]

This was different from the *Rolling Stone* controversy because taking a stand for Korean Americans meant effectively taking a stand against a Black artist giving voice to the rage in the African American community. In a December 12, 1991, letter to the president of Priority Records, Bradley expressed his support for the Korean Americans and decried "Black Korea," saying it crossed a line with lyrics that promoted racial hatred and violence and threatened to undo the "progress made thus far" in Los Angeles. He invoked the city's diversity, explaining that "our city has benefitted greatly from the rich ethnic and cultural diversity represented in our city. But at the same time, we must also share the responsibility of creating an environment of harmony rather than disharmony."[85] He continued, "As the most culturally rich and diverse city in the nation, we have the unique opportunity to showcase Los Angeles as a city where people from different ethnic backgrounds could live and work together harmoniously." Finally, Bradley called on Priority Records to "practice corporate responsibility by demonstrating greater sensitivity about the potential impact on the public by the products the company distributes."

The involvement of KAGRO, up until then an apolitical organization, was pivotal because unlike the KAC or BKA, it had the economic and political muscle to compel responses. Moreover, the Korean American response showed an intraethnic organizational unity that had been elusive previously. In November, as part of the larger boycott movement of *Death Certificate*, KAGRO approached the McKenzie River Corporation, the company that made St. Ides Premium Malt Liquor, which Ice Cube endorsed. After the company balked at their request to sever all relations with the rapper, KAGRO announced it would cease McKenzie's deliveries to its member stores. This boycott affected between five thousand and six thousand stores, and within a month, McKenzie folded, agreeing to stop using advertisements that featured Ice Cube and promising not to use him in any future promotions. In February 1992, Ice Cube met with KAGRO leaders and apologized in a written statement that explained he meant no malice toward Korean Americans as a group and sought only to voice the frustration that emanated from his own and his friends' experiences. He ended on a conciliatory yet direct note, promising, "When I tour the country, I will . . . discourage violence against store owners or anyone else. In return, I appreciate that you will work with members of your community to improve relations with the black community."[86]

Latasha, Rodney, Sa-I-Gu

The controversy over "Black Korea," which started in late 1991, was just one aspect of an unrelenting year of turmoil in Los Angeles. Also bringing things to the edge was the jury's verdict in the trial for Latasha Harlins' killing at Empire Liquor Market, located in Compton. In March 1991, Harlins was shot by Soon Ja Du, a middle-aged Korean immigrant who was not supposed to be working that day. Her son Joseph stayed home for fear of threats on his life by members of the Crips gang after he agreed to testify against them in a robbery case. Fifteen-year-old African American Latasha Harlins entered the store, and within minutes Du accused her of stealing. An altercation across the store counter broke out between the two, with Harlins punching and knocking down Du. Du then grabbed a gun and shot Harlins in the back of the head. She was later found to have had juice from the store in her backpack and money in her hand. On November 15, a jury handed down a manslaughter conviction for Du, for which she eventually served a suspended sentence along with probation and fines. Some Koreans rushed to defend Du, pointing out her Christian religiosity and involvement in her church.[87]

Black Angelenos were in disbelief and outraged. After the Empire Liquor Market shut down following the shooting, Danny Bakewell's organization, the Brotherhood Crusade, placed across the door a banner that read, "Closed for Murder and Disrespect of Black People." After the verdict, a writer for the *Los Angeles Sentinel* condemned Korean business owners as "poison pushing merchants who are apparently more outraged about being called names than they are about a dead Black child." The fallout over the

Harlins-Du trial, the "Black Korea" controversy, and division over Tae Sam Park and St. John's were paralyzing for the BKA. "Things were becoming more and more polarized so it was harder for us to get people to come together. And by then there was really very little place of equity to have a conversation," said Jai Lee. She remembered that in one BKA meeting, "An African American minister . . . used this analogy to open a meeting, saying, 'You know, when Koreans came to South LA, it was like when Europeans came to America. They came with ammunition. The ammunition the Europeans used were guns. With the Koreans it was money.'" Korean members felt constantly on the defensive. Against this deepening polarization even among BKA members, Lee and others grew pessimistic. "[By] the time the Rodney King beating happened and the verdict came," she recalled, "I was fairly sure that things would just get really awful."[88]

The event that eventually caused the powder keg to explode actually occurred outside of South Central and did not involve Black-Korean relations. Thirteen days after Harlins' death, a videotape of the beating of Black motorist Rodney King by LAPD officers was released to the public. Four officers went to trial over whether they had used excessive force, and the verdict, handed down about a year after the beating, acquitted them of all charges. Tom Bradley decried the jury's decision but was powerless to offer the solace people needed or deliver the justice they demanded. The Los Angeles uprising, which occurred from April 29 to May 4, was a collective spilling out of raw pain and outrage, sparked by the acquittal of the LAPD officers but tapping into years of building disillusionment. While violence flared in several parts of Los Angeles and elsewhere in the country, it concentrated in South Los Angeles and Koreatown, with the epicenter being Florence and Normandie in South Central. A disproportionate share of the destruction and damage was aimed at Korean-owned businesses.

Official responses to the unrest reflected the deep racial and class inequalities in American life, and the disregard for Korean and Black lives. Although their businesses were the most vulnerable to looting and damage, Korean merchants in South Central and Koreatown, along with everyone else in these neighborhoods, received virtually no police protection. The low priority assigned to the areas became evident when Chief Daryl Gates left the police headquarters to attend a political fundraising event at that very time rioting and arson were escalating. He justified his inaction and general lack of assistance and protection provided by his police force, saying, "There are going to be situations where people are going to go without assistance. . . . That's just the facts of life. There are not enough of us to be everywhere."[89]

Left on their own, some Koreans took matters into their own hands, taking up arms and improvising security forces. The resulting stories and dystopian images, which depicted Koreans as "Bitter, Armed, and Determined," were jarring and indelible. Seth Mydans of the *New York Times* called the pictures and videos of armed Koreans in front of stores and on rooftops in strip malls "gripping and, increasingly, controversial."[90] Especially searing, he said, was "a scene of two Korean merchants firing pistols repeatedly from a military stance. The image seemed to speak of race war, and of vigilantes taking the law into their own hands."

As the dust and smoke settled, people struggled to process and make sense of the uprising. Koreans in the United States and abroad called it Sa-I-Gu (4-2-9), which underscored the date the violence started (April 29). That they gave it a special name underscored the distinct trauma of the experience and immediate recognition of its place in their historical memory. Jan Jung-Min Sunoo, a Korean American employee with the Los Angeles County Human Relations Commission, said the events were "our worst nightmare come true." It was an American tragedy and extension of Korean people's history of war, violence, and trauma. It was also baptism by fire for being a racial minority in the United States. Taking in a broader view, the trenchant Los Angeles observer and historian Mike Davis saw the uprising as the inevitable outcome of the city's embrace of and centrality in the "Japan-California 'co-prosperity sphere,'" which "translated class contradictions into interethnic conflict." Culturally distinct middlemen—ethnic entrepreneurs and the like—were regarded by people in want as the representatives of "the invisible hand that has looted local communities of economic autonomy." In Los Angeles, Davis said, "it was tragically the neighborhood Korean liquor store, not the skyscraper corporate fortress downtown, that became a symbol of a despised new world order."[91]

Ki Suh Park was respected. Los Angeles architect whose accomplishments included designing Koreatown Plaza for his firm, Gruen and Associates. Having lived through the Korean War, he regarded the destruction of Koreatown in the 1992 uprising as a flashpoint in a succession of historical traumas endured by Korean people and said, "for the second time . . . someone must rebuild not only the buildings but the peace."[92] Koreatown Plaza was relatively spared, but Park was devastated as he surveyed the rubble, and he was resolute that his community would rebuild and move on. Moving on would be rebuilding Koreatown, and not returning to South Central.

CHAPTER 6

A Good Comeback

THE CNN TELEVISION SHOW *Parts Unknown* (2013–2018), hosted by chef and writer Anthony Bourdain, explored different parts of the world where he spotlighted unique foodways and cultures. In most episodes, Bourdain visited foreign countries, but Season One's second installment, which aired in April 2013, featured Los Angeles Koreatown.[1] Serving as local guides were the artist David Choe and the chef Roy Choi, whom Bourdain introduced as Koreatown's second-generation ambassadors. Brash, swaggering, and tattooed, Choe and Choi took the host on an eclectic tour of the neighborhood's culinary scene. Stops included Choe's childhood favorite Sizzler, Choi's Kogi taco trucks, and Beverly Tofu House, which "like so many of K-town's finer establishments is tucked away in the corner of a strip mall."

The show's handling of the Los Angeles uprising illustrated how, by the early twenty-first century, the event figured into Koreatown's post-1992 narrative as a great "comeback" story. Meanwhile, flashpoints like the death of Latasha Harlins and trial of Soon Ja Du, the boycott at St. John's Liquor Store, and the release of Ice Cube's recording "Black Korea" receded in the public memory. Koreatown was not only a site of commercial prosperity and cultural dynamism, Bourdain noted, but it was also a singular space of multicultural coexistence and convergence, embodied in the edgy and youthful personas of David Choe and Roy Choi. While the episode hinted at tension between Koreatown's consumer paradise image and its grittier social reality, it ultimately affirmed a celebratory—and familiar—depiction of Korean Americans as both tragic survivors of serial collective traumas and tenacious masters of self-reinvention.

The episode also captured a post-1992 conceptual and cognitive unlinking of Koreatown and South Central. Before the uprising, Korean immigrant business owners figured prominently in both areas' politics and media representations. Because of this, and due to the disproportionate violence and damage suffered in both areas, outside commentators sometimes confused or conflated them. But afterward, as Koreans' presence in South Central diminished, so too did the neighborhood in their consciousness and conception of their economic and social well-being. The post-1992 Koreatown-centered story of the uprising, as illustrated in shows like *Parts Unknown*, certainly acknowledged the tragedy of events leading to 1992 and nodded to the tumultuous history of Koreans and Blacks in South Central, but it sorted away those episodes in the rear view to instead marvel at what Koreatown had since achieved.

This chapter explores Koreatown's journey since 1992, regarding the rebuilding and emergence of its "comeback" narrative, and it examines how different groups attached themselves to competing interpretations of the uprising to guide the recovery and Koreatown's identity. It argues that the departure of Korean business owners from South Central was part of the symbolic unlinking of the fates of Korean America and Black America. Their wholesale dedication to rebuilding Koreatown entailed dependence on Latino immigrants, who were a majority of residents and the post-uprising economy's backbone. As a result, two disconnected Koreatowns emerged; the profitable ethnic playground on the one hand and the multiethnic, working-poor community on the other, contradictions that have only grown sharper in recent years.

Rebuild Los Angeles

The Watts riot of 1965—which the 1992 uprising was frequently compared to—occurred during the civil rights movement and war on poverty and on the cusp of the mass closures of factories after World War II. In its aftermath, Governor Pat Brown appointed a commission to study its causes and make recommendations to prevent future outbreaks. The McCone Commission, thus, sought to provide some level of government accountability for the problems of racial inequality and deterioration in inner cities. Besides a limited commission called by Tom Bradley to study the LAPD, no such public accounting took place in 1992, reflecting the erosion of the liberal principle that the state should intervene on social and economic problems. Instead, unstinting faith in the free market and private sector guided policymakers and leaders, evident when the city announced that its official rebuilding effort would be led by a private nonprofit corporation called Rebuild Los Angeles (RLA). RLA promised "to bring jobs and hope to the city's poorest neighborhoods" and spur recovery and revitalization.[2] The agency was composed of eleven task forces charged with responsibilities relating to issues from the media to race relations, and selected by Bradley and Governor Pete Wilson to lead it was Peter Ueberroth, a fifty-five-year-old Republican businessman from Laguna Beach best known for being the commissioner of Major League Baseball and director of the 1984 LA Summer Olympics. "Frankly," Ueberroth crowed, "America doesn't solve problems unless it's done by the private sector." He vowed that within five years, RLA's efforts would result in fifty-seven thousand new permanent jobs in the poorest areas, and unemployment would fall from as high as 60 percent to the teens.

By entrusting RLA with leading a recovery following urban unrest and enacting a plan to end poverty, the city staked its present and future on a neoliberal faith in the private sector to generate wealth and socially optimal outcomes. Most of its money went to administrative expenses such as rent for its downtown office near Little Tokyo and Skid Row, as it regarded its functions mainly to coordinate the flow of information and assistance. RLA spokespersons were emphatic that the agency was not a replacement for the government, and that it would advocate for people in need of services by working with agencies like the Federal Emergency Management Agency (FEMA) and the Small Business Administration (SBA). It eschewed direct financial assistance and social services and instead championed programs such as "enterprise zones" to help people become or remain entrepreneurs and generate their wealth. RLA prioritized attracting investments from corporate partners like Vons, Bank of America, Hughes Aircraft, Mattel, and Pioneer Electronics, which would revitalize the inner-city with jobs, big retail, business loans, training, and education. Ueberroth predicted that RLA's model would become a blueprint for cities everywhere and "revive urban America in a way that governments by themselves failed to do."[3]

The notion that urban renewal was good for business was not new, as it had been a tenet of CRA-led downtown redevelopment in the mid-twentieth century. RLA pushed the idea further by trying to convince companies that investing in the poor communities they traditionally avoided would be profitable. Intrigued by the prospect, one of its corporate partners, Von's grocery chain, promised to bring twelve stores and two thousand jobs to struggling areas, acknowledging its motivations were not simply charitable.[4] "First and foremost," said Roger E. Strangeland, the company's chairman, "it had to be a good business strategy. . . . If there had been no riots and no Rebuild LA, we probably would have gone about it in a fairly leisurely manner. But the civil disobedience placed a kind of magnifying glass over the whole issue and made it apparent to us that we ought to go at this as a fully articulated and fast-paced program."[5]

Things seemed to never go smoothly for RLA, and from its inception, it came under intense criticism. It suffered from internal instability, exacerbated rather than cleared bureaucratic red tape, and operated from what many deemed problematic and wrong-headed ideas about economic recovery. In November 1992 the *Los Angeles Times* reported that a quarter of RLA's corporate pledges could not be verified, raising early doubts about its promises. The board was bloated with eighty members, which resulted in infighting and inefficiencies. It also fended off criticism about a lack of minority representation, prompting leadership changes, including the replacement of Ueberroth with four cochairs representing different racial communities.[6] Repeated restructurings and regroupings aimed at better responsiveness caused further delays and confusion in Los Angeles's rebuilding. For instance, stories of small entrepreneurs stymied by hassles and red tape piled up. "Most businessmen, with the exception of major retail chain operators, said that they received absolutely no help from the RLA," reported Paul Feldman in a two-year retrospective in the *Los Angeles Times*.[7] By contrast, major chains faced fewer hurdles to secure financing; thus, the areas considered to be the greatest success stories also tended to have large concentrations of these chains.

Critics on the left had misgivings that went deeper than concerns about organizational inefficiencies. As they saw it, RLA was trying to impose a "failed formula of free markets" on disadvantaged communities and promoting an empty "mythology of messianic entrepreneurialism."[8] The sociologist and urban planning expert J. Eugene Grigsby argued that prioritizing capital accumulation was a mismatched strategy for poor neighborhoods struggling with basic problems like retaining capital and creating jobs.

Opening a supermarket chain may have been an "excellent service strategy," he said, but it was not economically sound. Most of the jobs in big retail paid minimum wage. They lacked benefits or advancement opportunities, thus offsetting any overall benefit to the community and instead likely producing a "net loss."[9] Grigsby suggested RLA should have instead made capital available to businesses already in the area to expand their workforces or even facilitate joint ventures between Koreans, Blacks, and Latinos. Others argued for New Deal–style initiatives in which the government provided jobs and built infrastructure, pointing out these had a record of success. However, such arguments made little impact on a city's leadership, which was dominated by people whose fealty was with the business sector. With organized labor, once a major player in Los Angeles politics, losing its seat at the table, little consideration went to needs like working conditions, benefits, and wages. Communities already deprived of resources were not much better off and, moreover, had to bear the burdens of providing affordable housing, health services, working for police reform, challenging zoning regulations, and coordinating legal assistance.[10] The priorities and shortcomings of RLA, thus, led the Korean American lawyer and activist Angela Oh to lament ominously that its legacy would be little more than strengthening the ties between corporations and politicians.[11]

RLA also failed to improve either the efficiency or capacity of the government agencies tasked with delivering direct assistance. Meeting records reveal that rather than forging a productive public-private partnership, RLA board members were frustrated with the SBA and FEMA for having restrictions they thought were too onerous, disbursing insufficient funds, and ineffectively disseminating information about its programs. The criticisms of RLA might have been tempered if it had delivered on its promise of jobs, but that did not come to pass. In a one-year update on recovery since the uprising, James Johnson, Walter Farrell, and Maria-Rosario Jackson concluded that, given the pace of its work and the economic downturn of the early 1990s, the RLA would fall short of the 57,000 jobs it promised. They estimated that 5,000 jobs had been created.[12] By the end of its five-year run, RLA had not ushered in an "LA Renaissance." The jobs had not materialized and the corporate partners had not rescued suffering communities. Companies donated goods and services and provided training but did not hire residents on a large scale or establish a sustained, transformative neighborhood presence. By 1997, the RLA's final year, an estimated 100,000 jobs had disappeared due to the uprising, and 26,000 were generated, but not all directly because of the agency.[13] Most of the new jobs, moreover, went to non-Hispanic whites, even though Blacks, Hispanics, and Asians incurred up to 85 percent of the job loss.

As disproportionately affected owners of the damaged businesses, Koreans were depicted as both sympathetic victims of tragedy *and* crucial linchpins to recovery. However, they too found themselves mired in the mess of rebuilding and were often neglected or insufficiently served through the official channels for assistance. Of the 4,500 stores destroyed, over 2,300 were Korean-owned or run, and nearly every building in Koreatown was damaged. The total damage to property was estimated to be between $785 million and $1 billion, with Koreans incurring between $350 million and $400 million of it in everything from grocery stores, swap meets, clothing shops, liquor stores, dry cleaners, electronic shops, gas stations, jewelry shops, restaurants, beauty salons, auto shops, furniture shops, and video shops. Most of the businesses were uninsured, moreover, and ten months after the uprising, just a quarter had reopened. The establishments in Koreatown that did stay open saw revenues decline by as much as 50 percent. The ripple effects of the destruction and shuttering of so many uninsured establishments included owners defaulting on their business loans and losing their homes due to nonpayment of mortgages.[14]

Dismayed by what he saw as a general disregard for the challenges that Korean business owners faced, Stuart Ahn of the Korean Chamber of Commerce appeared before the city's Ad Hoc Committee on Recovery and Revitalization in June 1992 and said that Koreatown was "devastated beyond repair." He characterized an initial Planning Department proposal for recovery as "grossly unfair to Korean small businesses." The plan required owners of existing businesses to rebuild without major entitlements and contend with a substantial public hearing process, which was stressful and onerous for people with limited English ability.[15] SBA loans that might have been a lifeline entailed long delays, arduous restrictions, and meager disbursements.[16] Another post-riot loan program required businesses to stay in their original location, which for many was impossible, particularly those that had operated stores in South Central.[17] Other hurdles included zoning and land-use limits on the types of businesses that could operate in damaged areas, franchise fees, and complicated permit requirements. Soon Chan Cha, for instance, had owned a shop for just ten months before it was destroyed. He learned that the neighborhood in which it was located had been rezoned from commercial to residential a year before he moved in, and he was told his only option was to build a three-unit apartment on his lot.[18]

Another impediment to the resumption of business-as-usual involved conversion initiatives aimed at rooting out establishments deemed harmful to health and safety. If they wanted to reopen, controversial businesses like gun stores, swap-meet type shops, pawn shops, and auto parts stores would have to comply with stipulations such as limiting store hours, adding parking, and hiring security guards. In this push to create more wholesome neighborhoods, the future of liquor stores—a longtime symbol of the exploitation of vulnerable Blacks in South Central—came under scrutiny. Prominent among the activists was future Congressional representative Karen Bass of the Community Coalition for Substance Abuse Prevention and Treatment. Also a former member of the BKA, Bass said South Central had an "over-concentration" of liquor stores compared to other parts of Los Angeles, which had deleterious effects on the life expectancies, rates of infant mortality, and AIDS infections among residents, who were disproportionately Latino and Black.[19] The racially targeted marketing of malt liquor and fortified wines, products associated with violence and high rates of alcoholism, was also troubling. "If you go into West Los Angeles," Bass said, "and ask for a 'short dog,' a 'Thunderbird,' or 'MD 20–20' you won't find these products."[20] She called for liquor stores not to be rebuilt and for merchants to be compensated and offered incentives to convert their businesses to more "wholesome" enterprises, such as laundromats, or franchises with companies like Meineke Car Care, Rally's Burgers, and Futurekids Learning Academy. The idea attracted buy-in from the City and community organizations and was formalized in a program conducted across several agencies and organizations including RLA, CDD, and the Wellness Foundation.[21] Providing assistance to Asian Americans were the Asian Pacific Planning Council, the Asian Pacific Americans for a New Los Angeles, and the Korean Youth Council (KYC). The KYC in particular was instrumental in helping Korean applicants through the processes of getting matched with a franchise, obtaining education for their next venture, and acquiring necessary city permits.[22]

Rebuilding was rocky and frustrating all around, for those willing to convert their business as well as those hoping to operate their old businesses under new sets of rules. Conversion required applying for city permits, a process in which people languished for up to a year.[23] In the uprising, 224 out of 723 liquor outlets in South Central were destroyed, and of these just a handful had been allowed to reopen. New zoning strictures aimed at preventing the return of small convenience stores with high volumes of liquor were especially daunting and discouraging for owners who thought they could simply resume their pre-1992 businesses. The Trojan Market, owned by Don Myung, was one of the few allowed to reopen, thanks to help from his landlords, the Wolf family, who presented petitions of support from customers at a public hearing. Myung agreed to hire a security officer, close by 10 p.m., and sell fresh meat and produce. While he was able to keep his business going, he was bitter. "Now I'm over 40 and starting new," he said. "I'm burned out and I have to start all over again. My whole life, I'll be a victim."[24] Adding security, which was required of businesses post-uprising, cut substantially into costs and threatened their viability, as shop owners might make $2,000 in profits per month while the cost of security guards exceeded that amount.

Conversion and other obstacles to resuming business inflamed new and old wounds. Koreans expressed feeling like scapegoats and collateral damage for the second time. Though they were not the only owners of liquor stores in South Central, they were the largest group affected by conversion, and some complained they were being singled out. For her part, Karen Bass insisted she was merely trying to draw a line between capitalism and community welfare and rightfully prioritize the latter, but to Korean merchants, these might as well have been fighting words. KAGRO president Yang Il Kim bristled at how he felt Koreans were being unfairly maligned, with regard to the uprising and now business conversion proposals to keep out liquor stores:

> The Korean American merchants did not initiate the problem. Before 1965, and Watts riots, the original license owners were Chinese, Japanese, Jewish, and even Afro American people. The Korean American merchants began buying the stores in the early part of the 1970s. Now almost 80 percent of South Central area liquor or market owners are Korean American merchants. That's why we are targeted right now. From a business aspect there is nothing wrong with that. Only some attitudes, or culture barriers, or language barriers comprise the current problem.[25]

That appeals to place community welfare above the pursuit of commerce sparked defensiveness and anger signaled that South Central's post-uprising era was not going to be marked by interethnic harmony and Black-Korean joint enterprises, which people in the wake of events continued to call for. At a symposium on Black-Korean dialogue on May 22 and 23, sponsored by the Korean Cultural Center and *Korea Times*, participants—which included activists and leaders from both communities and local officials— noted the same forces of inequality and division that led to the uprising showed no signs of abating. One speaker lambasted policies and politics beginning under Reagan that worsened people's suffering, and also scape- goated Black "welfare cheats" and Latino and Asian "foreigners." The thrust of many speakers' remarks was that minority communities should come together because they were all under assault and had their own separate and entangled histories of oppression and hardship. Though the scale and de- struction of the uprising was tragic, they knew cooperation was a possibility, and they could embark together in building a new world where Blacks and Koreans worked with, rather than avoided, one another on joint ventures and responsible development.[26]

One barrier on the path of intraminority solidarity was the unwillingness or inability of many Koreans to rethink their lives and what they were striv- ing for. In this regard, the lessons of Sa-I-Gu were not to practice interracial solidarity or care about the welfare of Black people. Besides, the uprising and then the politics of rebuilding seemed to underscore that their presence was not wanted in South Central. Soon, the media was predicting a mass exodus of and sell-off by Koreans from the area, echoing the departure of white merchants almost three decades earlier.[27] "Now, after the riots, some have nothing to stay for; their businesses burned. Others are willing to sell if they can find anything reasonably priced in Orange County."[28] In addition to Orange County, where there was already a large Korean population, San Diego and Garden Grove were named as likely destinations. Young Shim and Cheoljin Chung joined the exodus. Shim had operated the Right On Drive-in Hamburger Stand on 75th and Vermont, which served Chinese and American food and was destroyed in the riots.[29] Left with a burned out vacant lot, he put up this property for sale while reopening another business in East LA. Though business had been better in the old location, he did not want to go back. Cheoljin Chung's liquor store on Florence just east of Normandie had also burned down. He was expecting a $100,000 insurance check and told the *Korea Times* that once he received it, he would start over in Orange County. "I don't like the South LA area. I am not going back," he said.[30]

Rebuild Koreatown

Faced with obstacles and disincentives to returning to South Central, Korean business owners and associations threw their energies elsewhere, namely rebuilding Koreatown. As Timothy Tangherlini has observed, after the uprising, the streets became a locus for the reassertion of Korean Americans. It was where they had lost so much that they would take back and show their power. "Territoriality," he states, "[was] reinscribed at just the point it [was] threatened to be erased."[31]

Koreatown's recovery was fitful. On the one hand, by 1994, 82 percent of its damaged buildings had been rebuilt, compared to 50 percent in the city.[32] However, due to people's lingering trepidation and a sluggish state economy, tenants and customers were slower in returning, and many buildings sat empty. One building owner, a sixty-five-year-old Los Angeles man named Clifford Eng, did manage to rebuild his structure on 8th and Vermont after securing an SBA loan and other financing, but before it could be completed some of his former tenants had already moved on. Rental rates plunged to $1.50 per square foot from its pre-uprising level of $2.25. Tenants and Korean customers had to return, the overall economic climate had to improve, crime had to come down, and non-Korean consumers had to be brought into the fold. Despite the uncertainty, plans remained in place to move head with a $115 million, 587,000-square-foot development in Koreatown called the Pacific Trade Center.[33]

Community and business leaders resurrected their pre-1992 dreams for Koreatown as they embarked on the work of post-uprising rebuilding. They spoke again of Koreatown becoming a tourist attraction to rival Chinatown and Little Tokyo; Koreatown as an emotional and organizational home for Korean immigrants and Korean Americans alike; and Koreatown as a magnet for continuous investment and capital from Asia. By the end of the 1990s, a stunning transformation had indeed occurred, and talk of Koreatown's comeback seemed to have supplanted memories of its destruction. Three key developments are critical for understanding this comeback—the rise of David Lee, CRA status, and inflow of South Korean capital.

Koreatown business leaders and boosters hoped to secure the CRA status that eluded them before the uprising. As discussed in chapter 2, they did not show the same distrust toward the agency that other communities did, nor did they show much hesitancy about handing over to the CRA the latitude to exercise its powers in Koreatown, including eminent domain. Instead, they had welcomed it as the key to comprehensive development and symbolic recognition. Post-uprising, this became even more urgent due to the shortcomings of RLA. In July 1992, Stuart Ahn of the Korea Chamber of Commerce urged for CRA designation, saying it would bring to fruition the objectives of the Koreatown Specific Plan while also speeding the area's recovery. He resurrected the pre-uprising goals for Koreatown to have a cultural center, youth and senior services, and affordable housing, as well as fixed boundaries at 8th-Vermont-11th-Western. "We don't have to repeat 3 years of citizens advisory committee meetings and Environmental Impact Report which are completed for the Koreatown Specific Plan," he said.[34]

Finally, in December 1995, the City Council granted Koreatown CRA designation. The Wilshire Center and Koreatown communities had separately approached the council to request assistance, and the two areas were combined into a single redevelopment district. As part of an overall effort to promote redevelopment and recovery, it also approved a project in South Los Angeles. Together, these CRA projects were expected to generate $300 million for the communities over thirty years.[35] The plans focused on economic development in the Wilshire-Olympic-Vermont-Western area and rehabbing of the commercial and industrial corridors in South Los Angeles. The CRA said it would use $700,000 from a federal grant, and other funds would come from tax revenue generated by developments and improvements in the project areas. Development, scheduled to begin in late spring, would eliminate blight, improve transportation and city services, promote economic development, provide recreational facilities and open space, promote cultural diversity, and develop job training programs. For the Wilshire Center–Koreatown Recovery Redevelopment Project, Cooke Sunoo was named the project manager.[36] "If the residential area is more stable, then businesses are more willing to invest in the area," he said.

Also guiding Koreatown's comeback was a rising cohort of financial leaders and real estate developers. If there is a single figure associated with post-uprising Koreatown it is David Lee, who was once given the nickname "the Howard Hughes of the local Korean community."[37] Lee came to the United States in 1971 at the age of seventeen and lived in Pasadena and Encino while his family ran a grocery store in Koreatown. Like many children of immigrant shopkeepers, Lee chose a different path from his parents; he attended Northwestern University and then studied and practiced internal medicine. However, in the aftermath of the Los Angeles uprising, when the value of properties in Koreatown and mid-Wilshire tumbled, he saw financial opportunity.[38] As a hagiographic article about Lee in *LA Downtown News* said, "The chaos led many investors and property owners to flee the area. But a man named David Lee saw opportunity." Or as his daughter Jaime offered, "All the developers fled to suburbia and we came in."[39] In 1995, Lee established a company called Jamison, and, with eight other immigrant doctors and dentists, purchased his first Koreatown property, an office building on Wilshire Boulevard which they paid $6 million for. Lee and Jamison found plenty of property owners willing to sell their buildings on the cheap because they were so eager to leave the area. Also, due to the high rate of vacancies in Koreatown in the mid-1990s, insurance companies were selling half-empty buildings at low prices.[40] The initial Wilshire office building the group had purchased went up fivefold in value from 1995 to 2000, and Lee would repeat this formula many times over. By 2008 Jamison owned numerous properties in the Koreatown section of Wilshire, among them Equitable Tower.[41] He was able to draw investors by promising and delivering returns as high as 15 percent. As one of his partners Norman Lee explained, "We aggressively pursue assets that will have positive cash flow from day one."[42]

This model made a great deal of money for Lee and Jamison and facilitated the return of many merchants to Koreatown. But it also made for uneven development. By holding the underperforming properties it had purchased and putting meager resources into maintenance and renovations, the company could keep rents and costs low for tenants. This was especially helpful for small business owners and firms as well as prospective tenants that lacked the credit, English language skills, or other resources to acquire office space.[43] The "quiet tycoon" known for helping to lead Koreatown's resurgence also became known for the aged and dilapidated condition of his properties.

Koreatown's comeback was also indirectly an outcome of the 1997 Asian financial crisis, which saw the economic collapse of several Asian countries, including South Korea. To help restore a measure of stability in South Korea, the International Monetary Fund ordered the government to loosen its capital controls, one effect of which was an increased inflow of investments into Koreatown by South Korean corporations such as Hanil and private individuals seeking to take advantage of the depressed post-uprising real estate values there.[44] As the South Korean economy rebounded, the flow of money from Seoul to Los Angeles only grew, with much of it going into large, upscale commercial developments and high-rise condominiums targeting wealthy immigrants and middle- and upper-class people from the suburbs.[45] This transnational capital facilitated the post-uprising economic boom and helped to distance Koreatown from the events of 1992. One of the most potent symbols of the comeback and historical distancing was the opening of the Galleria in September 2001. Billed at the time as the largest Korean supermarket outside of Korea, it was constructed where a strip mall once stood, before it was destroyed in the uprising.

Another major project of post-uprising Koreatown that rode the wave of transnational capital and the politics of redevelopment was the Aroma Center shopping complex on Wilshire in the heart of Koreatown.[46] A CRA project aimed at boosting the economy of Koreatown as well as Los Angeles's development, its promoters said it would bring a new sense of place to regenerate Koreatown and attract further external capital and customers. In striking ways, it blurred the lines between local and transnational interests, as well as those separating the public from private sectors. For instance, Christopher Park, the architect behind the Aroma Center, was also the owner of a private Koreatown development company called Archeon, the lead planner for the Wilshire Center-Koreatown Recovery Revitalization Project, and chair of the Board of Zoning Appeals in Los Angeles. Primarily financed by the South Korean Hanil corporation and institutionally assisted by city government, the Center symbolized the alliance of local government, transnational capital, and ethnic placemakers and illustrated the idea that the future of Koreatown and the Korean American community would be inextricably tied to capital and economic values. The Aroma Center brought into focus the contradictions of Koreatown after 1992 and of redevelopment in Los Angeles more generally. Government-assisted redevelopment under CRA was supposed to create more, not less, equality and uplift local communities. The Aroma Center received Section 108 funds on the rationale—supported by the city—that its construction was necessary and appropriate to achieve economic development objectives. Section 108 allowed local governments to use Community Block Development grant money from HUD into federally guaranteed loans so long as they provided for physical and economic improvement of struggling neighborhoods. This was an important public investment tool for local governments to help spur or support revitalization. To be sure, Koreatown had suffered tremendous damage and areas needed sprucing up. But developers appropriated the rhetoric and exploited the tools of community development meant to aid the underserved in order to build a massive shopping and health center that catered to people with money. The Aroma Center provided no housing, did not help poor people, and was strenuously opposed at the grassroots.

Unlinking South Central

South Central was also in ruins after the uprising, so legislators called for rebuilding to repair the destruction and lift the area out of its decades-long malaise. A large proportion of the six hundred South Central businesses that were gutted or damaged lay along the Vermont-Manchester corridor. US Representative Maxine Waters envisioned transforming the area into a bustling thoroughfare recalling the "pedestrian-rich Old Town Pasadena or Santa Monica's Third Street Promenade," with coffee shops, bookstores, bakeries, and theaters. Council member Mark Ridley-Thomas, whose office was destroyed in the uprising, called for a revival of commerce as well as new affordable housing.

The Vermont corridor's heyday was the 1920s to 1950s when the area rivaled downtown. By the mid-1960s, white flight had taken hold, and with the closure of factories and relocation of large employers, an era of prosperity in the area came to an end. During the 1970s, other major institutions—cultural, educational, commercial—then followed the exodus from South Los Angeles, such as Pepperdine University and Sears. Remaining and new residents were increasingly Black and Latino, who suffered under the lack of jobs and services. Because of the departure of retail, South Los Angeles residents had little choice but to do their shopping in communities like Culver City. Thus, the 1992 uprising was just "the most recent malady" in the area's long-running struggles.[47]

Koreatown's recovery contrasted strikingly to that of South Central. The entire Vermont Avenue thoroughfare, encompassing Koreatown, Pico-Union, and South Central and roughly bisected by the Santa Monica freeway, suffered tremendous destruction and was left "broken and dispirited." But by 1994, a significant disparity was evident in recovery north or south of the freeway. Sixty-three percent of damaged commercial properties north of it had been rebuilt or were under construction. In Koreatown alone, that figure was 82 percent. To the south, by contrast, it was 44 percent.[48] According to the *Los Angeles Times* 1,100 buildings in South Central—most of them occupied by Korean-owned businesses—had suffered more than $500 million in damage.[49] Of those, about 500 had resumed operations in eighteen months.[50] This still left over 600 structures (technically 25 percent or more damaged) that remained inoperative and weed-strewn.[51]

Explanations for South Central's slow recovery included obstacles securing insurance and financing, residents' fear of crime and more strife, speculation by absentee landlords, and grassroots opposition to the return of liquor stores and other socially harmful businesses. Filling vacant properties with new buildings and occupants would just be a first step because of the neighborhood's overall impoverishment.[52] For instance, a microloan program funded by Disney and distributed through the AME Church was a salutary means of assisting business owners, or would-be business owners, and represented an important form of community reinvestment, but it did not directly address urgent needs like food, housing, and jobs. What modest rebuilding had occurred in South Central two years since the uprising was largely limited to the appearance of retail chains like Chief Auto Parts, Smart & Final, and Payless ShoeSource.

In March 1995, approaching the three-year anniversary of the start of the uprising, the *Los Angeles Times* announced that South Central was on the cusp of a rebirth, thanks to a combination of corporate investment, neighborhood initiatives, and federal and local government programs. As the area went neglected for decades by retail, a large untapped potential clientele with purchasing power remained, and companies and developers now wanted to cash in under the guise of rebuilding South Los Angeles. A Taco Bell, KFC, and Home Savings of America were among the new or returned businesses about to open their doors. Because of the ongoing shortage of supermarkets, the announcements of plans for an Alpha Beta grocery store on Adams on Vermont and a Vons on Vermont and Slauson were met with local excitement.[53]

For many locals, addressing the dearth of supermarkets and retail became a matter of justice; the problem symbolized the systematic government and corporate neglect of South Central and exacerbated economic, social, and health inequalities suffered by residents. Throughout South Central the number of supermarkets declined from 55 to 30 between 1965 and 1990, and overall, it had 25 percent fewer than the rest of the county. As noted above, South Central residents were forced to do much of their shopping for basic needs outside their community. The call to bring supermarkets to the neighborhood made odd but necessary bedfellows of community activists and business leaders. The deal to bring an Alpha Beta grocery store was touted as a particular game changer. In April 1994, Mark Ridley-Thomas announced plans for shopping development at Adams and Vermont that would be anchored by the grocery store (whose parent company was Food 4 Less). The property had sat empty for nine years after being purchased by Alpha Beta's parent company Food 4 Less. During this time, a group called the Southern California Organizing Committee successfully lobbied Ridley-Thomas and Food 4 Less—through actions like staging slowdowns at markets owned by the company—to finally do something about the lot. The planned $9 million supermarket would be top of the line—with a pharmacy, bakery, and deli—located in a development with an additional fourteen thousand square feet of retail space, and bring 150 new jobs. And with Danny Bakewell's development company being responsible for the construction, he would be a minority part owner.[54] Resident Lillian Marenco lived near the property and hoped the development would spark other business activity and lift South Central.[55]

South Central's path to recovery from the uprising after decades of setbacks was, thus, incremental and fitful and did not benefit from infusions of transnational capital going elsewhere. One controversial solution proposed shortly after the uprising was to make South Central a CRA area.[56] "We can't afford to toss the tools of redevelopment on the scrap heap," said the agency's administrator Edward Avila in August 1992. "The federal, state and local governments are strapped for cash." He warned that without incentives, "the private sector also will steer clear of the historic core, South-Central and other communities desperately in need of help."[57] Avila's successor John Molloy insisted that CRA and residents could reinvent development to be more grassroots and collaborative. He acknowledged the agency had lost its way, especially during the 1980s, and did more to hurt than help South Central. A new model, said Molloy, might mean spottier transformation, with new buildings here and there, but it could nonetheless be achieved. "It will turn on our ability to work with existing property owners and to get some grass-roots reinvention of capitalism, if you will, on the part of the people living there. It's not going to be this highly stylized, corporate lawyer sort of negotiation that we had in the past."[58] Using the power of CRA in South Central was also supported by Tom Bradley, Peter Ueberroth, and Assemblyman Chris Tucker (Inglewood).

The belief that CRA development undermined the autonomy of poor and working-class communities ran deep, and local activists had a legacy of fighting its encroachment. In 1989, over eight hundred community leaders and neighborhood activists from groups including the Concerned Citizens of South Central Los Angeles and Westwood-based Not Yet New York assailed the CRA, Mayor's Office, and City Council for exacerbating the divide between the haves and have-nots. CRA and urban redevelopment in general failed repeatedly to deliver on promised jobs, affordable housing, and economic development for poor communities.[59] Thus, many greeted with resistance the renewed efforts by CRA to extend its reach into South Central.[60] Residents were wary and believed a CRA for South Central would simply mean more displacement vis-à-vis construction of large industrial parks. The community activist Lois Medlock expressed her opposition to a bill introduced by Assemblyman Chris Tucker proposing a development area in his district and allowing CRA to bypass bureaucratic hurdles to development, saying CRA "are land-grabbers, and the money goes into the pockets of the developers."[61]

Resistance to CRA nonetheless started to show signs of weakening after 1992. Problematic as its legacy was, no other agencies were lining up to assist, so people were willing to give it a try. In October 1995, eager to develop the vacant lots dotting their community and uplift South Central in some appreciable way, leaders and stakeholders from the Vermont-Manchester area met with CRA and agreed to designate a community development zone. In early 1996, it was formally designated by the City. It encompassed 250 acres of commercial land on Manchester between Van Ness and Harbor Freeway and around Western between 85th and 89th and Vermont between 79th and 88th. The focus would be to revive the Manchester corridor by attracting new businesses and enrolling the participation of existing store owners.

This action was part of a process to not just physically revitalize South Central but also to conceptually reinvent the area, a process that eventually led to expunging the very name "South Central." In 2003, the City Council decided to eliminate "South Central" from LA city maps.[62] "South Central" by this time was geographically nebulous, though in the early 1900s it did describe a discrete neighborhood in the city. In its heyday of the 1920s and 1930s, the area was regarded as "LA's Harlem"; moreover, historian Josh Sides explains that the name "South Central" was "synonymous with a sense of black progress and accomplishment." By the 1980s and 1990s,

"South Central" denoted a larger area and a clustering of neighborhoods. But more concerning to city officials than its geographic nebulousness was the cultural and social baggage the name carried. "South Central" from the 1980s was synonymous with Black poverty and despair, and the 1992 uprising sealed this image in the national consciousness. Locals, thus, considered whether changing the name could help overcome the stigma that was impeding the area's progress. Community members proposed names that would highlight smaller neighborhood identities, such as "Newton," which was taken from a local police station. Instead of this approach, "South Los Angeles" was adopted, not just replacing but swallowing up South Central into a larger, more nondescript entity. "South Los Angeles" denoted a vast fifty-square-mile area encompassing 750,000 people. While the stigma attached to South Central might have been expunged, the possibility of forming local identities around place and neighborhood became more elusive. Residents, business owners, and activists pointed out that local namelessness would have consequences for investment and development as well as grassroots organizing. As business owner Vivian Bowers explained, "It's not that they don't want a name. . . . If you gave them a name, [residents] would wear it with pride."[63] The core neighborhoods around Central Avenue simply disappeared from geographical maps as well as people's mental maps, which made it easier for the public to forget the area's history and to ignore the high poverty affecting the predominantly Latino and Black residents.

Winners and Losers

Stories of Koreatown's rebirth celebrated—once again—Korean immigrants' tenacity and their civic and social integration into multicultural Los Angeles. By 2003, stories of their resurrection were appearing at a rapid clip. Koreatown's clientele now included domestic and international businesspeople, non-Asians, and young professional Korean Americans who were drawn to the area's new cosmopolitan character and its new bars, microbrews, and restaurants with eclectic menus. Another indicator of Koreatown's comeback was how expensive it was becoming; by 2007, the median home price there was $847,000, almost twice that of Los Angeles County and 50 percent more than Orange County.

The growing power of bankers, investors, and developers eclipsed other Koreatown stakeholders and shaped Korean American politics in Los Angeles. As Edward Park observed, "Koreatown [became] too important and too valuable for global investors for the American ethnic bona-fides to find firm footing. For Korean Americans who experienced the civil unrest and continue the quiet and time-consuming labor of building interracial and interethnic coalition, it is difficult to be seen and heard above the bright lights and the loud din of transnational spectacle."[64] In 2012, as Korean Airlines prepared to break ground at the site of the downtown Los Angeles Hilton, which it had purchased in 1989, for the $1 billion Wilshire Grand Center, it was clear that "Korean Americans did not need political engagement and grassroots coalition building to find a voice in Los Angeles—what they needed was South Korean money."[65]

As detailed earlier, this transformation relied on South Korean capital, but it would also not have been possible without low-wage workers from Latin America and Korea. The new Koreatown was a place of contradictions that developers, investors, consumers, and city leaders who were wedded to its glitzy incarnation could not reconcile. Koreatown had two faces, which, explains Kyongwan Park and Youngmin Lee, reflected its "hybrid spatiality" as both a "lived multicultural community" and "representational ethnic theme park."[66] This social two-facedness corresponded to the deep wealth disparities in Koreatown, which itself reflected the overall reorganization of Los Angeles's and the nation's economy. Propping up the restaurants, supermarkets, retail, and nightclubs that composed the transnational and moneyed spectacle of the post-riot era was a wage-earning nonunionized immigrant workforce. Supermarkets epitomized the new Koreatown economy, having gone from mostly small and family-owned enterprises to large-scale, corporatized entities. By 2005, six supermarkets dominated, most led by wealthy Koreatown business owners.[67] Due to their size, they employed about 700 workers, mostly Korean and Latino. Restaurants, by contrast, had not consolidated along these lines, as most employed ten people or less. Still, they had grown in number to about 550, the owners being predominantly Korean and Latino.

The synchronization of capital investment and low-paid service jobs produced intractable inequality. Unemployment in Koreatown was relatively low, but compensation was frequently unlivable and working conditions barely tolerable. Poverty belied the neighborhood's image, the success of its businesses, and low unemployment.[68] In 2005, 70 percent of Koreatown's population—the majority foreign-born—were the working poor, and over 30 percent lived below the poverty line.[69] Residents' median household income was $20,000 below the county average of $42,000.[70] Koreatown was also one of the densest and most expensive places to live in the United States. A minimum wage earner could afford to pay a monthly rent of $351, but the average rent for a one-bedroom apartment in Koreatown was $1,000.[71] It was common for multiple families to share an apartment.[72] Due to the demands of low-wage jobs in Koreatown—in restaurants and retail in particular—workers commonly suffered back and neck injuries, but just 3 percent of residents had health insurance through an employer.

Following the 1992 uprising, the arrival of new immigrants to Koreatown continued and brought even more ethnic diversity to the area. In 2005, residents represented Korea, China, Philippines, Vietnam, Pakistan, Bangladesh, Nicaragua, El Salvador, Mexico, and Peru. About 50 percent were from Mexico, Central America, and South America; 20 percent were Korean; 25 percent were white; and 5 percent were Black. Over 70 percent were "recent" immigrants who spoke a language other than English at home.[73] The ethnic representational landscape changed as well. For example, over the 1990s, Oaxacans expanded their residential and economic presence in Koreatown. Businessman Fernando Lopez seized an opportunity when he purchased the iconic VIP Palace in 1994 and converted it into an Oaxacan restaurant called La Guelaguetza. More recently a Little Bangladeshi has emerged within Koreatown.

While the availability of South Korean money obviated the need for grassroots political engagement and coalition-based activism to rebuild and further develop Koreatown, but the injustices and suffering that local workers continued to endure drove forms of insurgent activism that challenged the area's power structure and identity. In 1992, a few months before the outbreak of the uprising, a private nonprofit organization called the Korean Immigrant Worker Alliance (KIWA) was established by Korean Americans Roy Hong and Danny Park. It prioritized improving wages and working conditions, better government enforcement of labor laws, and advocating for health care, immigration status, and affordable housing. Though its original mission was to help Koreans employed in Korean businesses, it expanded to include non-Koreans because even then they made up the majority of Koreatown's workforce.[74]

KIWA elevated its profile after the uprising, especially in the late 1990s in a highly publicized Restaurant Worker Justice Campaign. Restaurants were one of Koreatown's largest employers and most notorious violators of worker rights.[75] A probe by the US Labor Department in 1998 of 43 Koreatown restaurants found that two hundred workers had been underpaid by $250,000 and all but two were in violation of labor laws.[76] Among its victories was the 1998 reinstatement of a cook who had been fired from Cho Sun Galbi. In another major case, KIWA represented immigrant Jorge Castillo, who had been employed in Baek Hwa Jung, where he worked six days per week, twelve hours per day, and was paid the equivalent of $2.43 an hour. According to Castillo, when he asked for a raise his boss threatened to report him to the Immigration and Naturalization Service before firing him. He sought $29,000 in back wages.[77] To raise awareness of labor abuses and support its clients, KIWA organized pickets of Koreatown restaurants and documented a range of abuses in the industry, including ageism in hiring, withholding wages, spying by owners, and failing to assist workers injured on the job.[78]

Though KIWA addressed problems that were endemic, not just to the structure of Koreatown but the entire national economy since the 1970s, its activism opened a painful rift in the Korean American community. Its members, mostly 1.5- and second-generation Korean Americans in their twenties and thirties were cast as arrogant upstarts waging war on the older Koreatown establishment.[79] Peter G. Lee, the owner of Chung Soo Oak restaurant asked in exasperation, "Why are these kids trying to destroy their parents' businesses?"[80] Critics accused KIWA of misplacing its focus and suggested that instead of attacking employers it could work to educate them on the labor laws. Kyung Ai Hah, the owner of Sa Rit Gol, said if she gave in to KIWA's demands, she would have to shut down her business. Roy Hong responded that Kyung was exaggerating, and that she "drives a Mercedes-Benz and plays golf everyday." Restaurant owners called KIWA leftist, disrespectful, and unpolished bullies who went to meetings in jeans and were bent on destroying the Korean American economy of Los Angeles. To some, the campaigns echoed the opposition and rancor of the liquor store boycotts of the early 1990s, except the attackers came from their own community.[81]

With the uprising and events of 1992 increasingly in the rear view mirror, Koreatown's identity and legacy remained under intense contestation. KIWA and the immigrant workers it represented presented an alternative—indeed radical—idea of Koreatown and the Korean American community, a key piece being the reality that Koreatown was not a monoethnic place that belonged only to Korean business owners and shoppers. This challenged the hierarchical mindset of many Korean immigrants and compelled them to acknowledge that their fate was linked to non-Koreans. By casting its lot with working class immigrants, KIWA also showed the need to reframe the idea of success that Korean Americans had long extolled and attached themselves to. It troubled the dominant representational project of Koreatown by highlighting labor abuses and the presence of non-Koreans as community stakeholders and argued that these realities should not be just acknowledged but also integrated in the story and identity of Koreatown. As Koreatown was home to "communities grappling with low-wage work and community poverty," KIWA believed tackling these problems would mean the area could be at the "forefront of the struggle to create a more just Los Angeles."[82]

At the same time, the fight to empower Koreans and Korean Americans as the stewards of Koreatown continued, as the political power that Koreatown leaders thought would come with successful placemaking remained elusive. In 2012, council redistricting, a process occurring every ten years, again brought attention to this dilemma. Koreatown residents and activists filed suit against the city over how a district represented by Herb Wesson was redrawn. They charged that the changes were meant to increase the percentage of Black voters in the new district at the expense of Koreans. "The city has diluted and negatively impacted the voting power of Koreatown residents by unnecessarily, unlawfully, and unconstitutionally dividing their community into two separate districts," said the suit.[83] Koreatown, said the activists, had grown into a valuable economic asset to the city but still lacked a political voice. Moreover, Wesson, they charged, using similar rhetoric to their counterparts in earlier redistricting fights, treated Koreatown as an ATM that he only cared about when he visited for campaign contributions. They demanded Koreatown be moved from Wesson's district and placed into one represented by Eric Garcetti, which would have combined it with Thai Town and Filipinotown and improved the chances of electing an Asian American. The mayor and Council rejected the proposal.

Questions about whom Koreatown is for, who gets to claim it, and what Korean Americans' relationship to it should be were driven by specific concerns arising in the changing world of the early aughts, but people had always asked and grappled with these questions in some way from the very inception of Koreatown, Los Angeles, starting with the earliest immigrant place entrepreneurs. Into the twenty-first century, Koreatown was at another crossroads. On the one hand, the community had pulled off an impressive recovery after the destruction and trauma of the 1992 uprising. The rebuilding was so successful that observers were remarking, "Visitors would be hard-pressed to guess the destruction that ravaged the community more than a quarter-century ago."[84] Koreatown was drawing Koreans and non-Koreans alike, and it was back on track to being a place that people wanted to visit that also instilled pride and a feeling of belonging for Koreans near and far. On the other hand, the long-present, marginalized working class that made recovery possible demanded their due, and many Korean Americans continued to complain about being ignored and voiceless in local government and the culture at large. The contestations over and contradictions in Koreatown and the accompanying debates about its relationship to Korean Americanness remain enduring and perhaps more defining than any stories of triumph and success.

The Americanization of Koreatown and the Koreatown-ification of Los Angeles

SINCE THE TURN of the twenty-first century, the Koreatown of the pre-uprising years, defined by its "cluttered ethnic flavor," has become a subject of nostalgia and wistfulness.[1] The area around Olympic Boulevard, where Hi Duk Lee opened VIP Palace and which immigrant place entrepreneurs envisioned a thriving commercial Koreatown to rival Chinatown and Little Tokyo, has grown "threadbare" and less identifiably Korean.[2] Many of the key figures who built and led Koreatown and Korean Americans in the 1970s have died or moved on to other pursuits.[3] Koreatown's center has moved north and west from Olympic and Normandie to Wilshire and Western, where "the big Korean money goes these days." Longtime residents and shopkeepers lament that Koreatown is losing its "charm and character" as old shops were replaced by chains like Coffee Bean & Tea Leaf, Cold Stone Creamery, and Nine West. Moreover, community banks that served the area and Korean Americans in Los Angeles since the 1980s—Hanmi, Nara Bancorp, Wilshire Bancorp, and Center Financial—had been eclipsed by mainstream US banks like Wells Fargo and Bank of America.[4]

In the last few years, the extremes of Koreatown have become even more pronounced. More "glitzy developments" have come in, as have young professionals and middle-class families who see the area as an affordable alternative to nearby Hollywood or downtown. The opening of three Metro Purple Line stops along Wilshire at Vermont, Normandie, and Western further boosted the neighborhood's value. By the late 2010s, real estate watchers declared Koreatown to be one of Los Angeles's hottest markets as it underwent a construction boom driven by residential and hotel projects.[5] An apartment retail complex above the Wilshire Vermont Station featured futuristic architecture, a multicolored entryway, and lush palm trees. The only reminder that one was in Koreatown was a picture of an empty rice bowl in the entryway.[6] Koreatown's evolution has made it even more inaccessibly expensive than before; rents are as high as $3,000 per month. But even this detail is taken as further proof of Koreatown's stunning comeback, as the *Real Deal*, an online real estate magazine explained, "Its reputation as a cultural hub has been growing. That reputation—built partly on karaoke bars and affordable Korean barbecue—has attracted a flood of redevelopment over the past six years." With such a rosy outlook, one might conclude that the neighborhood escaped "its tragic past," and was now "set . . . to enter a golden era."[7]

Continuing the patterns that emerged after 1992, Koreatown was not so much becoming an affluent area as it was turning into one of Los Angeles's most polarized and unequal neighborhoods. Many of the traditional denizens are still there: working class Koreans, Latinos, and other longtime residents and shopkeepers, some of whom welcome the glitziness of revived Koreatown as needed makeovers, some of whom lament it.[8] The pricing out and displacement of working class and poor people has only compounded poverty in Koreatown as well as the growth of its homeless population. Homelessness in Koreatown came to widespread public attention in 2018 when Mayor Eric Garcetti launched a plan to tackle the city's homeless problem with the construction of new shelters. Based on data about the locations of existing encampments, Koreatown, which had a homeless population of about four hundred—a very large number considering the small size of the area—was selected as one of the sites for a temporary shelter.[9]

The controversy that ensued after the site was announced shed light on social tensions and fissures long in the making as well as the evolving constituency of stakeholders vying to make their claims on Koreatown's identity and destiny. In the fight over homeless shelters, two movements emerged, a faction that opposed the shelter and another that supported it and decried the opponents as short-sighted and selfish. A group calling itself Koreatown for All represented a diverse wing of activists, and while it was multiethnic and intergenerational, the dominant spokespeople were by and large young, non-Korean, and new to Koreatown, or young second- and third-generation Korean Americans. The wing opposing the shelter was likewise diverse but primarily led by older immigrants and Korean Americans, thus representing and being dismissed as the unenlightened old guard. For many Koreans the controversy awakened a renewed resentment about their lack of political voice despite the vital economic role Koreatown has played for the city, now for nearly five decades. For others, it strengthened their commitment to working in coalition and viewing Koreatown as multiethnic and multiracial, as it had always been.

Another notable pattern to emerge, aside from the so-called gentrification or mainstream Americanization of Koreatown and heightened outside interest in it, is a Koreatown-ification of Los Angeles. It has outgrown its roots as a section in the city aspiring to be a stronghold for an emerging ethnic community. Its largest property owners have aggressively and profitably pursued their interests outside of Koreatown. In 2002, David Lee acquired his first downtown building, the nine-story Banco Poplar building for $6 million. He went on to acquire a hodgepodge of downtown properties, including an office center in Little Tokyo and Macy's Plaza Shopping Center. These and other acquisitions made Lee one of downtown's largest stakeholders, spending more than $600 million to acquire eleven buildings in the central city.[10] Through his real estate firm, Jamison Properties, Lee and his Korean partners became the biggest owners of commercial real estate not just in Los Angeles County but also in all of Southern California. In 2005 its holdings included seventy office buildings, thirteen medical buildings, and six shopping centers. In 2008 Lee's portfolio was worth more than $3 billion.[11]

Koreatown's growing place in the American cultural consciousness has converged with and paralleled the rise of *hallyu*, or the global popularity of South Korean film, television, and music. The two phenomena often get conflated and confused, but they have also had a synergistic relationship. Koreatown draws on the appetite for South Korean entertainment among diasporic Koreans as well as non-Koreans. This in turn impacts Korean American identity and makes room for more Korean American participation and representation in US media, while also resetting the relationship between Koreans and Korean Americans.

To bring this book to a close, I end with what for me has been among the most powerful and complex recent images of Los Angeles Koreatown. In 2020, the world was gripped by the novel coronavirus pandemic, which in the United States came with large helpings of government incompetence and anti-Asian racism. President Donald Trump's blaming of China for unleashing the virus and reckless remarks throughout the early months of the pandemic lit a match on the weeds of ignorance and racial resentment, with terrifying consequences. Disturbing videos of violent attacks on elderly Asians in broad daylight circulated on social media, and Asian Americans across the country reported record numbers of incidents of harassment, physical and verbal. In April 2021 shortly after news outlets reported that a white male gunman had shot and killed eight people at several Atlanta, Georgia, spas, the South Korean embassy confirmed that four of the victims were Korean women. In all, six of the eight victims were Asian women, and the Korean media reported that witnesses heard the gunman saying he wanted to "kill all the Asians."[12] Though people had been sounding an alarm about rising anti-Asian hostility from the start of the pandemic, the tragedy and horror of the killings were a turning point that prompted the upsurge of a movement to stop violence against Asians in America. Rallies were held across the country, activists spread the message to "Stop Asian Hate," and Asian Americans were newly awakened and politicized about the realities of racism against them.

The grief and fear of continued violence gripped Asian American communities across the country, including Los Angeles Koreatown, which still had a large concentration of Korean and Korean American residents. One of the many nationally reported attacks on Asian Americans in the early months of 2021 was the violent assault of 27-year-old Denny Kim in the heart of Koreatown by two men who yelled slurs about the "China virus" and told him to "go back to China."[13] As in other Asian enclaves, volunteers in Koreatown organized patrols to ensure the safety of residents, especially the elderly, and on March 27 they held a march to "Stop Asian Hate." Coordinated by the Korean American Federation of Los Angeles in partnership with several other organizations, the event drew over a thousand people and featured celebrities and elected officials including Mark Ridley-Thomas. It was reminiscent of the Korean Festivals that began in the 1970s when Koreans marched and performed down Olympic Boulevard to announce their community's presence to the rest of Los Angeles, but it was also tragically poignant that in 2021 they were holding signs reading "Stop Killing Us" and "Hate Is a Virus" and were taking to the streets to remind other Americans that their visibility merely reflected their membership in the larger civic community and should not invite resentment and harm.

The Koreatown rally culminated with a performance by a youth troupe of Korean traditional drummers who led hundreds of marchers down

Olympic Boulevard. Ending the procession at Normandie Avenue, the masked youths then broke into a traditional Korean drumming version of the hit song "Dynamite," which played over loudspeakers to back the performers. During summer 2020 "Dynamite" had reached #1 on the *Billboard* charts; the song is infectiously uplifting so helped to end the event on a hopeful note. It was probably no coincidence that the song was by a South Korean pop group, BTS, whose unprecedented global success is a story in itself. It was a snapshot of a paradoxical moment when Korean culture achieved untold acceptance and popularity in the US mainstream at a moment of rising anti-Asian violence and political mobilization.[14] The pathos and disorientation was captured in social media commenters remarking on their mixed feelings of pride, sorrow, and global connectedness to Koreans around the world.

In pondering how Koreatown informs what it means to be Korean in the United States, or the relationship between place and ethnic identity during the late twentieth and early twenty-first centuries more generally, it becomes clear how fluid and perpetually changing these subjects are. They illuminate our understanding of the lengths that newcomers have taken to remake their lives, become full participants in their adopted communities, and transform the places where they settle. They also bring attention to the messiness that accompanies migration and placemaking, how it often entails contestation, erasure, or uneasy coexistence with others. Place matters as an aspect of social identity because it is tangible, invested with symbolic meaning, and can confer legitimacy and acceptance to the people who claim it. Conceiving Koreatown and turning it into an economic niche and emotional home for Koreans in the United States that also attracted the interest and dollars of non-Koreans have been powerful forces throughout recent Korean American history and have also made for an unpredictable balancing act. And as long as race and ethnicity matter as factors shaping inequality and the struggle for inclusion, the relationship between place and identity will remain salient, for those inside and outside Koreatown, for immigrants and the US-born, the post-1965ers, the knee-highs, the BK Koreans, and everyone in between.

Notes

Introduction

1. Ivan Light and Edna Bonacich, *Immigrant Entrepreneurs: Koreans in Los Angeles, 1965–1982* (Berkeley: University of California Press, 1988), 200.

2. Sophia Kyung Kim, "Purchasing Power to Win Economic Gains, Urges Southland Grocers," *Korea Times Los Angeles*, October 16, 1983.

3. Earl C. Gottschalk Jr., "The American Dream Is Alive and Well in Koreatown," *Wall Street Journal*, May 20, 1985.

Chapter 1

1. Cindy Cheng provides a thorough discussion of Hyun's case. See Cindy I-Fen Cheng, *Citizens of Asian America: Democracy and Race during the Cold War* (New York: New York University Press, 2013), 126–130.

2. David Hyun, "Los Angeles: An East-West Ethnic Miracle of Global Proportions," *Los Angeles Times*, July 15, 1983, D7.

3. Pyong Gap Min, *Koreans' Immigration to the U.S.: History and Contemporary Trends*, Research Report No. 3, January 27, 2011 (New York: The Research Center for Korean Community, Queens College of CUNY), 7, www.qc.cuny.edu/Academics/Centers/RCKC/Documents/Koreans%20Immigration%20to%20the%20US.pdf.

4. Richard E. Meyer, "Exploding Ethnic Populations Changing the Face of LA," *Los Angeles Times*, April 13, 1980, B1, 4.

5. Robert Lindsey, "California Becomes Melting Pot of the 1980's," *New York Times*, August 1, 1981, 1:1.

6. Ray Herbert, "Downtown Pulls Foreign Capital to L.A.," *Los Angeles Times*, September 3, 1979, A1.

7. Letter to the editor, *Los Angeles Sentinel*, December 10, 1981, A6.

8. Thomas Borstelmann, *The 1970s: A New Global History from Civil Rights to Economic Inequality* (Princeton, NJ: Princeton University Press, 2011), 61.

9. During the 1970s, the GDP grew at an average rate of 2.9 percent while the previous decade it was over 4 percent. Barry Bluestone, "Foreword," in *Beyond the Ruins: The Meanings of Deindustrialization*, ed. Jefferson Cowie and Joseph Heathcott (Ithaca, NY: Cornell University Press), viii.

10. Bluestone, "Foreword," viii.

11. In 1971 the dollar was allowed to float against the value of other currencies, instead of being fixed in amount. Borstelmann, *The 1970s*, 54.

12. Domestic production fell after 1970, but consumption continued to rise, so production shifted to the Persian Gulf and North Africa. US dependence on imports went up fivefold over the 1970s. Borstelmann, *The 1970s*, 56.

13. Bluestone, "Foreword," ix.

14. Bluestone, viii.

15. Bluestone, ix.

16. Josh Sides, *LA City Limits: African American Los Angeles from the Great Depression to the Present* (Berkeley: University of California Press), 58.

17. Sides, *LA City Limits*, 180–181.

18. "Minorities' Influx Continues as Whites Leave, EYOA Says," *Los Angeles Sentinel*, February 18, 1971.

19. Mike Davis, "'Chinatown', Part Two? The 'Internationalization' of Downtown Los Angeles," *New Left Review* 1, no. 164 (July–August 1987): 74.

20. Davis, "Chinatown," 70.

21. William Julius Wilson, *The Truly Disadvantaged: The Inner City, the Underclass, and Public Policy* (Chicago: University of Chicago Press, 1987).

22. Sides, *LA City Limits*, 7.

23. Manuel Pastor, "Keeping It Real: Demographic Change, Economic Conflict, and Interethnic Organizing for Social Justice in Los Angeles," in *Black and Brown in Los Angeles: Beyond Conflict and Coalition*, ed. Laura Pulido and Josh Kun (Berkeley: University of California Press, 2013), 46.

24. Pastor, "Keeping It Real," 46.

25. Pastor, 46.

26. Pastor, 16.

27. Davis, "Chinatown," 74.

28. This comes from a quote by Jim Downs, who spoke at the 1955 IDEA conference on urban redevelopment. See Alison Isenberg, *Downtown America: A History of the Place and the People Who Made It* (Chicago: University of Chicago Press), 188.

29. Isenberg, *Downtown America*, 188.

30. Mara A. Marks, "Shifting Ground: The Rise and Fall of the Los Angeles Community Redevelopment Agency," *Southern California Quarterly* 86, no. 3 (Fall 2004): 242.

31. Davis, "Chinatown," 69.

32. Marks, "Shifting Ground," 260–261.

33. Marks, 241.

34. Marks, 274.

35. Davis, "Chinatown," 70.

36. Davis, 71.

37. Jan Lin, "Globalization and the Revalorizing of Ethnic Places in Immigration Gateway Cities," *Urban Affairs Review* 34, no. 2 (November 1998): 313.

38. Herbert, "Downtown Pulls Foreign Capital," A1.

39. Marks, "Shifting Ground," 278.

40. Davis, "Chinatown," 76.

41. Isenberg, *Downtown America*, 188.

42. Isenberg, 189.

43. Frederick D. Sturdivant, *The Ghetto Marketplace* (New York: Free Press, 1969), 153.

44. Davis, "Chinatown," 74.

45. Madeline Y. Hsu, "The Disappearance of America's Cold War Chinese Refugees," *Journal of American Ethnic History* 31, no. 4 (Summer 2012): 20.

46. Those designated "immediate family" members were exempt from numerical restrictions, thus considered nonquota, and initially occupied the two highest preferences categories, the first being limited to spouses and unmarried children of US citizens and the other to spouses and unmarried children of permanent residents. The remaining preference categories, which were subject to the twenty-thousand annual ceiling, were naturalized citizens' married children (fourth) and siblings (fifth), and occupational immigrants divided into professional/technical/administrative/managerial (third) and other (sixth).

47. While it helped relieve nationwide labor shortages, the entry of foreign medical workers contributed to the segmentation of the medical industry, with American-born white doctors working in the suburbs for profitable private and group practices and immigrants working in city-run hospitals in less prestigious specializations. In turn, an institution like the Veterans Administration, the largest centrally directed medical complex in the United States, would become, by 1980, the largest employer of immigrant doctors.

48. Illsoo Kim, *The New Urban Immigrants: The Korean Community in New York* (Princeton: Princeton University Press, 1981), 28–29.

49. Kevin F. McCarthy, "Immigration and California: Issues for the 1980s,"

January 1983. Santa Monica: The Rand Corporation, Tom Bradley Administration Papers, Box 4052, Folder 6, University of California at Los Angeles Special Collections, Los Angeles, CA.

50. McCarthy, "Immigration and California," 10.

51. "Minority Contractors Assured of Participation in L.A.'s Urban Renewal," *Los Angeles Sentinel,* October 19, 1972, A16.

52. "City Pledges to Help Minority Contractors Achieve Goals," *Los Angeles Sentinel,* August 3, 1972, A18.

53. "Dymally Forms Ethnic Commission," *Los Angeles Sentinel,* November 4, 1976, A2.

54. "Dymally," *Los Angeles Sentinel,* A2.

55. "Dymally," A2.

56. Wilson, *Truly Disadvantaged,* 60.

57. Ray Zeman, "Orientals Are Non-Political," *Los Angeles Times,* March 3, 1966, A4.

58. William Overend, "Asians: Minority or Not Minority," *Los Angeles Times,* May 17, 1979, 12.

59. Overend, "Asians," 13.

60. Harold Brackman and Stephen P. Erie, "Beyond 'Politics by Other Means'? Empowerment Strategies for Los Angeles' Asian Pacific Community," in *Asian American Politics: Law, Participation, and Policy,* ed. Don T. Nakanishi and James S. Lai (New York: Rowman & Littlefield, 2003): 241.

61. Lin, "Globalization and the Revalorizing," 314.

62. Yung-Hwan Jo, "Problems and Strategies of Participation in American Politics," in Yu, Phillips, and Yang, *Koreans in Los Angeles,* 205.

63. Davis, "Chinatown," 79.

64. Davis, "Chinatown," 79; Jeff Wilson, "Homeless Retreat as Police Conduct Skid Row Sweep," *AP News,* June 5, 1987.

65. William Overend, "Koreans Pursue the American Dream . . ." *Los Angeles Times,* September 10, 1978, H1.

66. Eui-Young Yu, "Koreans in Los Angeles: Size, Distribution, and Composition," in Yu, Phillips, and Yang, *Koreans in Los Angeles,* 23.

67. Kenneth Hahn Papers, Box 94, Folder 3b, Huntington Library Manuscript Collection, San Marino, CA.

68. Nancy Yoshihara, "Koreans Find Riches, Faded Dreams in L.A.," *Los Angeles Times,* February 1, 1976, SG1.

69. Won Moo Hurh, *The Korean Americans* (Westport, CT: Greenwood Press, 1998), 40.

70. For more, see chapter 3 in Kim, *New Urban Immigrants.*

71. Since the late nineteenth century, the adoption of Western medical practices,

including antibiotics and immunization, reduced the mortality rate and increased the fertility rate. Then, after World War II, about 2.3 million Koreans who had been living abroad in places like Japan and Manchuria, returned, some 80 percent of them to the South.

72. Hurh, *Korean Americans*, 41.

73. Hurh, 41.

74. Militarization in South Korea was well underway before Park Chung-hee's presidency. The Korean War and the US support directly led to military buildup in the country.

75. White-collar workers in Asia faced career immobility. Asian countries meanwhile had been fostering education for their own professional management stratum and could not always absorb all their highly trained people, and the United States offered higher salaries or possibilities. US education was still more accessible in South Korea. Kim, *New Urban Immigrants*, 34.

76. Selective emigration prohibited certain groups from leaving, namely former prisoners, alcoholics, those unable to perform physical labor, and draft evaders—later, people with a lot of money and status. Government passed a law in 1975—on the heels of the post-Saigon exodus—that prohibited military officers and retired generals, high-ranking government officials, and people who owned more than $100,000 in property from emigrating. Kim, *New Urban Immigrants*, 52.

77. The schemes fell short due to shabby treatment in some of the countries, mismatched expectations between migrants and host countries, and a shortage of willing receiving countries. Korean workers in West Germany, for instance, were denied a pathway to citizenship and expelled during economic recessions. In Latin America the generally educated and urban backgrounds of migrants made them a poor fit for farming, and they would leave the countryside for cities like Sao Paulo and Buenos Aires. Kim, *New Urban Immigrants*, 54; Won K. Yoo, *Global Pulls on the Korean Communities in Sao Paolo and Buenos Aires* (New York: Lexington, 2015), 34, 37.

78. Hurh, *Korean Americans*, 49.

79. Kim, *New Urban Immigrants*, 11, 33.

80. Min, *Koreans' Immigration to the U.S.*, 9.

81. Occupational preferences used by Koreans fell to 22 percent in 1975. Min, *Koreans' Immigration to the U.S.*, 33. Hurh, *Korean Americans*, 40; Kim, *New Urban Immigrants*, 149.

82. Kim, *New Urban Immigrants*, 25.

83. Specifically those who entered between 1966 and 1975. Kim, *New Urban Immigrants*, 39.

84. Diana Sherman, "Largest Outside Korea: Korea Town's Population, Extent Grow Daily," *Los Angeles Times*, February 25, 1979, I1.

85. Eui-Young Yu, "Korean Community in the United States: Socioeconomic Characteristics and Evolving Immigration Patterns," in *Korean Economy and Community in the 21st Century*, ed. Eui-Young Yu et al. (Los Angeles: Korean American Economic Development Center, 2009), 35. In 2000, 44 percent of Koreans lived in western states, compared with 22 percent of the US population at large. By the mid-1990s, New York had about 150,000 Koreans.

86. Jack Smith, "L.A. with a Korean Accent," *Westways*, May 1976, 33.

87. Smith, "L.A. with a Korean Accent," 36; Yu, "Koreans in Los Angeles," 23.

88. Smith, 36; Yu, 23.

89. David S. Kim and Charles Choy Wong, "Business Development in Koreatown, Los Angeles," in *The Korean Diaspora: Historical and Sociological Struggles of Korean Immigration and Assimilation in America*, ed. Hyung-chan Kim (Ann Arbor: University of Michigan Press, 1977), 235.

90. Kim and Wong, "Business Development," 229, 234; Edna Bonacich and Tae Hwan Jung, "A Portrait of Korean Small Business in Los Angeles," in Yu, Phillips, and Yang, *Koreans in Los Angeles*, 82.

91. At the time, there were two Korean banks in Los Angeles, one concerned with international trade and the other with local businesses. Government provides matching funds to help a local community purchase a community center building. Edna Bonacich, Ivan H. Light, and Charles Choy Wong, "Koreans in Business," *Society* 14 (September/October 1977): 54–59.

92. Paul Ong, Edna Bonacich, and Lucie Cheng, "Introduction," in *The New Asian Immigration in Los Angeles and Global Restructuring*, eds. Paul Ong, Edna Bonacich, and Lucie Cheng (Philadelphia: Temple University Press, 1994), 3–38.

93. Overend, "Koreans Pursue the American Dream."

94. Bonacich and Jung, "Portrait of Korean Small Business," 82.

95. Yoshihara, "Koreans Find Riches."

96. Randy Hagihara interview with author, June 25, 2015.

97. Julian Hartt, "Dual Culture Poses Problem for Koreans of Southland," *Los Angeles Times*, June 4, 1967, G1.

98. Smith, "L.A. with a Korean Accent," 33.

99. Overend, "Koreans Pursue the American Dream."

100. Overend.

101. Overend.

102. Bonacich and Jung, "Portrait of Korean Small Business," 86.

103. Kim and Wong, "Business Development," 234.

104. "Korean Storeowners in Slum Ghetto Trying to Cope with Prevailing Crime," *Pacific Citizen*, January 20, 1978, 1.

105. "Korean Storeowners," *Pacific Citizen*, 1.

106. Kim and Wong, "Business Development, 234; Edna Bonacich, "The Social

Costs of Immigrant Entrepreneurship," *Amerasia* 14, no. 1 (1988): 119–128; Davis, "Chinatown," 73.

Chapter 2

1. A copy of the book was provided to the author by Pyong Yong Min of the Korean American National Museum in Los Angeles. Sonia S. Suk, *Life on Two Continents* (Seoul: Dong A. Printing, 1984).

2. Steve Chanecka, "Sonia Suk, Dean of Korea Town Realtors," *Koreatown Weekly*, December 3, 1979, 3.

3. According to her memoir, Suk went to North Carolina on the advice of a US military commander whom she met while working at a radio station. Suk, *Life on Two Continents*, 51.

4. Chanecka, "Sonia Suk."

5. Sherman, "Largest Outside Korea."

6. It is unclear what she meant by this, but the California Alien Land Law was invalidated and McCarran-Walter Act was passed in 1952, when Democrat Harry S. Truman was president. However, the governor at the time, Earl Warren, was a Republican, and when the Alien Land Law was formally repealed in 1956, Dwight D. Eisenhower, a Republican, was president. Suk, *Life on Two Continents*, 111.

7. Overend, "Koreans Pursue the American Dream," H1.

8. Lin, "Globalization and the Revalorizing," 314.

9. Overend, "Koreans Pursue the American Dream," H1; "Koreatown Rejuvenated Los Angeles Inner City," *Asian Week* 8, no. 25 (February 6, 1987): 102.

10. John Pashdag," Where East Meets West," *Los Angeles Times*, August 16, 1977.

11. Overend, "Koreans Pursue the American Dream," H1.

12. David Holley, "Koreatown Suffering Growing Pains," *Los Angeles Times*, December 8, 1985.

13. Sherman, "Largest Outside Korea"; Holley, "Koreatown Suffering Growing Pains."

14. Ivan Light, "Immigrant Place Entrepreneurs in Los Angeles, 1970–99," *International Journal of Urban and Regional Research* 26, no. 2 (June 2002): 215–28.

15. For example, Jun Kim recommended certificates of appreciation for Gene Kim in 1975 and Hi Duk Lee in 1983. Sonia Suk was appointed to the Human Relations Commission. City of Los Angeles, Inter-Departmental Correspondence, April 7, 1983, Tom Bradley Administration Papers, Box 4267, Folder 5; Office of the Mayor Office Memorandum from Jun Kim to Kojima, September 25, 1975, Box 4267, Folder 4, Bradley Administration; Memo from Kojima to Bradley, November 13, 1974, Tom Bradley Administration Papers, Box 998, Folder 3.

16. Lee, *Echo of Komerica*, 160.

17. Overend, "Koreans Pursue the American Dream," H1.

18. Lee, *Echo of Komerica*, 165–66.

19. Smith, "L.A. with a Korean Accent," 33.

20. Randy Hagihara, interview with author, June 25, 2015.

21. Overend, "Koreans Pursue the American Dream," H1.

22. Sherman, "Largest Outside Korea."

23. Holley, "Koreatown Suffering Growing Pains"; "$25-Million Koreatown Shopping Mall to Rise," *Los Angeles Times*, April 21, 1985.

24. "$25-Million Koreatown Shopping Mall to Rise," *Los Angeles Times*, April 21, 1985.

25. Remarks by Councilman David Cunningham, December 10, 1979, Tom Bradley Administration Papers, Box 4052, Folder 10.

26. Remarks by Councilman David Cunningham, Tom Bradley Administration Papers.

27. Steve Chanecka, "Koreans Plan for 'Korea City,'" *Koreatown Weekly*, December 17, 1979; Hyun, "Los Angeles."

28. Chanecka, "Koreans Plan for 'Korea City.'"

29. Sherman, "Korea Town's Extent."

30. Holley, "Koreatown Suffering Growing Pains."

31. Sam Kaplan, "Koreans in Search of an Identity," *Los Angeles Times*, September 20, 1979.

32. Chanecka, "Koreans Plan for 'Korea City.'"

33. Chanecka.

34. Chanecka.

35. Cooke Sunoo, interview with author, August 14, 2015.

36. Smith, "L.A. with a Korean Accent," 35.

37. Cooke Sunoo interview with author, August 14, 2015.

38. Steven Zuckerman, "Parade Blends Korean Culture, U.S. Traditions," *Los Angeles Times*, September 24, 1979.

39. Office of the Mayor Office Memorandum from Jun Kim to Kojima, September 25, 1975, Tom Bradley Administration Papers, Box 4267, Folder 4.

40. Steven Zuckerman, "Parade Blends Korean Culture, U.S. Traditions," *Los Angeles Times*, September 24, 1979.

41. Sherman, "Korea Town's Extent."

42. Zuckerman, "Parade Blends Korean Culture, U.S. Traditions."

43. "Korean-Americans Parade, Celebrate L.A. Bicentennial," *Los Angeles Times*, September 22, 1980.

44. Letter from Tom Bradley to Rev. Song Cha Kim, August 11, 1975, Tom Bradley Administration Papers, Box 2469.

45. Letter from City of Los Angeles Office of the Mayor to Korean Festival

Committee, August 11, 1977, Tom Bradley Administration Papers, Box 4269, Folder 293.

46. In 1979 the grand marshal was John Ferraro. Also among attendees were State Senator David Roberti and wife, City Council member Arthur K. Snyder, and State Assembly member Mike Roos and wife.

47. Office of the Mayor, Office Memorandum from Jun Kim to Kojima, September 25, 1975, Tom Bradley Administration Papers, Box 4267, Folder 4.

48. Judith Michaelson, "Broom-Toting Koreans Take to the Streets," *Los Angeles Times*, August 16, 1979, C1.

49. Michaelson, "Broom-Toting Koreans," C1.

50. Letter to Tom Bradley from Ki Sung Kim, Korean Association of Southern California, November 2, 1978, Tom Bradley Administration Papers, Box 4270, Folder 3.

51. Kaplan, "Koreans in Search of an Identity."

52. Ivan Light, *Deflecting Immigration: Networks, Markets, and Regulation in Los Angeles* (New York: Russell Sage Foundation, 2008), 124.

53. The photograph is reprinted in Katherine Yungmee Kim, *Los Angeles's Koreatown* (Charleston: Arcadia, 2011), 98–99.

54. Light, "Immigrant Place Entrepreneurs," 222.

55. Gottschalk, "American Dream."

56. Gottschalk.

57. Gottschalk.

58. Letter to Tom Bradley from Sea O. Choi of Koreatown Development Association, November 3, 1978, Tom Bradley Administration Papers, Box 293, Folder 4270.

59. Letter to Tom Bradley from Ki Sung Kim, Korean Association of Southern California, November 2, 1978, Tom Bradley Administration Papers, Box 4270, Folder 3.

60. Sherman, "Korea Town's Extent."

61. Smith, "L.A. with a Korean Accent," 36.

62. Gottschalk, "American Dream."

63. Gottschalk.

64. It was to be located at 1100 S. Bronson Avenue. First phase was to be 10 three-bedroom units. The developer was Chong Lee Investment Co. Priced at $109,000 to $119,000. "Affordable Town Houses Open in Mid-Wilshire/Koreatown," *Los Angeles Times*, October 2, 1983.

65. Letter from undersigned to Jun Kim, assistant to the mayor, November 2, 1978, Tom Bradley Administration Papers, Box 4270, Folder 3.

66. Letter from Jung Su Lee, president of commerce, Korean Chamber of Com-

merce of Southern California to Jun Kim, assistant to the mayor, November 2, 1978, Tom Bradley Administration Papers, Box 4270, Folder 3.

67. Letter to Tom Bradley from Sea O. Choi of Koreatown Development Association, November 3, 1978, Tom Bradley Administration Papers, Box 293, Folder 4270.

68. Lee, *Echo of Komerica*, 188.

69. Holley, "Koreatown Suffering Growing Pains."

70. Sixteen percent were white, 6 percent were Black, 12 percent were Korean, 5 percent were Japanese, 3 percent Filipino, and 7 percent other Asian. Holley, "Koreatown Suffering Growing Pains."

71. Gottschalk, "American Dream."

72. There was no information on women.

73. Kenneth Hahn Papers, Box 94, Folder 3b.

74. Maria L. La Ganga, "Once-Booming Koreatown Goes Downhill," *Los Angeles Times*, August 15, 1982.

75. Chanecka, "Koreans Plan for 'Korea City.'"

76. Kaplan, "Koreans in Search of an Identity."

77. James Rainey, "Explosion of Mini-Malls Spurs a Maxi-Dispute," *Los Angeles Times*, September 23, 1985.

78. Holley, "Koreatown Suffering Growing Pains."

79. Holley.

80. Sherman, "Korea Town's Extent."

81. Holley, "Koreatown Suffering Growing Pains."

82. Holley.

83. Yeo-Chun Yun, "City Zone Changes Opposed at Hearing," *Korea Times Los Angeles*, February 24, 1984.

84. Chanecka, "Koreans Plan for 'Korea City.'"

85. La Ganga, "Once-Booming Koreatown Goes Downhill."

86. Holley, "Koreatown Suffering Growing Pains."

87. Lee, *Echo of Komerica*, 229.

88. La Ganga, "Once-Booming Koreatown Goes Downhill."

89. La Ganga.

90. Penelope McMillan, "Koreatown Hopes for Some Recognition in Grant Form," *Los Angeles Times*, November 7, 1984.

91. They had formed the Committee for Koreatown Community Planning (CKCP). Yong-Pil Pak, "Koreatown CARE Project Begins with Help from PACE and CKCP," *Korea Times Los Angeles,* January 24, 1985.

92. Sophia Kyung Kim, "Revitalization for Koreatown Proposed," *Korea Times Los Angeles*, September 20, 1984.

93. Kim, "Revitalization"; Yong-Pil Pak, "Koreatown CARE Project Begins."

94. McMillan, "Koreatown Hopes for Some Recognition."

95. The staff had to submit at least twelve loan proposals to city by July. In the last eighteen months, they submitted nine, three of which were accepted.

96. Yong-Pil Pak, "Koreatown CARE Project Begins."

Chapter 3

1. The terms *1.5* and *knee-high* refer to immigrants who came to the United States as children.

2. Sophia Kim, interview with author, August 8, 2015.

3. Kim, interview.

4. Kim, interview.

5. Matthew Frye Jacobson, *Roots Too: White Ethnic Revival in Post-Civil Rights America* (Cambridge, MA: Harvard University Press, 2008), 3.

6. Jacobson, *Roots Too*, 2–3, 10.

7. K. W. Lee, "Editorial," *Koreatown Weekly*, December 1982, 2.

8. Eddie Iwata, "Koreans: Recalling the Pioneers," *Los Angeles Times*, September 3, 1980, 6.

9. Carolyn Ayon Lee, "I Speak English But I'm Still a Korean," *Koreatown Weekly*, December 1, 1981, 1.

10. Julie J. Suhr, "Growing Up with Asian Stereotypes," *Koreatown Weekly*, June 14, 1982, 2.

11. "It's Rewarding Work Helping Confused Kids," *Koreatown Weekly*, August 10, 1981, 6.

12. KASCON held its first meeting in 1980 and KAYF in 1982. K. W. Lee, "Reunion of American-born Like a Page out of History," *Koreatown Weekly*, September 8, 1980, 4; Gloria Hahn, "Reunion Preparation More Than Worth It," *Koreatown Weekly*, November 3, 1980, 3.

13. K. W. Lee, "Reunion."

14. Lee, "I Speak English."

15. K. Connie Kang, "New Koreans a Mystery to First Generation," *Koreatown Weekly*, December 1982, 2.

16. K. W. Lee, "Reunion," 4.

17. Iwata, "Koreans," G1.

18. Hahn, "Reunion Preparation," 4.

19. K. W. Lee, "Tai B. Chung: 'No Free Lunch in U.S.'" *Koreatown Weekly*, January 14, 1980, 9.

20. K. W. Lee, "Tai B. Chung," 9.

21. K. W. Lee, 4.

22. K. W. Lee, "Reunion," 4.

23. Tong Soo Chung, "Glimmers of Hope for 1983," *Korea Times Los Angeles*, December 30, 1982.

24. Iwata, "Koreans," 6.

25. Iwata, 7.

26. Iwata, 7.

27. "Korean Language Classes Sprouting Up," *Koreatown Weekly*, November 3, 1980, 1.

28. "Korean-American Convention," *Los Angeles Times*, August 12, 1980, F6.

29. Kenneth Hahn Papers, Box 402, Folder 9.

30. "Korean Language Classes Sprouting Up," *Koreatown Weekly*, 9.

31. "Speakers to Oppose Commission Closure," *Korea Times Los Angeles*, November 1, 1982.

32. Others to be closed were the Mexican American Education Commission, Afro American Education Commission, Asian-American Education Commission, and Special Education Commission.

33. Yeo-Chun Yun, "Activists Pledge to Continue Efforts to Keep AAEC Alive," *Korea Times Los Angeles*, November 12, 1982.

34. "Speakers to Oppose Commission Closure," *Korea Times Los Angeles*.

35. "It's Time to Seek Our Heroes Here," *Koreatown Weekly*, February 11, 1980, 1.

36. "It's Time," *Koreatown Weekly*, 1.

37. "It's Time," 1.

38. "It's Time," 1.

39. Hahn, "Reunion Preparation," 3.

40. Jacobson, *Roots Too*, 7–8.

41. Iwata, "Koreans," G1. Gloria Hahn said there were sixteen.

42. Iwata, G1.

43. B. Y. Choy, "Few Class Distinctions among Early Immigrants," *Koreatown Weekly*, October 6, 1980, 9.

44. Choy, "Few Class Distinctions," 9.

45. "Philip Jaisohn—Our George Washington," *Koreatown Weekly*, February 11, 1980, 2.

46. Luisa March-Hyun, "A Korean Exile Ends His Long Journey Home," *Los Angeles Times*, November 5, 1975. Additionally, organizational and spatial practices secured their legacies and place in the historical memory. A group of Korean American doctors established the Philip Jaisohn Foundation in 1975 in Philadelphia to help new Korean immigrants in the area. Community leaders announced plans to turn independence activist and community leader Ahn Chang Ho's family home, which sat on land owned by the University of Southern California since the 1960s,

into a Korean American memorial. John H. Lee, "Patriot Ahn Honored 50 Years After Death," *Korea Times Los Angeles*, March 29, 1988.

47. Song was elected to the California State Senate in 1962 and served for sixteen years. Alvina Lew, "Col Kim Tribute: History in the Making: Nikkei, Koreans Join Hands," *Asian Week*, September 4, 1987.

48. Gloria Hahn, "Thoughts of Community in Rapid Transition—Us," *Koreatown Weekly*, December 1, 1980, 5

49. K. W. Lee, "Isn't Yellow a Colored Person?" *Koreatown Weekly*, November 19, 1979, 5.

50. K. W. Lee, "Chicago Yi Family Helped Koreans," *Koreatown Weekly*, December 10, 1979, 3.

51. "We Salute Pioneers Roh, Suk, Yoo," *Koreatown Weekly*, December 3, 1979, 2.

52. Hahn, "Thoughts of Community," 5.

53. David Hyun, "Greetings," *KAC Newsletter*, April 1983, 2.

54. Hyun, "Greetings," 2.

55. Tong Soo Chung, "Glimmers of Hope."

56. "Korean-American Convention," *Los Angeles Times*, F6.

57. Editorial, *Korea Times Los Angeles*, April 5, 1988 (USC).

58. Yeo-Chun Yun, "Coalition Formed to Fill Community Gaps," *Korea Times Los Angeles*, February 18, 1983.

59. Tong Soo Chung, "Our Long Term Future," *Korea Times Los Angeles*, October 28, 1982.

60. Kapson Lee, "Actor, Politician Pull No American Punches," *Korea Times Los Angeles*, September 8, 1982, 1.

61. Jin Choe, "Voter Street Drive Gets 100 Names; Most Registering By Phone," *Korea Times Los Angeles*, July 30, 1984 (USC).

62. Sophia Kyung Kim, "Voter Registration Enters Computer Age," *Korea Times Los Angeles*, December 4, 1985.

63. "Koreans Dominate 'New Voter' Figures for Asian Community," *Joong Ang Daily*, November 1, 1984; "KAC Primed for Voter Sign-Up; Need Volunteers," *Korea Times Los Angeles*, June 5, 1984; "Older Citizens Most Responsive to Voter Registration Drive," *Korea Times English*, July 2, 1984; Choe, "Voter Street Drive"; Jae Song, "8,000 Korean Americans Will Have Voice in Government," *Korea Times Los Angeles*, November 11, 1984.

64. Mike Davis, "Who Killed Los Angeles: Part Two, the Verdict Is Given," *New Left Review* 1, no. 199 (May/June 1993): 44.

65. The Alatorre plan realigned fifteen council boundaries, but one in particular—that of Mike Woo, the only Asian American on the council—was most affected. Woo represented Hollywood, Chinatown, and predominantly Latino areas in Northeast Los Angeles. In the new configuration, he would lose his

Hollywood base of support as his district would move eastward and become more Latino. Asian American groups expressed concern because if Woo had to run for reelection in the newly configured, more Latino district, he would face another council incumbent, John Ferraro. Woo still opposed because it created a district tailored for election of a second Latino in central Los Angeles. This would come at the expense of John Ferraro and Michael Woo, who would be thrown into the same Hollywood-Wilshire district and forced to run against each other. A compromise plan was passed by the council that created a predominantly Latino district that Woo would not have to compete in. Alvina Lew, "Remap Plan," *Asian Week*, August 1, 1986; Janet Clayton, "Asian Groups Warn of Strife over Alatorre Remap," *Los Angeles Times*, July 9, 1986.

66. Richard Simon, "City Denies Koreatown Residents' Demand for Council District Status," *Los Angeles Times*, August 28, 1986; Lew, "Remap Plan."

67. Kapson Lee, "Immigrants Unaware of Voting Potential," *Korea Times Los Angeles*, July 12, 1982.

68. Lee, "Immigrants Unaware."

69. Randy Hagihara, interview with author, June 25, 2015.

70. In May 1991, it had 350 members in a city with 250,000 Koreans. James S. Kim, "KAC Committees Incorporate 1st, 2nd Generation Koreans," *KoreAm Journal*, May 1991.

71. Kim, "KAC Committees."

72. Also running was thirty-year-old Adam Schiff. Bill Stall, "Election for Roos' Seat in Assembly Attracts 14," *Los Angeles Times*, April 23, 1991; "Attorney Tong Soo Chung: Community Activist Challenges for Koreatown Assembly Seat," *KoreAm Journal*, April 5, 1991, 28.

73. "Attorney Tong Soo Chung," *KoreAm Journal*, 31.

Chapter 4

1. Suk, *Life on Two Continents*, 124.

2. Katherine Baber and James Spickard, "Crafting Culture: 'Tradition,' Art, and Music in Disney's 'It's a Small World,'" *Journal of Popular Culture* 48, no. 2 (2015): 226.

3. Baber and Spickard, "Crafting Culture," 2.

4. "Bradley Honors Korea Delegation," *Los Angeles Sentinel*, December 22, 1977.

5. Every doll in the exhibit had to have identical faces, be of children, and made of anti-electricity material.

6. Jay Matthews, "Gateway to America Now Faces the Orient," *Washington Post*, July 1, 1984.

7. Matthews, "Gateway."

8. Matthews.

9. Matthews.

10. Matthews.

11. Matthews.

12. Matthews.

13. "Attention Is Now Being Paid to the New Glitter of Downtown L.A.," *Los Angeles Times*, July 22, 1984.

14. Matthews, "Gateway to America."

15. Hyun, "Los Angeles."

16. Hyun.

17. Hyun.

18. Notes in a letter dated October 13, 1976; trade between two nations has grown remarkably over the last ten years. Director was Myung Jin Cheun. Edmund Edelman Papers, Box 365, Folder 4, Minorities Korean, Huntington Library Manuscript Collection, San Marino, California. "L.A. Unit Asked by Korean Bank," *Los Angeles Times*, January 16, 1967. "Korean Bank Opens Office," *Los Angeles Times*, September 10, 1967.

19. "L.A. Firm Gets Korea Pact," *Los Angeles Times*, July 14, 1968.

20. "L.A. Firm," *Los Angeles Times*.

21. Kenneth Hahn Papers, Box 402, Folder 9.

22. They became sister cities as part of the federal Sister Cities program in 1968 but were not formally recognized by the city until 1971.

23. "A Nixon Doctrine for Los Angeles," *Los Angeles Times*, April 7, 1971.

24. Letter from Office of Mayor, City of Busan, to Tom Bradley, January 11, 1974, Tom Bradley Administration Papers, Box 1616, Folder 2.

25. A group had traveled there in 1968 when the cities' relationship was informal.

26. Jessie Mae Brown, "Your Social Chronicler," *Los Angeles Sentinel*, November 24, 1977.

27. Letter to Bradley from Ministry of Health and Social Affairs, Republic of Korea, June 9, 1977, Tom Bradley Administration Papers, Box 4269, Folder 12.

28. Letter to Bradley from Seoul Metropolitan Government, Office of the Mayor, June 8, 1977, Tom Bradley Administration Papers, Box 4269, Folder 12.

29. Letter from Bradley to Ja Choon Koo, June 5, 1977, Tom Bradley Administration Papers, Box 4269, Folder 12.

30. Letter from Korean Cultural Service to Jun Kim, January 4, 1982, Tom Bradley Administration Papers, Box 4269, Folder 7.

31. Press release from Korean Cultural Service about rededication, Tom Bradley Administration Papers, Box 4269, Folder 7.

32. In 1971, Richard Nixon announced the removal of twenty thousand US troops—a third of its total—from South Korea and, the following year, opened relations with Communist China. His announcement that all US troops would be

withdrawn from Vietnam in 1973 sent "tremors" through South Korea for fear that they would be next.

33. On Koreagate see Shelley Sang-Hee Lee, "The Party's Over: Sex, Gender, and Orientalism in the Koreagate Scandal of the 1970s," *Frontiers: A Journal of Women's Studies* 39, no. 3 (2018): 1–28.

34. Matthews, "Gateway to America."

35. Letter from Bradley to Min Soo Park, consulate general, March 24, 1982, Tom Bradley Administration Papers, Box 4269, Folder 7.

36. Don Shannon, "Asian Bloc Supports L.A. Bid for Olympics," *Los Angeles Times*, October 14, 1969.

37. Matthews, "Gateway to America."

38. Brad Pye Jr., "Stop Begging," *Los Angeles Sentinel*, May 14, 1984.

39. Joseph and Sharon Rosendo, "Looking to L.A. and the Olympics," *Washington Post*, October 2, 1983.

40. "Attention Is Now Being Paid to the New Glitter of Downtown L.A.," *Los Angeles Times*, July 22, 1984.

41. "Olympians Carry on the Tradition," *Los Angeles Sentinel*, July 5, 1984.

42. *Korea Times Los Angeles*, July 14, 1984.

43. City of Los Angeles, Inter-Departmental Correspondence, January 4, 1985, Tom Bradley Administration Papers, Box 4267, Folder 6.

44. "Attention Is Now Being Paid," *Los Angeles Times*.

45. "Attention Is Now Being Paid."

46. Tong Soo Chung, "Thoughts of the Times," *Korea Times Los Angeles*, August 14, 1984.

47. Tom Bradley Administration Papers, Jun M Kim, Box 4267, Folder 6.

48. Letter from Tom Bradley to Yong Nae Kim, mayor of Seoul, July 13, 1988, Tom Bradley Administration Papers, Box 4269, Folder 12.

49. David S. Wilson, "Olympics Bring Pride to Koreatown," *New York Times*, September 19, 1988.

50. K. Connie Kang, "NBC Coverage of Games Typical Old American News," from USC KAC boxes, KTLA, 1988.

51. "Attention Is Now Being Paid," *Los Angeles Times*.

52. Letter to the editor, *Los Angeles Sentinel*, May 10, 1979.

Chapter 5

1. Claude Reed Jr., "A Conversation with Marla Gibbs," *Los Angeles Sentinel*, January 6, 1983.

2. Brenda Stevenson, *The Contested Murder of Latasha Harlins: Justice, Gender, and the Origins of the LA Riots* (Oxford: Oxford University Press, 2013).

3. June Shiver Jr., "Minority Hopes Dashed as West Olympia Bank Fails," *Los Angeles Times*, February 15, 1984.

4. "Banks on the Brink," *Black Enterprise*, January 1981.

5. Shiver, "Minority Hopes Dashed."

6. "Banks on the Brink," *Black Enterprise*.

7. "Soulvine," *Los Angeles Sentinel*, September 9, 1982.

8. James H. Cleaver, "Shakeup Rocks Bank of Finance," *Los Angeles Sentinel*, February 18, 1982.

9. Phyllis Bailey, "Bank Works on Image," *Los Angeles Sentinel*, February 3, 1983.

10. James Cleaver, "West Olympia Bank Shuts Down Branch," *Los Angeles Sentinel*, October 20, 1983.

11. Bailey, "Bank Works on Image."

12. Cleaver, "West Olympia Bank."

13. Cleaver.

14. Betty Pleasant, "Whither the Black Branch of Wilshire State Bank," *Los Angeles Sentinel*, December 5, 1985; Betty Pleasant, "Wilshire Bank Executive Fired," *Los Angeles Sentinel*, July 26, 1984.

15. Stanley G. Robertson, "Who's Kidding Whom?" *Los Angeles Sentinel*, May 21, 1981.

16. Jim Cleaver, "Another Kind of Racism in this Nation," *Los Angeles Sentinel*, May 22, 1980.

17. Letter to the editor, *Los Angeles Sentinel*, January 21, 1982.

18. Stanley G. Robertson, "Can Blacks Ignore 'Immigration Issue'?" *Los Angeles Sentinel*, May 2, 1985.

19. Robertson, "Who's Kidding Whom?"

20. A. S. Doc Young, "Commitment to Mediocrity," *Los Angeles Sentinel*, May 15, 1980.

21. A. S. Doc Young, "The Winning Way," *Los Angeles Sentinel*, August 18, 1977.

22. Young, "Commitment to Mediocrity."

23. Young, "Winning Way."

24. Young, "Commitment to Mediocrity."

25. Von Jones, "Blacks, Koreans Struggle to Grasp Thread of Unity," *Los Angeles Sentinel*, May 1, 1986.

26. James H. Cleaver, "Asian Attitudes Toward Blacks Cause Raised Eyebrows," *Los Angeles Sentinel*, August 18, 1983.

27. Sandy Banks, "Korean Merchants, Black Customers—Tensions Grow," *Los Angeles Times*, April 15, 1985.

28. Cleaver, "Asian Attitudes Toward Blacks," *Los Angeles Sentinel*.

29. Banks, "Korean Merchants, Black Customers."

30. Jones, "Blacks, Koreans Struggle to Grasp Thread of Unity."

31. Banks, "Korean Merchants, Black Customers."
32. Shiver, "Minority Hopes Dashed."
33. Pleasant, "Whither the Black Branch of Wilshire State Bank."
34. Banks, "Korean Merchants, Black Customers."
35. Jones, "Blacks, Koreans Struggle to Grasp Thread of Unity"; Banks, "Korean Merchants, Black Customers."
36. Banks, "Korean Merchants, Black Customers."
37. Banks.
38. Banks.
39. David Hyun and Charles Kim, "African American–Korean American Relations in Los Angeles," *Asian Week* 13, no. 10 (October 25, 1991): 2.
40. Hyun and Kim, "African American–Korean American Relations," 2.
41. "Message to Our Community," May 14, 1991, Tom Bradley Administrative Papers, Box 4247, Folder 9; Letter from County of Los Angeles Commission on Human Relations to Michael Antovich, chairman of LA county board of supervisors, Tom Bradley Administrative Papers, Box 4247, Folder 21.
42. According to KAGRO, 9 percent of members had businesses in predominantly Black neighborhoods. Draft Press Statement, June 11, 1991, Tom Bradley Administrative Papers, Box 4248, Folder 7.
43. A community forum was held on May 14, 1991, at Trueway Baptist Church. Flyer, Tom Bradley Administrative Papers, Box 4247, Folder 21.
44. Banks, "Korean Merchants, Black Customers."
45. Helen Zia, *Asian American Dreams: The Emergence of an American People* (New York: Farrar, Straus and Giroux), 179.
46. Jai Lee interview with author. June 15, 2015.
47. "Message to Our Community," May 14, 1991, Tom Bradley Administrative Papers, Box 4247, Folder 9.
48. Banks, "Korean Merchants, Black Customers."
49. On October 5, 1989, he hosted breakfast at City Hall (with help from the BKA) where leaders in the Korean community were invited to "discuss important topics that are of interest to our business community." Letter from Office of Mayor, September 25, 1989, Tom Bradley Administrative Papers, Box 4248, Folder 16.
50. "Mayor's Merchant Conference," Tom Bradley Administrative Papers, Box 4247, Folder 21.
51. "Meeting with Benjamin Hong, CEO/President of Hanmi Bank," Tom Bradley Papers, Box 4248, Folder 2; Bankers Meeting Briefing, October 31, 1991, Tom Bradley Administrative Papers, Box 4248, Folder 3.
52. Op-Ed Contribution, Tom Bradley Administrative Papers, Box 4248, Folder 5.
53. December training for Korean merchants, Tom Bradley Administrative Papers.

54. BKA Code of Ethics Committee, Tom Bradley Administrative Papers, Box 4247, Folder 5.

55. Briefing from Ron Wakabayashi, Tom Bradley Administrative Papers, Box 4247, Folder 10.

56. Jones, "Blacks, Koreans Struggle to Grasp Thread of Unity."

57. Banks, "Korean Merchants, Black Customers."

58. Meeting notes, June 27, 1991. Tom Bradley Administrative Papers, Box 4247, Folder 21.

59. Hyun and Kim, "African American–Korean American Relations," 2.

60. Itabari Njeri, "Blacks: Enraged or Empowered?" *Los Angeles Times*, July 12, 1990.

61. Sheila Benson, "Asians React to Film Images," *Los Angeles Times*, May 10, 1980.

62. Benson, "Asians React to Film Images."

63. Benson.

64. "Criticism of 'MASH' Played Up in *LA Times*," *Korea Times Los Angeles*, February 8, 1983; "Local Radio Show Airs Koreans' Views of MASH," *Korea Times Los Angeles*, February 28, 1983.

65. Kurt Anderson, "Los Angeles: The New Ellis Island," *Time*, June 13, 1983.

66. Ben Cate was the bureau chief and Joseph Kane was the author. "Asian Protest 'Biased' Portrayal of Immigrants," *Asian Week* 4, no. 42 (June 16, 1983): 1.

67. Quoted in "Korean Paper Calls for Boycott of *Time*," *Asian Week* 4, no. 48 (July 28, 1983): 3.

68. Patrick Andersen, "Koreans, Blacks Continue Dialogue," *Asian Week*, October 28, 1983.

69. Tong Soo Chung, "Animosity between Blacks and Asians Must Go," *Koreatown*, January-March 1984.

70. Sophia Kim, "Seeking a Dialogue by Koreans, Blacks," *Los Angeles Times*, June 8, 1984.

71. The others were Mike Young, described as "a black community activist from New York, and Oaksook Kim, who worked for the County Commission on Human Relations. Kim, "Seeking a Dialogue."

72. Kim, "Seeking a Dialogue."

73. P. J. O'Rourke, "Seoul Brothers," *Rolling Stone*, February 11, 1988.

74. "Asians Call Magazine Article on Korea 'Racist,'" *Hokubei Mainichi*, February 10, 1988.

75. *KAC Position Paper*, Tom Bradley Administrative Papers, Box 4244, Folder 10.

76. *KAC Position Paper*, Tom Bradley Administrative Papers.

77. Karen Lew, "'Rolling Stone' Concedes to Three Korean Demands," *Asian Week*, March 18, 1988.

78. All concessions were eventually met except for the article about Korean Americans because the commissioned article by Korean American journalist Jeannie Park was deemed not up to par. Sophia Kyung Kim, "Rolling Stone Mag. Apologizes to KAs," *Korea Times Los Angeles*, February 6, 1988; Sophia Kyung Kim, "Rolling Stone Mag. Agrees to Specific Concessions," *Korea Times Los Angeles*, March 17, 1988; Sophia Kyung Kim, "Asian American Groups Chisel Awareness in The Rolling Stone," *Korea Times Los Angeles*, January 28, 1989.

79. Korean American Coalition, November 4, 1991, Tom Bradley Administration Papers, Box 4248, Folder 9; Memo to Bradley from Yoon Hee Kim, November 4, 1991, Tom Bradley Administration Papers, Box 4248, Folder 9.

80. Jeff Chang, "Race, Class, Conflict and Empowerment: On Ice Cube's 'Black Korea,'" *Amerasia Journal* 19, no. 2 (1993): 94.

81. Chang, "Race, Class, Conflict and Empowerment," 91.

82. Memo to Bradley from Yoon Hee Kim, November 4, 1991, Tom Bradley Administration Papers, Box 4248, Folder 9.

83. Letter to Bradley from KAC, November 4, 1991, Tom Bradley Administration Papers, Box 4248, Folder 9.

84. Letter from Dan Kim of the Korean Restaurant Owners Association of Southern California, Tom Bradley Administrative Papers, Box 4248, Folder 9.

85. Letter from Bradley to Bryan Turner, Priority Records, December 12, 1991, Tom Bradley Administrative Papers, Box 4248, Folder 9.

86. Statement from O'Shea Jackson to Yang Kim, National Korean American Grocers Association, February 8, 1992. Tom Bradley Administrative Papers, Box 4245, Folder 24.

87. For a comprehensive overview of the killing of Latasha Harlins and background on the lives of Harlins, Du, and the judge presiding over the trial, Joyce Karlin, see Stevenson, *Contested Murder*.

88. Jai Lee Wong, interview with author. June 23, 2015.

89. Robert Reinhold, "Riots in Los Angeles," *Los Angeles Times*, May 5, 1992.

90. Seth Mydans, "A Target of Rioters, Koreatown Is Bitter, Armed, and Determined," *New York Times*, May 3, 1992, 2.

91. Mike Davis, "In L.A., Burning All Illusions," *The Nation*, June 1, 1992.

92. Duane Noriyuki, "One Man's Vision," *Los Angeles Times*, June 26, 1994.

Chapter 6

1. *Parts Unknown*, Season 1 Episode 2, "Los Angeles," directed by Michael Steed, written by Anthony Bourdain, featuring Anthony Bourdain, David Choe, and Roy Choi, aired April 21, 2013, on CNN, Zero Point Zero Production.

2. Davis, "Who Killed Los Angeles, 49; Richard W. Stevenson, "Patching Up LA—A Corporate Blueprint," *New York Times*, August 9, 1992, 6.

3. Stevenson, "Patching Up LA," 6.

4. Stevenson, 6.

5. Stevenson, 6.

6. James H. Johnson Jr., Walter C. Farrell Jr., Maria-Rosario Jackson, "Los Angeles One Year Later: A Prospective Assessment of Responses to the 1992 Civil Unrest," *Economic Development Quarterly* 8, no. 1 (1994).

7. Paul Feldman, "Vacant Lots a Stark Tribute to 2nd Anniversary of Riots," *Los Angeles Times*, April 22, 1994.

8. James Johnson of the Center for Study of Urban Poverty at UCLA; Stevenson, "Patching Up LA," 6; Davis, "Who Killed Los Angeles," 49.

9. J. Eugene Grigsby III, "In Planning There Is No Such Thing as a 'Race Neutral' Policy," *Journal of the American Planning Association* 60, no. 2 (1994): 241.

10. Angela E. Oh, "Rebuilding Los Angeles: One Year Later or Why I Did Not Join RLA," in *Los Angeles—Struggles Toward Multiethnic Community: Asian American, African American, and Latino Perspectives*, ed. Edward T. Chang and Russell Charles Leong (Seattle: University of Washington Press, 1994), 158.

11. Oh, "Rebuilding Los Angeles," 158.

12. Johnson, Farrell, and Jackson, "Los Angeles One Year Later," 21.

13. James H. Spencer, "Los Angeles since 1992: How Did the Economic Base of Riot Torn Neighborhoods Fare after the Unrest?" *Race, Gender & Class* 11, no. 2 (2004): 98.

14. March/April 1993 newsletter, Roberti Papers, Box 152, Special Collections, Loyola Marymount University.

15. Speech, June13, 1992, Tom Bradley Administration Papers, Box 4245, Folder 21.

16. RLA/KYCC Meeting Minutes, July 14, 1993, Rebuild LA Collection, Series 5, Box 151, Folder 724, Department of Archives and Special Collections, Loyola Marymount University Special Collections.

17. SBA loans were meant to help impacted areas revitalize, but "given the local politics, Korean American merchants with SBA approvals are not in a position to go back to the location of their former businesses. Therefore, they are simply stuck." Rebuild LA board of director meeting notes, April 28, 1993, Rebuild LA Collection, Series 5, Box 151, Folder 724.

18. Anthony Duignan-Cabrera, "Trapped in Red Tape," *Los Angeles Times*, June 25, 1993.

19. At the time they made up about half of the residents of South Central.

20. Eui-Young Yu, ed., *Black-Korean Encounter: Toward Understanding and Alliance* (Los Angeles: Regina Books, 1994), 71.

21. Liquor Store Business Conversion Program Overview, September 7, 1993, Rebuild LA Collection, Series 5, Box 156, Folder 798, Loyola Marymount University Special Collections.

22. RLA/KYCC Meeting Minutes, July 14, 1993, Rebuild LA Collection, Series 5, Box 151, Folder 724, Loyola Marymount University Special Collections.

23. RLA/KYCC Meeting Minutes, July 14, 1993; Duignan-Cabrera, "Trapped in Red Tape."

24. Feldman, "Vacant Lots a Stark Tribute."

25. Yu, *Black-Korean Encounter*, 98.

26. Yu, 81.

27. John Needham, "Koreans May Lead Post-Riot Exodus," *Korea Times Los Angeles*, June 29, 1992.

28. Needham, "Koreans May Lead."

29. Feldman, "Vacant Lots a Stark Tribute."

30. Needham, "Koreans May Lead."

31. Timothy R. Tangherlini, "Remapping Koreatown: Folklore, Narrative, and the Los Angeles Riots, *Western Folklore* 58, no. 2 (Winter 1999): 152.

32. Linus Chua, "Koreatown Businesses Still Nursing Post-Riot Wounds," *Los Angeles Times*, April 28, 1994.

33. Feldman, "Vacant Lots a Stark Tributes."

34. Letter to Mark Ridley-Thomas, July 13, 1992, Tom Bradley Administration Papers, Box 4245, Folder 21.

35. The South LA project encompassed about 2,900 acres south of Santa Monica freeway while the Wilshire-Koreatown area encompassed 1,200 acres especially impacted by the 1992 riots.

36. "Revitalization Efforts Approved by Council," *Los Angeles Times*, December 22, 1995.

37. Anna Scott, "The Quiet Tycoon," *LA Downtown News*, May 19, 2008, http://www.ladowntownnews.com/news/the-quiet-tycoon/article_734049fe-fc76-5b77-a56c-47c8a0355e99.html.

38. Scott, "Quiet Tycoon."

39. Gregory Cornfield, "Neighborhood Spotlight: Escaping its Tragic Past, Koreatown Embarks on a Golden Era," *The Real Deal*, September 21, 2018, https://therealdeal.com/la/2018/09/21/neighborhood-spotlight-escaping-its-tragic-past-koreatown-embarks-on-a-golden-era/.

40. Scott, "Quiet Tycoon."

41. Kevin Roderick, "Hidden Power of L.A. Real Estate," *LA Observed*, October 20, 2005.

42. Scott, "Quiet Tycoon."

43. Roderick, "Hidden Power"; Light, "Immigrant Place Entrepreneurs," 223.

44. Edward J. W. Park, "From an Ethnic Island to Transnational Bubble: A Reflection on Korean Americans in Los Angeles," *Amerasia Journal* 38, no. 1 (2012): 45.

45. Kyonghwan Park and Youngmin Lee, "Rethinking Los Angeles Koreatown: Multi-scaled Geographic Transition since the Mid-1990s," *Journal of the Korean Geographic Society* 42, no. 2 (2007): 198.

46. Park and Lee, "Rethinking," 212.

47. Stephen Gregory, "From the Ground up the Comeback Corridor," *Los Angeles Times*, March 26, 1995.

48. Feldman, "Vacant Lots a Stark Tribute."

49. Feldman."

50. The structures sustained less than 25 percent damage.

51. Gregory, "From the Ground."

52. Feldman, "Vacant Lots a Stark Tribute."

53. Vons said it was planning a $100 million expansion into traditionally underserved areas.

54. Gregory, "From the Ground."

55. Gregory.

56. Edward Avila, "Redevelopment in Los Angeles," *Los Angeles Times*, August 23, 1992.

57. "Jump-Starting Neighborhoods," *Los Angeles Times*, November 21, 1995.

58. "Jump-Starting Neighborhoods," *Los Angeles Times*.

59. Jill Stewart, "Mayor, Council, Redevelopment Agency Blamed for LA Ills," *Los Angeles Times*, March 13, 1989.

60. State Assembly member Chris Tucker's (D-Inglewood) introduced bill allowing the CRA to bypass certain bureaucratic hurdles (including citizenship oversight and environmental controls) to speed reconstruction in riot-torn neighborhoods, including South Central. Chris Tucker proposed a development area to address $427 million worth of damage to 1,053 structures. He argued it would benefit development by waving specific procedures.

61. Jerry Gillam, "Rebuilding Bill Scrapped amid Distrust of CRA," *Los Angeles Times*, August 29, 1992.

62. Jill Leovy, "Former South Central Struggles," *Los Angeles Times*, July 10, 2008.

63. Leovy, "Former South Central Struggles."

64. Park, "Ethnic Island," 47.

65. Park, 46.

66. Park and Lee, "Rethinking," 214–215.

67. "Koreatown on the Edge: Immigrant Dreams and Realities in One of Los Angeles' Poorest Communities," A report prepared by the Korean Immigrant Workers Advocates (2005), 12, KIWA Archive, Box 6, Folder 8, Southern California Library for Social Studies and Research, Los Angeles, California.

68. "Koreatown on the Edge," KIWA Archive, 6.
69. "Koreatown on the Edge," 2.
70. Its cost of living is 140 percent of other metropolitan areas in United States. "Koreatown on the Edge," 2.
71. "Koreatown on the Edge," 7.
72. "Koreatown on the Edge," 8.
73. "Koreatown on the Edge," 6.
74. KIWA materials, Tom Bradley Administration Papers, Box 4245, Folder 7.
75. Toward the end of the decade, there were about three hundred Korean-owned restaurants and cafes that employed nearly two thousand workers, about a third of whom were Latino. K. Connie Kang, "Activism Opens Generational Rift in Koreatown Workplaces," *Los Angeles Times*, September 6, 1998.
76. Kang, "Activism Opens Generational Rift."
77. Booklet, no date, Restaurant Workers Justice Campaign, Southern California Library.
78. Kang, "Activism Opens Generational Rift."
79. Kang.
80. Kang.
81. Kang.
82. "Koreatown on the Edge," 3.
83. "Redistricting Fight Moves to Federal Court," *Los Angeles Times*, July 31, 2012.
84. Cornfield, "Neighborhood Spotlight."

Epilogue
1. Gerrick Kennedy, "Two Worlds Blend Uneasily in Koreatown," *Los Angeles Times*, August 23, 2009.
2. Sam Quinones, "The Koreatown That Never Was," *Los Angeles Times*, June 3, 2001.
3. Sonia Suk died in 1996 at the age of 83. In her obituary, the *Los Angeles Times* called her one of the founders of Koreatown and reported that the community honored her with a three-day funeral observance. Hi Duk Lee died in 2019 at the age of 79, running a plant nursery as late as 2016. Tong Soo Chung faded from public life as a Korean American activist after his unsuccessful run for office and pursued a career as a lawyer in South Korea. K. W. Lee remains active in the Korean American community, and a leadership institute in Los Angeles for Korean American youths was named after him. "Sonia S. Suk; Koreatown Community Leader," *Los Angeles Times*, July 18, 1996; Alejandra Reyes-Velarde, "Hi Duk Lee, Visionary Who Founded Los Angeles' Koreatown, Dies at 79," *Los Angeles Times*, March 21, 2019.

4. Quinones, "Koreatown That Never Was."

5. Jamison was behind three of the ten largest projects filed with the planning department.

6. Kennedy, "Two Worlds Blend Uneasily."

7. Cornfield, "Neighborhood Spotlight."

8. Kennedy, "Two Worlds Blend Uneasily."

9. Avishay Artsy, "In L.A.'s Koreatown, Homeless Rift Has Historic Roots," KQED, June 28, 2018, www.kqed.org/news/11677728/in-l-a-s-koreatown-homeless-rift-has-historic-roots.

10. Scott, "Quiet Tycoon."

11. Scott.

12. Regina Kim, "Atlanta Spa Shootings: What Korean-Language Media Told Us That the Mainstream Media Didn't," *Rolling Stone*, March 31, 2021, www.rollingstone.com/culture/culture-news/atlanta-shootings-what-korean-language-media-told-us-that-the-mainstream-media-didnt-1149698.

13. Sarah Moon and Claire Colbert, "Attack on Asian Man in LA's Koreatown Being Investigated as a Hate Crime," *CNN*, February 26, 2021, www.cnn.com/2021/02/26/us/asian-american-man-attack-koreatown-los-angeles-trnd/index.html.

14. BTS WorldWide, "A BTS Tribute at the #StopAsianHate Rally in Ktown LA Today!!!," YouTube video, March 28, 2021, www.youtube.com/watch?v=zz9fscqQ8lU.

Bibliography

Archival Collections

David A. Roberti Papers, Department of Archives and Special Collections, Loyola Marymount University, Los Angeles, CA

Edmund Edelman Papers, Huntington Library Manuscript Collection, San Marino, CA

Kenneth Hahn Papers, Huntington Library Manuscript Collection, San Marino, CA

Korean American Coalition, East Asian Studies Library, University of Southern California, Los Angeles, CA

KIWA Archive, Southern California Library for Social Studies and Research, Los Angeles, CA

K. W. Lee Papers, University of California at Davis Special Collections, Davis, CA

Tom Bradley Administration Papers, University of California at Los Angeles Special Collections, Los Angeles, CA

Rebuild LA Collection, Department of Archives and Special Collections, Loyola Marymount University, Los Angeles, CA

Newspapers and Magazines

Asian Week
Associated Press (AP) News
Hokubei Mainichi
KoreAm Journal
Korea Times Los Angeles
Koreatown Weekly

Los Angeles Sentinel
Los Angeles Times
The Nation
New York Times
Pacific Citizen
Rolling Stone
Wall Street Journal
Washington Post
Westways Magazine

Books, Articles, Dissertations

Abelmann, Nancy, and John Lie. *Blue Dreams: Korean Americans and the Los Angeles Riots.* Cambridge, MA: Harvard University Press, 1997.

Baber, Katherine, and James Spickard. "Crafting Culture: 'Tradition,' Art, and Music in Disney's 'It's a Small World.'" *Journal of Popular Culture* 48, no. 2 (2015): 225–239.

Bonacich, Edna. "The Social Costs of Immigrant Entrepreneurship." *Amerasia* 14, no. 1 (1988): 119–128.

Bonacich, Edna, Ivan H. Light, and Charles Choy Wong. "Koreans in Business." *Society* 14 (September/October 1977): 54–59.

Bonacich, Edna, and Tae Hwan Jung. "A Portrait of Korean Small Business in Los Angeles." In Yu, Phillips, and Yang, *Koreans in Los Angeles*, 75–98.

Borstelmann, Thomas. *The 1970s: A New Global History from Civil Rights to Economic Inequality.* Princeton, NJ: Princeton University Press, 2011.

Brackman, Harold, and Stephen P. Erie. "Beyond 'Politics by Other Means'? Empowerment Strategies for Los Angeles' Asian Pacific Community." In *Asian American Politics: Law, Participation, and Policy*, edited by Don T. Nakanishi and James S. Lai, 231–246. New York: Rowman & Littlefield, 2003.

Callinicos, A. T. "Meaning of Los Angeles Riots." *Economic and Political Weekly* 27, no. 30 (July 25, 1992): 1603–1606.

Chang, Edward T., and Russell Charles Leong, eds. *Los Angeles—Struggles toward Multiethnic Community: Asian American, African American, and Latino Perspectives.* Seattle: University of Washington Press, 1995.

Chang, Jeff. "Race, Class, Conflict and Empowerment: On Ice Cube's 'Black Korea.'" *Amerasia Journal* 19, no. 2 (1993): 87–107.

Cheng, Cindy I-Fen. *Citizens of Asian America: Democracy and Race during the Cold War.* New York: New York University Press, 2013.

Chung, Angie Y. "Giving Back to the Community." *Amerasia Journal* 30, no. 1 (2004): 107–124.

———. *Legacies of Struggle: Conflict and Cooperation in Korean American Politics.* Stanford: Stanford University Press, 2007.

———. "'Politics without the Politics': The Evolving Political Cultures of Ethnic Non-Profits in Koreatown, Los Angeles." *Journal of Ethnic and Migration Studies* 31, no. 5 (September 2005): 911–929.

Cowie, Jefferson, and Joseph Heathcott, eds. *Beyond the Ruins: The Meanings of Deindustrialization.* Ithaca, NY: Cornell University Press, 2003.

Davis, Mike. "'Chinatown', Part Two? The 'Internationalization' of Downtown Los Angeles." *New Left Review* 1, no. 164 (July–August 1987): 65–86.

———. "Who Killed Los Angeles: Part Two, the Verdict Is Given." *New Left Review* 1, no. 199 (May/June 1993), 29–54.

Grigsby III, J. Eugene. "In Planning There Is No Such Thing as a 'Race Neutral' Policy." *Journal of the American Planning Association* 60, no. 2 (1994): 240–241.

Hsu, Madeline Y. "The Disappearance of America's Cold War Chinese Refugees." *Journal of American Ethnic History* 31, no. 4 (Summer 2012): 12–33.

Hurh, Won Moo. *The Korean Americans.* Westport, CT: Greenwood Press, 1998.

Isenberg, Alison. *Downtown America: A History of the Place and the People Who Made It.* Chicago: University of Chicago Press, 2005.

Jacobson, Matthew Frye. *Roots Too: White Ethnic Revival in Post-Civil Rights America.* Cambridge, MA: Harvard University Press, 2008.

Jo, Yung-Hwan. "Problems and Strategies of Participation in American Politics." In Yu, Phillips, and Yang, *Koreans in Los Angeles*, 203–218.

Johnson, James H., Jr., Walter C. Farrell Jr., and Maria-Rosario Jackson. "Los Angeles One Year Later: A Prospective Assessment of Responses to the 1992 Civil Unrest." *Economic Development Quarterly* 8, no. 1 (1994): 19–27.

Joyce, Patrick. *No Fire Next Time: Black-Korean Conflicts and the Future of America's Cities.* Ithaca, NY: Cornell University Press, 2003.

Kim, Claire Jean, and Taeku Lee. "Interracial Politics: Asian Americans and Other Communities of Color." *PS: Political Science and Politics* 34, no. 3 (September 2001): 631–637.

Kim, David S., and Charles Choy Wong, "Business Development in Koreatown, Los Angeles." In *The Korean Diaspora: Historical and Sociological Struggles of Korean Immigration and Assimilation in America*, edited by Hyung-chan Kim, 229–245. Ann Arbor: University of Michigan Press, 1977.

Kim, Elaine H. "'At Least You're Not Black': Asian Americans in U.S. Race Relations," *Social Justice* 25, no. 13 (Fall 1998): 1–6.

Kim, Illsoo. *The New Urban Immigrants: The Korean Community in New York.* Princeton: Princeton University Press, 1981.

Kim, Katherine Yungmee. *Los Angeles's Koreatown.* Charleston: Arcadia, 2011.

Kim, Nadia. "A View from Below: An Analysis of Korean Americans' Racial Attitudes." *Amerasia Journal* 30, no. 1 (2004): 1–24.

Laws, Glenda. "Globalization, Immigration, and Changing Social Relations in U.S. Cities." *ANNALS of the American Academy of Political and Social Science* 55, no. 1 (1997): 89–104.

Lee, Dong Ok. "Koreatown and Korean Small Firms in Los Angeles: Locating the Ethnic Neighborhoods." *Professional Geographer* 47, no. 2 (1995): 184–195.

Lee, Hi Duk. *Echo of Komerica.* Seoul: Yang Jung Sa, 2006.

Lee, Shelley Sang-Hee. "The Party's Over: Sex, Gender, and Orientalism in the Koreagate Scandal of the 1970s." *Frontiers: A Journal of Women's Studies* 39, no. 3 (2018): 1–28.

———. "Where Others Have Failed: Korean Immigrants and the Reinvention of Entrepreneurship in 1970s and 1980s America." *Journal of Asian American Studies* 21, no. 3 (2018): 341–366.

Lee, Taeku. "Riot, Remembrance, and Rebuilding: Some Longer-Term Aftereffects of Sa-I-Gu." *Amerasia Journal* 38, no. 1 (2012): 39–43.

Light, Ivan. *Deflecting Immigration: Networks, Markets, and Regulation in Los Angeles.* New York: Russell Sage Foundation, 2008.

———. "Immigrant Place Entrepreneurs in Los Angeles, 1970–99." *International Journal of Urban and Regional Research* 26, no. 2 (June 2002): 215–28.

Light, Ivan, and Edna Bonacich. *Immigrant Entrepreneurs: Koreans in Los Angeles, 1965–1982.* Berkeley: University of California Press, 1988.

Lin, Jan. "Globalization and the Revalorizing of Ethnic Places in Immigration Gateway Cities." *Urban Affairs Review* 34, no. 2 (November 1998): 313–339.

———. "Los Angeles Chinatown: Tourism, Gentrification, and the Rise of an Ethnic Growth Machine." *Amerasia Journal* 34, no. 3 (2008): 110–126.

Margulis, Harry L. "Asian Villages: Downtown Sanctuaries, Immigrant Asian Reception Areas, and Festival Marketplaces." *Journal of Architectural Education* 45, no. 3, (May 1992): 150–160.

Marks, Mara A. "Shifting Ground: The Rise and Fall of the Los Angeles Community Redevelopment Agency." *Southern California Quarterly* 86, no. 3 (Fall 2004): 241–290.

Min, Pyong Gap. *Caught in the Middle: Korean Communities in New York and Los Angeles.* Berkeley: University of California Press, 1996.

Oh, Angela E. "Rebuilding Los Angeles: One Year Later or Why I Did Not Join RLA." In *Los Angeles—Struggles Toward Multiethnic Community: Asian American, African American, and Latino Perspectives*, edited by Edward T. Chang and Russell Charles Leong, 158. Seattle: University of Washington Press, 1994.

Ong, Paul, Edna Bonacich, and Lucie Cheng, eds. *The New Asian Immigration in Los Angeles and Global Restructuring*. Philadelphia: Temple University Press, 1994.

Park, Edward J. W. "Competing Visions: Political Formation of Korean Americans in Los Angeles, 1992–1997." *Amerasia Journal* 24, no. 1 (1998): 41–57.

———. "Friends or Enemies?: Generational Politics in the Korean American Community in Los Angeles." *Qualitative Sociology* 22, no. 2 (1999): 41–57.

———. "From an Ethnic Island to Transnational Bubble: A Reflection on Korean Americans in Los Angeles." *Amerasia Journal* 38, no. 1 (2012): 43–47.

Park, Kyeyoung. "An Analysis of Latino-Korean Relations in the Workplace: Latino Perspectives in the Aftermath of the 1992 Los Angeles Civil Unrest." *Amerasia Journal* 38, no. 1 (2012): 143–169.

———. "Use and Abuse of Race and Culture: Black-Korean Tension in America." *American Anthropologist* 98, no. 3 (1996): 492–499.

Park, Kyonghwan, and Youngmin Lee. "Rethinking Los Angeles Koreatown: Multi-scaled Geographic Transition since the Mid-1990s," *Journal of the Korean Geographic Society* 42, no. 2 (2007): 196–217.

Parson, Don. "'This Modern Marvel': Bunker Hill, Chavez Ravine, and the Politics of Modernism in Los Angeles." *Southern California Quarterly* 75, no. 3/4 (Fall/Winter 1993): 333–350.

Pastor, Manuel. "Keeping It Real: Demographic Change, Economic Conflict, and Interethnic Organizing for Social Justice in Los Angeles." In *Black and Brown in Los Angeles: Beyond Conflict and Coalition*, edited by Laura Pulido and Josh Kun, 33–66. Berkeley: University of California Press, 2013.

Sides, Josh. *LA City Limits: African American Los Angeles from the Great Depression to the Present*. Berkeley: University of California Press.

Spencer, James H. "Los Angeles since 1992: How Did the Economic Base of Riot Torn Neighborhoods Fare after the Unrest?" *Race, Gender & Class* 11, no. 2 (2004): 94–115.

Stevenson, Brenda. *The Contested Murder of Latasha Harlins: Justice, Gender, and the Origins of the LA Riots*. Oxford: Oxford University Press, 2013.

———. "Latasha Harlins, Soon Ja Du, and Joyce Karlin: A Case Study of Multi-cultural Female Violence and Justice on the Urban Frontier." *Journal of African American History* 89, no. 2 (Spring, 2004): 152–176.

Stewart, Ella. "Communication between African Americans and Korean Americans: Before and after the Los Angeles Riots." *Amerasia Journal* 19, no. 2 (1993): 23–54.

Sturdivant, Frederick D. *The Ghetto Marketplace*. New York: Free Press, 1969.

Suk, Sonia S. *Life on Two Continents*. Seoul: Dong A. Printing, 1984.

Tangherlini, Timothy R. "Remapping Koreatown: Folklore, Narrative and the Los Angeles Riots." *Western Folklore* 58, no. 2 (Winter 1999): 149–173.

Twomey, Jane L. "Newspaper Coverage of the 1992 Los Angeles Uprising: Race, Place, and the Story of the 'Riot': Racial Ideology in African American and Korean American Newspapers," *Race, Gender & Class* 8 no. 4 (October 2001): 140–154.

Wilson, William Julius. *The Truly Disadvantaged: The Inner City, the Underclass, and Public Policy*. Chicago: University of Chicago Press, 1987.

Yoo, Won K. *Global Pulls on the Korean Communities in Sao Paolo and Buenos Aires*. New York: Lexington, 2015.

Yu, Eui-Young, ed. *Black-Korean Encounter: Toward Understanding and Alliance*. Los Angeles: Regina Books, 1994.

———. "'Koreatown' Los Angeles: Emergence of a New Inner-City Ethnic Community." *Bulletin of the Population and Development Studies Center* 14 (1985): 29–44.

Yu, Eui-Young, Peter Choe, Sang Il Han, and Kimberly Yu. "Emerging Diversity: Los Angeles' Koreatown, 1990–2000." *Amerasia Journal* 30, no. 1 (2004): 25–52.

Yu, Eui-Young, Earl H. Phillips, and Eun Sik Yang, eds. *Koreans in Los Angeles: Prospects and Promises*. Los Angeles: Koryo Research Institute, Center for Korean-American and Korean Studies, California State University, 1982.

Zia, Helen. *Asian American Dreams: The Emergence of an American People*. New York: Farrar, Straus and Giroux, 179.

Index